HUMANIZING SCHOOLS

new directions, new decisions

HUMANIZING SCHOOLS

new directions, new decisions

DOUGLAS H. HEATH
Haverford College

HAYDEN BOOK COMPANY, INC., NEW YORK

To Harriet and David
For Russell, Wendilee, and Annemarie

1   2   3   4   5   6   7   8   9   PRINTING

71 72 73 74 75 76 77 78   YEAR

Contents

Preface

What a paradox! Sputnik spawned stormy years of educational change and improvement. Billions of dollars have been spent to improve educational facilities, consolidate schools, purchase thousands of yellow school buses, expand pupil personnel services, modernize curricula (particularly in the sciences), offer advanced placement and other enrichment courses, provide elaborate language laboratories, computer, and other expensive educational technologies, and reeducate and improve the lot of teachers.

Yet today, many of our schools are in a hurricane of protest, strikes, disaffection, and calumny that make the Sputnikian days halcyon by comparison. Teachers are apprehensive and bewildered, uncertain about the relevance of what they are doing, and increasingly resented by their students. Administrators feel trapped between implacable forces: local Birch types attacking sex education programs; seditious students rebelling against any authority; parents complaining about school taxes and the breakdown in school discipline; and older and younger teachers splitting, not just on issues of curriculum and discipline, but on the purposes and worth of education itself.

And students? Who can make sense of them these days? Certainly, increasing numbers of them are much more knowledgeable, impressively alert to the currents of the world, morally sensitized and perceptive, and less imprisoned in the illusions and myths we adults have long taken for reality. Yet, increasing numbers are also bored and apathetic, even gloomy and despairing, resentful and lost, uncommitted and privatistic. They increasingly reject the claims of traditional authorities and the way of life of their achieving, puritanical, but joyless, middle class parents. The hippie and drug route speak to the suppressed needs of more youth than we are willing to admit. And what do they think of their schools? Irrelevant, boring, repressive, joyless. The more articulate say that they are prisoners of a dehumanized "system" that treats them like "niggers." Increasing numbers repudiate requirements, grades, achievement, and competition. Witness this poignant comment of a Berkeley senior who had the highest grade-point average of his graduating class:

> The first thing I would like to say to you is that it was not worth it . . . [in the pursuit of grades, he had become] subject to a paralyzing mental machinery: if I did not study twelve hours a day, compose at the speed of 1000 words an hour while writing a paper, go through required reading at 33 pages an hour, I was a failure. I pushed myself until I was more enchained than a Russian factory worker in the 1930s. [His longing for human contact, he said] would come at night as I walked home from the library. I would look at the lights in the windows and think to myself: behind those windows are people—real, live, human, fleshy, thinking, feeling, loving, despairing people. I am out here and they are in there. They will never come out here to me, and they would never allow me to come inside to them (McGuire, *Time*, June 7, 1968).

The paradox can be understood partly in terms of the changing character of our students, being caused by forces now in process in our society. Part I examines those character changes that are alienating them from their emotional needs, from each other, and from traditional communal sources of values. Boredom, loneliness, and meaninglessness are the emerging leitmotifs. I speak of trends I detect in our affluent middle class suburban and metropolitan youth. They may or may not apply to an increasing number of black and other deprived groups. I just don't know.

Some social scientists will object to my hypothesis that the character of our youth is changing. They will cite Aristotle's observations about the fractiousness of Athenian adolescents, the alienation of students throughout history, and the similarity of much contemporary student behavior to that of students of the twenties, for example (Lipsett 1970). But I disagree with the implication that "human nature" is static and immutable. The ways we express impulses or relate to others and to social institutions are not biologically given; they are not unaffected by profound societal upheavals and institutional changes.

Part II suggests that such character changes are caused by changes in the power of certain social institutions today to have educative and maturing effects on the young. Intimate, face-to-face, primary groups like the family, neighborhood, and church are losing their educative role. Increasingly, conforming, impersonal, secondary agencies like the mass media, peer culture, and the school are controlling and shaping the development of young people. These institutional changes are in turn related to more pervasive societal trends. Increasing affluence, complexity, interdependence, rate of change, incoherence, and pragmatic rationality prefigure the emerging society of 1984 which we must prepare a youth to cope with. I use the title of Orwell's book, *1984,* to symbolize some features of the society we are unwittingly creating, into which today's youth will go when they leave school. By pointing out some of the unhealthy effects that society may have, I hope to alert us to the necessity of making changes in our schools now to moderate such effects before it is too late.

Because we have been blind to these major trends and shifts in power and their human consequences, we have grievously misidentified how young people need to develop. We have, instead, supported structural and policy changes in schools that have compounded the deepening alienation of students. And we have become only more confused about what our principal educational goals should be.

Parts III, IV, and V make explicit what I believe is the beginning of a consensus about educational goals and changes needed to implement them. Our principal goal should be to further the educability of youth, that is, to help him become the agent of his own growth. I use a model of healthy growth, formulated from years of research (1965, 1968b) for identifying the kinds of educational experiences youth need. From such a model and research come insights into what kind of school and what kind of curriculum are necessary to counter the deepening alienation of youth and prepare them for their emerging society.

I don't delude myself that the proposals I make are novel. What this book may contribute is a systematic rationale for introducing certain changes judiciously and effectively.

To write about youth, society and its future, and schools is to risk superficiality, overgeneralization, inadequate documentation, and bias. I accept these risks. To be more forceful, I have abandoned the "mays," "mights," and "could be's" my academic conscience otherwise insists upon. I expect much disagreement with my analysis and proposals. I expect to be "proved" wrong-headed. The radical student will condemn me for not placing greater emphasis on the evils of society that justify his behavior. The radical educational critic will accuse me of selling out to the "system." I have tried to go beyond slogans and polemics to propose practicable changes — if we have the will to make them practicable.

This book has other limitations. It has grown out of conversations with elementary, secondary, and college teachers, students, and parents in many parts of the country. But since this is too broad a range to cover, I speak primarily to the secondary school world. The analysis and proposals, however, will be useful to any person interested in humanizing his school.

I have deliberately avoided discussing technical, curricular, and other educational topics that do not bear directly on the theme of the book. Similarly, I have ignored political and economic considerations, the role of government, and other important issues that are peripheral to my argument.

A more critical limitation is that the book deals primarily with the problems of predominantly white suburban schools. They are in as much difficulty, though perhaps of a different kind, as our city schools. My limited experience with the complexities of the problems of youth from dis-advantaged backgrounds makes me much less confident that my analysis and proposals are as appropriate for them as they are for our deprived suburban youth.

Because I concentrate on issues of educability, health, maturity, and the liberation of educators from a narrowly defined academicism, I risk being misunderstood. I value intellectual discipline and mastery very highly. I hold my own students to as high intellectual achievement as their abilities permit. But such expectations are damaging if they are not integrated into a larger vision of how a youth matures. Our failure to maintain such a vision has produced better *educated,* but less *educable* students, who are increasingly turned off by our schools and our academic values.

Because I seek to synthesize and make articulate trends and ideas that many observers have been noting, I am embarrassed about how to thank the many persons whose ideas I've so assimilated that I no longer recall who originated them. The literature about the topics of this book is immense. I have not had the time to read all of it. My thought has been shaped by the Zeitgeist, the critical tenor of the times, to which perceptive observers and critics like Mead, Goodman, Kozol, Kohl, Leonard, Holt, Friedenberg, and a host of others have contributed. Because I refer sparingly, if at all, to their specific thoughts or to the contributions of Keniston, Rogers, Sanford, Newcomb, Bruner, and others does not mean that this book has been unaffected by them. I have referred to the beginning of a consensus about our problems and their solutions. This consensus is being shaped by principals like Alan Glatthorn (1970), university deans like Dwight Allen, independent studies of our schools like the Four-School Study Report (1970), specific experimental institutions like the Philadelphia Advancement School, and the provocative ideas of Carl Rogers (1969) and the leaders of the human growth potential movement.

My own sojourn at Esalen and Kairos confirmed my hunches about the importance of developing a more integrative educational experience. I am grateful to Aaron Hillman, George Brown, and William Schutz for their example and advice, and to the Friends Council on Education and the National Association of Independent Schools for underwriting my visits to the centers to learn what they had to offer schools.

I don't know how to thank the many schools, public and private, large and small, nursery, elementary, secondary, and college, rich and poor, suburban and rural, East and West, American and Canadian that have asked me to work with their students and faculties in the past several years. The critical questions of hundreds of anonymous listeners have forced me to sharpen and distill my ideas over and over again. To single out just one school of those whose atmosphere convinced me of the singular importance of a humanistic environment for the growth of students, I mention Friends Boarding School, Barnesville, Ohio, whose spirit so obviously reflected that of the directors, Tom and Nan Brown. The ideas of this book have been tested against the experience of faculty, students, counselors, administrators, school board members, and parents. It has been their responsiveness and growing agreement that have given me the temerity to put them in print.

Another principal source of ideas for this book is my own research on adolescents for the past fifteen years, both at Haverford College and abroad. Much of this research has been supported by the National Institute of Mental Health, particularly one grant, #411227.

There are others who have contributed in other ways to this book, though they, of course, are not responsible for its deficiencies. It was Henry Scattergood who involved me initially in the problems of our schools. The Friends Council on Education has made it possible for me to visit most of the Quaker schools in the country. As the Four-School study independently discovered, their humane and caring atmospheres, as those of other schools I could mention, provided me with that glimmer of what a humanistic school could be like.

Of the many who have read earlier drafts, I am grateful to students like William Loughrey, teachers like David Denman, and thoughtful educators, as well as superb editorial critics like Robert Boynton for their constructively critical review of the book. Rodman Furnald deserves a very special word of thanks. His perceptive comments, stringent criticisms, and constant prods to complete the book gave me the support every author needs

No person can be as fortunate as I to have had as faithful and incomparably efficient secretary and research assistant as Emily Kingham. She has patiently typed the many drafts of the speeches out of which this book developed and the book itself.

Haverford College provided not only funds for some of the studies and the preparation of the manuscript, but also a leave of absence that made it possible for me to get deeply immersed in the problems of our schools.

Those who know David Mallery, Director of Program for the Friends Council on Education and the National Association of Independent Schools, can understand why I am indebted to him. I know of no other educator who has visited so many private and public schools, knows so well so many teachers and students and their problems (1962), and is as conversant with most of the innovative efforts being made in elementary and secondary schools. As a catalyst, author, and teacher, his infectious enthusiasm and his supportive and loving concern for others has served as the model of the mature and educable teacher I speak of in this book.

But for many reasons, it is my family which has made this book really possible. They have put up with the many days and nights I've been away, either visiting schools or writing. As a teacher of young children, my wife's loving patience, sensitivity, and understanding of how and why they grow wholly and healthily have shaped my ideal of an elementary school teacher. My children have taught me much about these times. This book is for them—a father's hope that they will grow up in more human schools and a healthier society.

Douglas Heath

Part I

The Deepening Alienation of Youth

We must begin where our youth are. Most of us are bewildered by their restlessness and apparent rejection of us and our traditions. We have been so preoccupied with their long hair, skirt lengths, psychedelic beads and sandals, pot parties, obscenity, underground newspapers, and confrontations that we have not clearly seen the more fundamental character changes occurring that make pot, long hair, and confrontations inevitable. So we've become confused about how to respond. We fight the trivial battles of beards and dress and ignore the important personal changes that affect our students' educability and maturing.

The magnitude and type of societal changes we have experienced since World War II have affected no group more than our youngsters. They are less protected by their memories and values than we from the effects of such changes. When uptight about my sixteen-year-old son, I try to erase every memory *I* formed before 1955. And then I ask "What would I be like if I hadn't experienced the insecurity my parents felt when they lost everything during the Depression? Hadn't known the patriotic fervor Pearl Harbor sparked in most Americans? Nor enjoyed the more leisurely school pace that never cast doubt on my being accepted in college?" "But if I were my son," I ask, "what would I be like if I had suffered the assassinations of three heroes? Witnessed the interminable violence of Vietnam on TV? Suffered the guilt of continued injustice to blacks? Vaguely sensed my country had betrayed its ideals and honor? Endured for years the SAT ogre and the inescapable presence of college? And turned when bored always to the ubiquitous and bizarre world of television?" More than our lives, those of our children reflect directly the psychological effects of our changing society.

Our children are very much aware that these changes affect them differently. In fact, they no longer talk of a "generation," symbolic of change, in terms of the traditional thirty or even twenty years. Current college seniors complain that they can't understand freshmen who seem to be different in ways they find difficult to describe. *Life* recently reported this conversation,

> "Well, maybe you want to come out here and help us," said one of the older kids to several younger kids.
> "Why should we help you? You've never done anything for us," said Matthew's friend, a twelve-year-old.
> "You're the older generation," said Matthew.
> "Four years isn't a generation," said a seventeen-year-old boy.
> "That's by your line of reasoning," said my thirteen-year-old boy.

Part I tries to understand what has been happening to our youth within a sufficiently long period of time—two decades—to identify basic trends. Understanding such trends will help us see more clearly the emerging realities of the present and glimpse the potential effects our technological, secular, and affluent society may have on all of us in the years ahead.

I must be very clear at this point. I believe that the trends I identify have now become so prominent in some youth, particularly our brightest and most sensitive, that we can no longer ignore them. Although I report psychological test information from two decades of white middle class suburban and metropolitan seventeen-year-old males to support my hunches, I rely much more heavily on my experience with young people and with adults who have worked closely with them in most parts of the country. Their consistent confirmation of the ideas of Part I gives me the temerity to generalize about long-term character changes.

Our society has developed a truly national culture since World War II, one that is pervasively and intrusively homogenizing the values and attitudes of young people. More than we, they do live in McLuhan's global village. Wherever I've traveled, I have found that students share similar cultural experiences. The mass media, television, the current popular singers and groups, and movies like *Easy Rider* reflect and affect the tastes and beliefs of almost all young people. A senior in a forty-four-student school in New Hampshire and a freshman at the thirty-thousand-student University of Texas both read the currently popular author (be it Camus or Vonnegut), react to the deaths of Janis Joplin and Jimi Hendrix, feel rootless, and are antagonistic toward the "system." During the past twenty years, students at Haverford College have become more similar in their interests and personal styles, even though recent students come from many more states, public schools, and religious groups. Some colleges no longer seek geographic diversity, having found that students from one section don't bring the social and psychological diversity they used to. These findings confirm those of a national survey of adolescents: ethnic, regional, and even social class differences are becoming less powerful determinants of personality differences (Douvan and Adelson 1966). Increasingly, variations in attitudes and values due to religious differences are also lessening (Hoffman 1970).

If adolescents are becoming more alike, it is reasonable to search for some common character changes among them. Although I speak primarily about trends and *don't intend to imply that they describe a majority of young people today,* they will, I predict, tomorrow. In fact, if we are to believe the Harris survey for the American Council on Education in 1970, some aspects of the deepening alienation I speak of later already apply to a majority, at least, of college students. Fifty-seven percent of these surveyed in 1970 respect a young man if he resists the draft. Only 29 percent in 1968 and 49 percent in 1969 so respected a resistor. The majority agree today that America has "become a highly repressive society, intolerant of dissent," that "basic changes in our system are necessary," that "war protestors have not been given fair trials," and that black revolutionaries "could not receive a fair trial in the United States." This deep disenchantment with our country reflects profound underlying changes in our students.

Within the past several decades, three trends have emerged with great clarity that describe increasing numbers of young people: boredom, belonginglessness, and meaninglessness. Each manifests a disturbance in a human being's principal modes of relating. Boredom is symptomatic of being cut off from part of one's self, particularly one's emotional needs. Belonginglessness results from an increasing dilution of one's emotional ties to other people, groups, and social institutions like the family, church, or nation. And meaninglessness comes from a deepening disenchantment with the authority of one's traditions, particularly religious and political "truths." Such is the real meaning of the "deepening alienation" of today's youth.

Chapter 1

Boredom

I have been impressed by the number of young people who tell me how bored and "turned off" they are. As a Harvard student recently said, "Everybody's bored. A professor can't keep people interested for 60 minutes if he does a song and dance act." Teachers agree. Those who have taught for many years say that it's increasingly difficult to keep students' attention these days. They have to change their pace more quickly, present information in shorter periods of time, assign more vivid, if not bizarre reading. More than ever, a teacher must draw upon his histrionic skills to excite his students.

That young people may be bored is not new. Much of life for vast numbers of people has always been tedious, monotonous, and drab. Man has created wars, Saturnalia, and the gaudy color of a Catholic mass to wake him up to life. Young people now create riots, Woodstocks, and psychedelic pageantry. Yet I see boredom as a key to the understanding of a wide range of youthful behavior.

First, expectations about being bored have changed. Our youth do not expect to be bored. They have developed an expectation, actually a value, of not being bored. They value having their "kicks," "peak experiences," or "highs" more frequently than we did. They actively seek to avoid being "down."

Second, whereas other generations, just to survive, had to learn to expect and endure boredom and tolerate its frustrations and tedium, younger people don't. Their survival is guaranteed by our affluence. They know they don't need to work at a boring job to stay alive. They know they can find a new job or not work at all. There is always the security of welfare if, as some hippies do, they simplify living to the barest necessities and learn how to hustle. Youth is freed of the need to work to survive.

4

One young man wrote me,

> We want creative, fulfilling, and meaningful work which makes an
> impact. This eliminates about 90 percent of today's jobs. We are
> well aware that most jobs are unexciting, unfulfilling, and unimpor-
> tant. Because of affluence and television, we have not experienced
> drudgery, hard work, and long hours, and thus we have little pa-
> tience and tolerance for this.

Increasing numbers of young people no longer value sustained, persistent,
but boring and tedious effort if it doesn't bring pleasure or guarantee some
immediate pay-off.

Third, boredom is produced by prolonged stimulation, to which a
person very quickly learns to adapt. He then seeks out even more intense
stimulation to arouse him to the same degree. The Eisenhower years, as
hectic as they were at the time, now seem halcyon and quiescent in comparison to the Kennedy and Johnson years. The Nixon era is boring to
many youngsters. Consider reactions to the Apollo moon landings. I was
struck by the blaséness of adolescents with whom I followed the televised
coverage of the first landing on the moon. Several didn't even bother to
watch at the critical moments. Few youngsters in our neighborhood
bothered with the second or third landings at all. Or more personally, I
recall in college how intent a group of us were to find a way to "borrow"
an illegal copy of Henry Miller's *Tropic of Cancer* from the locked cage of
the library. Twenty years later, satiated by the sexualization of most
advertising, books like *Portnoy's Complaint,* and X-rated movies, I returned
to *Tropic of Cancer* and found it to be too boring to complete. Although many viewers are shocked by the movie of the book, soon the
same movie may seem quite tame. If our world had been only that of our
youngsters since 1955, just what would "turn us on" if we were they?

Fourth, boredom results from encountering sameness and familiarity
rather than novelty. But what is novel to our children these days? They
have explored by way of television so much of the world by the time they
reach adolescence that there is little they don't know something about.
They've been to Biafra, Greenland, and viewed earth from the moon. How
routine! They've not only seen the posed mayhem and savageness of men
on TV programs like *The Wild Wild West,* but they have experienced
revengeful assassinations, murders, and Vietnam killings for real, instantaneously. They've witnessed the birth of a child, been in a Chicago riot,
heard about the technology of abortion, participated in a Kennedy funeral,
and died with a dying cancer patient. But all only vicariously.

Fifth, boredom occurs when consciousness is not well integrated with one's emotional needs. Too overdeveloped a consciousness, particularly an awareness of one's self, inhibits spontaneity and playful self-abandon. We become bored when we are only detached spectators, voyeurs of life, even of our own. In contrast to the image that television, *Time*, *Life*, and many commentators project about contemporary youth, the seeming impulsivity of our flower children or rioteers is not a pressing problem to educators. Our dilemma is how to help our youth reintegrate into their consciousness their suppressed child-like spontaneity. Increasingly more of this younger generation are very inhibited, overcontrolled, detached, and passive. I know that statement violates the stereotypes of many adults and the idealized self-image of many adolescents. So I must explore it in detail.

Note the themes in the following excerpt from a talk of a senior who was chosen by his graduating class to speak for them about themselves to a larger community:

> And we're distanced from people. Quite often, I think, projects like joining the Peace Corps, or working with slum kids are attempts to bridge a gap. Not just a sociological gap, but a gap of the heart. Because these people seem to operate on a more fundamental level than we do. Somehow their actions are more spontaneous and less embalmed by reflection. We worry about relating to people; but, for better or worse, they relate. There is a naturalness—often crude, but a naturalness nonetheless—about them. And too often it is obscured in us. And if this is the burden of the intellectual—if his cross is always to be separated from other men, almost as an observer—then I say he is not an intellectual at all. He is an academician. But nothing more. Because there is something precious in the unenlightened man; something viable in his ignorance. And that something—hard to define but recognizable, I think by feeling—is his unsophisticated unreflected-upon vulnerability to emotion. His ability to forget himself.

Let's first examine the consciousness of today's youths and then the way they control their impulses.

At no time in history has a generation had the means to so symbolize or make conscious its own experience and to become so aware of its own and others' existence. The insights of Freud about the disguises all of us use to protect ourselves from knowing parts of ourselves and others have released many to explore more consciously their unconscious wishes. Awareness that I can defensively protect myself by means of projection, rationalization, and repression opens me to the possibility of recovering the forbidden. The Yippies and New Left use other means to expand *our* consciousness. Obscenities, threats to levitate the Pentagon, nomination of a pig for president, and tumultuous confrontations to focus attention on issues we prefer not to face and strip away our "false" awareness are some of them. No longer will our more radical young allow us to use the defense of denial, that is, to not see what we in fact do see. No longer will they allow us to live with our racial prejudices, not "seeing" the unjust consequences of our beliefs and acts. No longer will they allow us to destroy another society, Vietnam, for example, to "save" it, and yet condemn those few youth who destroy our property in protest against our hypocrisy.

Some young people so deify expanding their consciousness that they risk their sanity to find more powerful ways to "expand" their minds. Drugs like marijuana are with us to stay for many reasons, one of which is that their use rivals more effortful ways of approaching insight and knowledge—at least so young people believe. Even this generation's music sensitizes consciousness. Young people not only have new powerful technological means available by which to expand their consciousness. They also have larger vocabularies and new symbols by which to expand their knowledge further and express it more vividly. The young are also adept at creating new symbols. Pop art, pins, clothes, hair styles, and psychedelic posters provide other symbols by which to channel their newly sensitized consciousness. Robert Finch, former head of the Department of Health, Education, and Welfare said,

> Long before . . . [a child] enters kindergarten, he's been exposed to thousands of hours of viewing, to an enormous range of information—unstructured, to be sure, but still raw information. So when he starts school he's already long past the "See Jane run" stage... When I was a kid, it was okay for the school system to stuff information into children like they were sausages. But it just won't work that way any longer (*Life*, January 24, 1969, p. 21).

It's not just that more young people now command new tools for symbolizing experience; more also value and seek to exploit the possibilities for knowledge such tools offer. It's a generation that values being honest, of seeing and telling everything like it is. It's not a generation content with the glossiness of fine manners, linen napkins, and the pink icing which most of us use to coat the less attractive sides of our lives and our world. Youths see more important values to live by—and they are right. They value going to the root of a matter. They become "paranoid" in their language, if they sense that we, the "system," conceal the truth from them by hiding behind our age, status, or experience. They delight in forcing into consciousness anything and everything, whether it is scatalogical expressions or the most repressed of our adult taboos. They try to show us (and more often themselves) that we (and they) have nothing to fear. I know of no adult secrets I cannot discuss quite comfortably with most teenagers I know. Our imagined devils, like our Communists, aren't as frightening as we think. Sixty-nine percent of the 1970 college undergraduates said that Communism was not our biggest threat; they said that 71 percent of their parents thought differently! Some young people are even missionaries to us heathens. None of us is to be left alone in our darkness. Nothing is to be left out of awareness.

If we believe that this heightened consciousness is characteristic of only our young adults, we are very mistaken. The night I was to talk to a group of senior high school students, the principal called to ask me to talk also to his middle school children. I had never talked to this age group as a group before and so asked my son, who was in seventh grade, "What do they want to hear?" Without any hesitation he said, "Tell them about LSD." Being more timid than he, and having just read Berne's *Games People Play,* I thought I would turn my adversity into some playful fun. So I titled the talk *Games Children Play* and asked the kids the next day, "What games have you learned to use to psyche out your parents and teachers to get what you want?" A forest of hands went up and we were excitedly off for the full forty minutes. The teachers winced, and so did I, to hear how astutely these youngsters had figured us out and were aware of how they did it. One of the foremost strengths of our youth is their psychological-mindedness. We adults dare not try to manipulate them. They know how to read us.

I am no longer surprised when junior and senior high school students ask me in public about all forms of sexually deviant behavior. Our young people have grown up in a culture infused with sexual images and preoccupations. Have we adults ever listened carefully to the lyrics of the Beatles, the Doors or other rock groups? Twenty years ago when we were in school would an eleventh grade girl have dared to ask in a school assembly, "Do you think girls my age should have lesbian relationships?" Even the seventh graders knew what she was talking about. Would an eleventh grade boy preface his question by, "I am a latent homosexual"? High school girls and boys interviewed by David Susskind freely and without embarrassment discussed their own premarital sexual standards. Even just ten—no, maybe five—years ago, would the musical *Hair* have kept in its score a song that begins like this (which has been recorded and is available to any ten year old who wants to buy it)?

Sodomy, fellatio, cunnilingus, pederasty.
Father, why do these words sound so nasty?
Masturbation can be fun.
Join the holy orgy, Kama Sutra, everyone.*

I have suggested that one cause of the boredom so many adolescents now complain of is their too-sensitized consciousness, which inhibits their emotional spontaneity and robs them of the ability to feel and act intensely and passionately. Like Hamlet, they are "sicklied o'er with the pale cast of thought."

This is the "cool" generation, which flocks to the low-keyed, detached, almost diffident style of the intellectualized, introspective, political candidate. When Humphrey impulsively kissed the image of his wife on the television screen upon hearing of his nomination in 1968, he "turned off" millions of young people. Other words like "uptight," "hung-up," and "boxed-in" reflect their awareness of their imprisonment by their inhibitions. Even life is a "game" to be "psyched out" and played "coolly."

I find the word "cool" to be very expressive of the character of many young people. It has diverse meanings but the one I prefer refers to the mode of impulse control. To be cool is to give the impression that one has complete control of one's emotional reactions. Self-control is singularly valued by this generation. To keep your status you must keep your cool. If you "blow your cool" you lose status, you become "vulnerable," you can be "shot down" or "cut up." Students are afraid to be too enthusiastic or too interested. They must appear to be "bored," particularly with school. To appear sophisticatedly cynical is to be "in." Though, as one high school girl said, "The only time I found life could be beautiful was when I blew my cool."

The fear of abandoning one's self to one's childlike feelings results in a prematurely serious, humorless, even grim, demeanor. One Stanford girl said in a *New York Times* interview, "We're so serious about everything. The other night we were sitting around in the dorm, telling old jokes, and we were laughing and laughing. It had been a long time since we had laughed like that" (June 7, 1970, p. 75). It's true that the world is a frightening place now in which to grow up. It's also true that we educators have forced our students to commit more of their time to education. They work harder and longer, at least until they get into college. They are more conscientious and responsible, as well as efficient and organized, in their academic work. With the assistance of Freudian, hip, and beat language, they have learned how to intellectualize away any feelings that suggest sentimentality, nostalgia, weakness, dependency, childlike naiveté, affection, or tenderness. The net effect of being cool is to feel inwardly empty and dead. Increasing numbers of youth say they don't feel alive anymore.

(Perhaps due to the drug experience that is beginning to loosen up many young people, there are signs of an erosion of the value of being cool. Increasingly, more youngsters are willing to express their hostility and anger more directly. And I have noted a few signs in several schools, perhaps due to the increasing impact of sensitivity groups, that affection and tenderness are being expressed more demonstratively.)

Associated with this fear of expressing feelings directly and openly has been a deepening passive orientation toward life. We so structure the lives of our students in secondary schools that it is not until they encounter the greater freedom of college that their inability to cope actively with freedom becomes apparent. College freshmen don't fail because of inadequate academic preparation or low ability; they fail because they aren't able to use freedom maturely. They don't know how to direct their own growth. Studies of the graduating seniors of Stanford University revealed that less than 25 percent had developed any intrinsic intellectual interests during their four college years and that their most salient characteristic was a deeply entrenched passive attitude toward their own educational experience (Katz and Associates 1968).

The increasing passivity of youth is seen in many other ways as well. The principal forms of recreation of this generation are film and folk rock, both passive spectatorship activities. The intense interest by some in film-making, television, and photography may reflect in part a passive voyeuristic attitude toward life. A person can vicariously participate without commitment—like a detached psychiatrist or objective researcher or the photographer in *Medium Cool.* Although many young people now enjoy listening to a rock band, they increasingly do not participate in or enjoy group singing (from 49 percent in 1948 to 77 percent in 1968 in my study) which is dying out in our peer culture. Glee clubs are losing their appeal in some schools. Although Haverford College has increased in size, we have fewer entering seventeen-year-olds now participating in the glee club than we have had for two decades. Coaches in different parts of the country have in the past two years told me that fewer students are interested in team sports. One men's college of twelve hundred students has had to discontinue its junior varsity football team. Some schools now *require* their students to go to pep rallies. There is a growing decline in student participation in extracurricular activities and seemingly "adolescent" types of play, like social events and Halloween parties. Increasing numbers of

young people do not like crowds and parties (from 35 to 60 percent) or
engaging in stunts at parties or in dramatics (from 20 to 34 percent in my
samples). Boarding schools report that their weekends are gloomy and
boring; the students do not seem to know how to entertain themselves.
In all of these situations, a youth risks the spontaneous and open expression of his feelings, the loss of his cool. It's not that young people don't
have an intense need to be emotional and demonstrative; they fear being
vulnerable.

We humans are not built to suppress our tensions and cool our feelings. We have tear glands to cry with (though males are discouraged from
crying in our society), facial muscles to express our feelings with (though
a youth is expected to play it cool and detached), and voices to laugh and
shout with (though teachers value a quiet classroom). We also have large
and small muscles to work with (though our society provides little physical
work any longer for adolescents), and to play and fight with (though both
are losing their status among some youth).

How then does a youngster express himself? Freud long ago noted
that if tension is not reduced through action or emotion, then it may be
partially reduced through fantasy, particularly dreams. Interestingly, in the
past several decades there have been slight, but consistent, increases in the
number of seventeen-year-olds who report that they dream (from 60 to 75
percent), that they dream frequently (from 30 to 60 percent) and repeti-
tively (15 to 30 percent). The content of their dreams has become more
frankly sexual (from 25 to 45 percent); proportionately more are worried
about their sexual feelings (5 to 20 percent). Drug-induced fantasies and
LSD trips provide other ways for the inhibited to express tension in start-
lingly pleasurable and occasionally nightmarish ways. More now (from 15
to 40 percent) have fantasies about doing something shocking or harm-
ful; over half of one entering group of freshmen said it had the desire to
destroy property.

To value not being bored, to have few goals that make the tedium of
achieving them tolerable, to live in too-exciting times, to exhaust novelty,
and to be hung up by a too-sensitized awareness that inhibits emotional
spontaneity may produce acute boredom. Boredom is painful. How do
adolescents react to boredom these days? Contemporary youths don't yet
accept the fact that much of their lives may necessarily be boring. Nor
have I encountered any number who are willing to endure boredom to
achieve certain goals. I expect that the frenetic search by our mass media,
advertisers, and ourselves for novelty will continue. Finding means to de-
inhibit, to anesthetize our hyperconsciousness will be the most practicable
way to avoid boredom.

At this point I need to explain the discrepancy between the seemingly indiscriminate, pleasure-seeking behavior of youth and my thesis that this is a very uptight generation. My hunch is that much of the impulsive and "free" behavior of some of our youth is compensatory. Their restless attacks on rules, the flight into drugs, and the use of confrontations are ways of destroying their inhibitions, which many are not able to let go spontaneously. Behavior that is compensatory is frequently indiscriminate, excessively driven, and tense. It may also be erratic, unpredictable, and inconsistent with a youth's past values. Finally, compensatory behavior seldom is childlike, delightful, or joyful. For example, an erratic, explosive, violent outbreak on a college campus among groups of very self-conscious, intellectualized students reveals by its very diffuseness and excess an underlying severe inhibition of hostility that has temporarily broken down.

Try to keep these clues of compensatory behavior in mind while I examine some of the ways current students seek to deal with their boredom. The clues may clarify why I propose that increasing numbers of our youth are deeply inhibited and passive in their orientation to living, why they are increasingly dependent upon something "out there" to excite them. I must highlight one caution, however. Human beings are very complex. They don't act just out of boredom. Other motives as well as societal provocations are involved in what adolescents do.

A bored youngster will ordinarily seek out intense stimulation to "turn him on." A favorite method by which to "turn on" is to turn up the decibel level of one's stereo. I visited an electric music hall recently. I saw hundreds of teenagers sitting on benches listening to electronic music that blasted them from innumerable speakers. There was no dancing and very little movement. The music was so loud that I couldn't talk with my wife. I began to feel the physical force of the music in my groin, to experience the vibes, a deep pulsation in my abdomen. I felt I was being erotically seduced by some demonic power. No wonder folk rock is called "hot." We fled after twenty minutes; the intensity of the experience became physically painful. But young people can endure this throbbing massage for hours.

Drugs like pot, speed, and acid have become the preferred ways for increasing numbers (now for 21 and 34 percent of high school and college students respectively, according to a national survey of 14 to 25 year olds, *Philadelphia Inquirer,* September 9, 1970) to "turn on" and escape boredom. There are other reasons, of course, that predispose a youth to drugs. With drugs you can have it both ways. You can expand your consciousness, so it is believed, and also "blow your mind," that is destroy your hang-ups and inhibitions. For many, the drug experience enhances their feelings and makes living seem "beautiful." Some feel more alive. Some secure a vision of how beautiful life is if they abandon their cool. Perhaps the drug experience will have the constructive and healthy effect of teaching some youths that if they allow themselves to give in to their emotional, affectionate feelings, they really may not be as vulnerable in their relations with others as they had thought. Unfortunately, the pot experience, in particular, tends to encourage passivity, to sap a person's will to assert himself and cope. Extensive use of pot may only entrench an already deep passivity in many adolescents. It could lead some, in the long run, to seek more intense types of experiences to avoid the boredom that comes with frequent drug use. Already taking pot is being called boring by some youths. What will provide the thrills tomorrow?

The increased potential for boredom, receptivity to more intense forms of stimulation, and passivity provide the psychological conditions predisposing a youth to participate anonymously in a confrontation or riot. Either is more appealing than working in some sustained, active, disciplined effort to produce social change. A riot is fun until the police bust occurs. And perhaps as students become more accustomed to confrontations, riots will not become fun *until* a bust is provoked. A riot can be a peer-group-sanctioned way to blow one's cool without guilt. It provides an outlet for much of the suppressed frustration and hostility so endemic in many older adolescents these days. The confrontation and its potential violence have been used by the SDS and blacks to induce needed social change. We may well see increasing numbers of other young people initiate and participate in a riot. Their purpose will not be to achieve just the ostensible list of non-negotiable demands. Their less conscious purpose may well be to blow their cool and enjoy the process of feeling "alive" for a day—as so many youngsters report of their confrontation experience.

The attraction to violence by bored youth is not confined to American college and high school students. The leader of a socio-drama experiment in a small, isolated Canadian town, Madoc, summarized her impressions of the imaginative themes of her children this way.

> Eleven-year-olds are invariably fascinated with violence because it is equated with action and excitement. It's a release. But I must say, I've never seen as much of it as I have here in Madoc. These Grade Sixers apparently feel excitement and action are missing in their part of the world (*The Globe and Mail,* April 18, 1970).

Increasing numbers of young people are exploring another way to de-inhibit themselves, as suggested in the following letter I received from a woman student in California.

This entire problem of the inability to really feel for others, to forget yourself, and to have spontaneous emotions and true compassion has been bothering me for months. I've been trying to do something about it by joining a sensitivity group, letting my defensive self-control drop, and just trying to become more aware of people and their feelings. (I don't believe in using pot, LSD, and never have even tried them or alcohol.) However, I keep returning to my old self-centered, unemotional insensitive self. So, as the man says, "Where to now, boss?," i.e., Help!

How would you answer her cry for help?

Why have the Esalen, *T*, encounter, marathon, and sensitivity groups become so popular in the past few years—and not just among young people? Why do Julian Beck's Living Theater and his *Paradise Now* as well as the almost compulsive "happening" or pursuit after de-inhibition as occurs in the frank sexualization of dancing to rock music, appeal to this generation? Because each frees us from being "uptight" so we can be more spontaneously emotional. Each helps us recover the muted child within. We have created a society in which we now need institutionalized ways to learn how to abandon our cool and be more honest about our feelings. The so-called sensitivity procedures will continue to flood into our schools, churches, and communities because they meet some deep needs of all of us. Our challenge as educators is to learn to use such procedures wisely to help young people integrate their emotional needs with their hyperconsciousness. Hopefully, they will then be more able to deal with boredom in the future.

Chapter 2

Belonginglessness

The second underlying character change becoming prominent is belonginglessness a not very elegant term to describe the growing estrangement of many youth from other persons and groups. It's ingredients are rootlessness, noncommitment, detachment, privatism, and loneliness. Recall the words of the graduating senior quoted earlier: "And we're distanced from people. Quite often, I think, projects like joining the Peace Corps, or working with slum kids are attempts to bridge a gap. Not just a sociological gap, but a gap of the heart." After describing the different forms this increasing alienation is taking, I will turn to the ways young people are trying to overcome the loneliness that accompanies the lack of enduring emotional bonds.

Feelings of belonging are nurtured by the clarity and intensity of one's identification with the social groups and traditions of society. An Italian, for example, has a clear order of identifications. He is of the Luigi or Robigilio family first, a Tuscan or Sicilian second, a Catholic, perhaps, third, and an Italian last. The order of an American's identifications is much more confused: a Jones, American, Southerner, and Baptist; or an American, Irish-Catholic, New Englander, and De Lancey. For increasing numbers of young people, the order of their primary identifications is even more confusing and the intensity of the identifications they do have is being diluted. Many youth feel that they don't belong to any group, even their families. They don't feel any loyalty to or affection for their local neighborhoods, churches, ethnic tradition, or, certainly, their schools, and increasingly, their own country.

Take, for example, the symbols of affection for and loyalty to one's school and country. The "old school tie," the school team, the fraternity membership, the graduating ceremony of "sharing the cup" that confirmed being an Amherst man in the 1950's, the Choate image, the high school reunion, the Star Spangled Banner and God Bless America, the Pledge of Allegiance, "my country right or wrong," Memorial Day, and "honor the flag" no longer appeal to our increasingly uncommitted youth. Few have any political loyalties or serious church attachments. Traditional establishment-oriented groups like the A.M.A., Rotary, and Daughters of the American Revolution will hold little interest for increasing numbers of this generation when they become adults. The feeling of rootlessness, of not being attached to anything anywhere, of being adrift, is captured nostalgically in the Beatles last album, *Let It Be,* in which the hope of finding and returning home is so noticeable. But where is home for this generation of adolescents? "We're like the Indians, always retreating and retreating. Hopefully, sometime we'll be able to put down roots. The only thing you can grasp onto is the earth," said a woman student (*The New York Times,* June 7, 1970, p. 75).

Commonly shared values also express and strengthen ties to others. Many of our traditional values and myths are ignored, if not rejected, by people. For example, our socio-religious tenet that a man is his brother's keeper is no longer shared by many who value instead, "doing their own thing." There is an unwritten compact which says, "I will ignore what you want to do, no matter how bizarre, perverse, or suicidal (as long as you don't hurt me), *if* you won't interfere with what I want to do." Some call it tolerance; others call it indifference. A film called *The Detached Americans* shows 38 of us safe in our apartments watching Kitty Genovese being murdered on the street below. None of us intervene; none of us call the police to get help. Our youth increasingly do likewise. A child falls down the steps in his school. No other child stops to ask if she is hurt. Or a child is able to come to school with a cast on his leg if he can use his crutches to climb the stairs. No other child wants to carry his books for him from class to class. So he stays home for an extra week. Or a youth is facially disfigured by a birth injury. A group of adolescents pick on him. He commits suicide. When asked about it, an acquaintance replies, "Well, he did mention suicide last week. I didn't believe him. Besides what could I do about it?" Or a boy trips regularly on acid, slowly destroying himself. His friends don't intervene, seek help, or even feel concerned. "It's his trip," they say, after he is hospitalized. The doubling of the adolescent suicide rate within the past decade and, so my hunch goes, the doubling of it again in the next five years, is symptomatic of the increasing number whose affectional ties with, or concern for, others are quite fragile. One hundred thousand collegians threatened suicide in 1966. About a thousand attempt suicide every month. (Ross, *The New York Times,* April 26, 1969.)

But we are confronted by a paradox. What of those young people who trudged through the New Hampshire snow for McCarthy, those who were buried in the earthen Mississippi dam while seeking justice for others, and those whose hands have reached out to children wherever want and misery exist? Or what of those who worked for the Peace Corps, who as medical students set up free clinics for our poor, and who marched at Selma, Chicago, and Washington? Or of those increasing numbers of young adults who reject the lucrative New York law firms to work for social justice in the ghettos? Fifty percent of the entering freshmen of one Columbia University class said it wanted to teach (Silver 1969). Studies show that the youths of the sixties were more concerned about social and political issues than those of the fifties. There is a sharper sense of justice and a heightened moral consciousness in more students today than formerly. There is probably a larger, though still small, proportion of youth working actively for social change.

I really am puzzled about how to interpret this paradox, primarily because I'm not certain I can rely on the image of youth that the mass media project. The extent and depth of their social commitment is questionable. Of the more than 11,000,000 college students who have been eligible for the Peace Corps, only about 50,000 have participated. Studies done in 1968, shortly after the extensive civil rights activities of the mid-sixties, showed that no more than 2 to 10 percent of the students on *any* college campus had participated in *any* social or protest activity—whether civil rights, Vietnam, or campus issues (Katz and Associates 1968; Peterson 1968). About 10 percent more were involved in selected specific issues. More frequently, the issues that galvanized those students into action were self-serving ones dealing with dress and parietal rules. Reporting in 1969, Gallup found that 28 percent of college students had participated in some kind of demonstration at some time in their lives (*The New York Times,* May 25, 1969). In the turbulent year of 1969, 11.5 percent of college freshmen said they had demonstrated about racial injustice as seniors in high school, 6.5 percent about our military policy, and 23.2 percent for changes in high school administrative policies (*The New York Times,* December 21, 1969). How many of these were the same students is not reported.

Other signs question the depth of this generation's commitment. Tutorial programs mounted in the mid-sixties have not survived in a number of cities, primarily because the young people don't sustain their commitment over a long enough period of time. My own college has a program for course credit in which students live in a black community and work with its elementary school children for a semester. Despite the enthusiasm of former participants, no more than seven students, and occasionally none, have participated in the program in a semester. The March on Washington in 1969 attracted hundreds from our campus. One month later, no more than thirty called on local congressmen or leafletted. And while hundreds of thousands of students participated in the Cambodia uproar, few maintained their commitment in the subsequent primaries.

> By the end of May, it had become clear, Mrs. Schoenbrod said, that both in numbers and accomplishments the volunteers were not living up to expectations (to unseat Congressman Rooney of the 14th Congressional District in New York City). A couple of hundred have shown up...but most of them work a day or two and don't come back. There are only 50 or 60 hard core workers that we can depend on. Originally we had 400 or 500 names of people who had volunteered through the movement, but when we call up, half of them tell us that they're "too busy." . . . Now it looks like the Cambodia crisis is over, and most of them are turning out to be just like their parents (Buckley 1970, p. 34).

Where does this leave us? Obviously, there are diverse patterns evolving that show the futility of generalizing. But I have a hunch. Are we witnessing a growing cleavage between words and actions, between the awareness of evil and the ability and willingness to do something about it? A sympathetic college president has noted the same discrepancy:

> For all the current attention paid to the indignities, repressions, and wrongs inflicted by institutionalized processes, isn't there an appalling absence of concern for one's fellow man as a single man? Isn't there a failure to love him or see him as a human, a failure to care for him? Instead of caring, are we beginning to be careless about people? (Plimpton 1968, p. 5.)

Our society is creating a very dangerous contradiction in its youth. On the one hand, we have developed a generation exquisitely aware of and sensitive to every evil of our world, committed to liberal social values, and eager to find justice and equality for all. On the other hand, we have neither provided our youth with the opportunities to learn the patience and skills to implement that idealism nor worked vigorously ourselves to eliminate the evils they see so clearly. The consequence? Impotence. Few feelings are more devastating to adolescents already uncertain of their own identities and loyalties. To protect themselves, they either become corrosively cynical about the hypocritical "system" that robs them of their power, or they withdraw from it to create their own Woodstock Nation, in either case compounding their alienation.

This contradiction is aggravated by the third principal change that is occurring in their mode of relatedness to others. Increasing numbers of youth do not know how or are unable to develop and maintain organized cooperative group activities for a sustained period of time to achieve a common goal. More of them value neither democratically created group norms and expectations nor group activities (Perloe 1970). Symptomatic of this trend may be the disbandment of the Beatles who became victims of their own "do your own thing" philosophy. I've mentioned the decline in interest in and commitment to cooperative team sports. Increasingly, students want to live in single rooms. Except for their desire to cohabit, they want privacy and freedom to live by themselves without the frustration of accommodation to someone else. Fraternities, which demand cooperative living skills, are losing their appeal. A dean of a graduate school told me that his students fought to get on faculty committees last year. Now they don't attend after the first few sessions when they find how tedious and time-consuming the committee process is. Even those deeply committed to political action, like the leaders of SDS, complain that they can't get their members to work together. One leader at a national SDS conference was quoted as saying,

> The process now is increasing fractionalization and intolerance of other people's views. They're engaged in a mishmash of the worst type of positions. Anyone who has some coherent politics is a threat because the politics they have is extremely manipulative and anti-democratic (*New York Times,* December 29, 1968).

The current espousal of anarchy may be a rationalization for an inability to accommodate one's needs to those of others. The demise of representative student government in the schools and colleges is one sign of this form of alienation. Each person wants his voice to be heard; he doesn't want someone else to represent his unique viewpoint. Hence, the demand for "town meetings," even for several thousands.

I am somewhat bemused by those of the Far Left who idolize Chairman Mao and Castro. These leaders certainly wouldn't tolerate those students' anarchistic interpretations of how society should be organized. A *New York Times'* article of March 31, 1969 on a student conference, titled "Student Unity Crumbles over Tactics," began, "After four days of argument, 450 participants in a student power conference here could agree today on almost nothing except that things were getting worse, more people were more alienated than ever . . . "

A fourth manifestation of the increasing social alienation of youth is the changing quality of their personal relationships with each other.

Because this change is so central to their feelings of belonginglessness, I describe it in detail. A teacher of creative writing at the University of North Carolina was struck by the "stories of isolation and of almost total passivity" of his students. He cited the following story of one of his students to illustrate that "gap of the heart" the graduating senior mentioned.

> . . . a young man uses his lunch hour by going into a waterfront museum to look out across a river through a powerful telescope in which he drops a quarter every five minutes. In another city, six miles away across the river, he finds through his telescope a certain building on the fifth floor of which is a window where an old man stands each day staring back at him, with naked eye, across the six miles.
>
> One day, in swinging the telescope into place, the young man spots on the street below the museum a quite attractive woman entering. When she appears at his side he is uncomfortable and almost speechless. But while she looks at the city through his telescope, he is able to talk to her and to make a date with her for the evening. When she leaves he watches her through the telescope and through the telescope she becomes real.
>
> He goes to his rendezvous avoiding looking at the mannequins in the store windows, walking near the curb to be as far away from them as possible. On the steps of the library he waits for her, and when she appears and tells him he [sic] cannot keep the date because her boy friend may find out, he strikes her. At his touch she becomes a mannequin and he flees, back to his telescope, where at the end he is searching for the old man who will be staring back from the fifth floor window of a building six miles away (Steele 1968).

Is not the story suggesting, among other things, that preoccupation with the generation gap, as wide as it may be for some, is a way to avoid confronting the more critical gap between one young person and another? "Alienation" is, for this generation, a feeling of not being able to make genuine contact with another human being. To reach out and touch another is to risk destruction. The following table underscores the growing isolation of more and more students. It reports the percentage of replies of "true" by a different group of seventeen-year-old males every four years since the late forties to only a few of a number of similar questions. Note the trend.

	Percentage Agreeing in:					
	'48	52	56	60	64	68
When I was a child I didn't care to be a member of a crowd or gang.	33	35	35	38	49	47
I could be happy living all alone in a cabin in the woods or mountains.	23	28	31	38	33	45
My worries seem to disappear when I get into a crowd of lively friends.	71	69	73	68	58	55

What is the consequence of this growing estrangement? Loneliness. All of us have been lonely at times, though some of us much more so than others. But this younger generation is more aware of its isolation and loneliness, for unlike its parents, it does not have to preoccupy itself with long hours of work to survive. Our affluence guarantees the satisfaction of its survival needs. It is freed to be concerned about less pressing issues such as the quality of its relationships with others. Studies of men graduating from Berkeley revealed that 50 percent of them had not had a meaningful relationship with a woman and that 36 percent had formed no such relation with a man; at Stanford, a strong fraternity college, 37 percent and 22 percent respectively answered similarly. About a third of the men and a quarter of the women reported having no dates during the year (Katz and Associates 1968). These figures are not atypical. About 30 percent of several successive graduating senior classes in my own college reported in interviews that what they regretted most about their college experience was that they had not formed any close friendships. Forty percent of a recent entering freshman class, many of them leaders in their schools and busily involved in the lives of others, said they were basically lonely. When I asked William Glasser, the psychiatrist, what problem emerged most saliently from his visits to public schools in Los Angeles, he replied, "Loneliness."

Many young people distrust others. They fear being vulnerable. It isn't that they don't want to love and to be loved. They are afraid to initiate friendships. To be too open is to risk being "shot down," misunderstood, or considered odd.

I got the following note from a fifteen-year-old boy while I was writing this chapter.

> I don't know how to be with people or how to show that I really
> like somebody. I think that once I get past a superficial relationship
> I tend to shy off or away from the person . . . I just get feeling
> very uneasy when the person is around . . . I don't really know
> hardly anything about friendship under the superficial level or
> about love. I feel uncapable of certain kinds of love . . . I want
> to know everything about everybody and have a complete under-
> standing of individuals and humanity as a whole.

After I spoke to some parents one evening, a mother, who had raised
her children in a Latin culture, came up to me with tears in her eyes. She
asked, "What am I to do? My daughter has always had close friends. She's
a freshman at college. I got a letter from her today saying other girls are
calling her a lesbian because she wants to have close friendships with other
girls. What am I to write her?"

As friendly as most Americans are, few of us accept our need to be
affectionate, tender, and in physical contact with each other. Our society
places formidable taboos on emotional relationships, particularly between
members of the same sex. We are a touchless society. One of the powerful
attractions of Esalen and other human growth centers is that they help
people accept their need to touch and be touched. Our fear of being close
to each other has intensified in the last decades. I am intrigued by the
current dancing styles where young people barely touch or even look at
their "partner". A youth, out of fear of being labeled a homosexual, cannot violate the touch barrier with his own sex. The only exceptions our
society permits occur when contact is masked by aggressiveness, as in playful wrestling, mutual hugging in the excitement of winning an athletic con-
test, or drunkenness. To call someone a fag or a queer is one of the more
damning indictments we can make in our culture, similar in force to
"nigger" or "kike." One boy who comforted a friend whose roommate
had just committed suicide, by putting his arm around him, was called a
fairy the next day by another student.

In Turkey, the young men publicly sprawl on each other, hug each
other, and walk hand in hand, arm in arm, without such affection being
thought "sexual" or perverted. American young men visiting Latin and
Arab countries report how much "freer" they've felt emotionally. By
providing few culturally sanctioned ways, particularly for boys, to care
for and comfort another emotionally, we teach our youth that their caring and affectionate needs are not to be trusted. No wonder then that that
fifteen-year-old—and he's not atypical—becomes "uneasy" when he gets
too close to another. No wonder so many youth protect themselves against

their attraction to and need for others by cutting them up or being ero-
sively critical, deprecating, and sadistic. Until recently, girls have been freer
of such taboos in our society. But in visits to girls' schools in the past few
years, I have been struck by the number who are now becoming uptight
about being affectionate with each other. They are not as openly and un-
self-consciously demonstrative as girls used to be in this society. Lesbian-
ism has become a more conscious fear in the past few years.

Our uneasiness about our own tenderness has historically been aggravated by equating affection with sexuality and sensuousness. Psycho-
analytical theory, now widely known, reinforces this equation by claiming
that affection is only masked sexuality. And because we are afraid of our
own sexual feelings for people of both sexes, we repress our affectionate
and caring feelings for each other, particularly for persons of the same sex.
Our obsession with sex in the past decades has compounded our uneasiness about our more tender feelings. Interestingly, there has been a progressive decrease in the number of young men who say they enjoy reading
love stories since the end of World War II (from 55 to 25 percent). There
has been an increase, however, in the proportion who say they dream of
sex and think of women primarily in terms of sex (29 to 43 percent). What
earlier generations may have euphemistically called love, the current more
"sophisticated" one may be frankly calling sex—or their feelings may be
increasingly erotic ones not fused with tenderness.

Could not another sign of our fear and repudiation of our own sexuality be the strong reaction of adults to long hair on boys? Kinsey tells us
that a male's erotic reactions become easily attached to different objects
in the environment. Adult males grew up in days when only girls had long
hair, which has, throughout much of history, been an erotic stimulus to a
man. Cutting off a woman's hair — upon entering a nunnery or a punishment for collaborating with the enemy — "desexes" her. So what happens
when a man encounters a young male with reasonably groomed long hair?
He becomes anxious. The arousal of his erotic feelings threatens his concept of maleness because of our cultural hang-up about sensuous reactions
to other males. So he unconsciously protects his threatened masculinity by
forcing the youth to cut his hair or by attacking him in other ways. Violence between the generations has many hidden roots.

This discussion does not explain why young people have become less
able to form intimate relationships in recent years. We must look to early
adolescence when the alienation I've described is aggravated in our changing society. As Sullivan has described (1953), early adolescence is the time
when intimacy skills become stabilized. In this chum or pal stage, a youth
learns to develop cooperative skills, like organizing and sustaining neigh-

borhood baseball or football games, accommodating one's need to those of another, learning about others and their feelings, including their sexual feelings, and sharing more openly and trustingly their fledgling awarenesses of themselves. Such skills are learned in a playful, exploratory way with members of one's own sex before one must confront the more mysterious sex when erotic impulses become imperious.

One reason that adolescents today have difficulty in "getting along with each other" and forming healthy relationships is that they have assimilated our cultural hang-ups about sexuality and affection too early in their development. Junior high school boys know what it means to be a male in our society and are particularly ruthless about labeling someone else a homo. A young adolescent's, particularly a boy's, sexuality is readily aroused by a diffuse range of stimuli, including members of the same sex. Formerly, such transitory sexual reactions (the so-called homosexual phase of development) were casually and blindly accepted and lived through. Nowadays, many youths become hyperconscious of their own excitability and, fearing that they may be queer, remain aloof from too close relations with others. This trend, combined with reduced opportunities for playing with others and for forming neighborhood gangs that dilute, but also sanction, playful relationships, means that increasing numbers of boys are not drawn into intimate relationships. They don't learn how to trust their affectionate feelings. So fewer may be learning how to care and trust and respond to another's needs. If intimacy skills are to be learned, in our type of society, they need to be learned before the anxieties about sexuality complicate them. When sex begins to command increasing attention, it becomes too risky to learn how to become close to a person of the same sex. A youth can lose his control too readily if his basic social skills are not well stabilized. By confusing affection, loyalty, consideration, and friendship with sexuality and sensuality, an increasing number of young people inhibit all tenderness, thus robbing themselves of the opportunity to learn the difference. As I shall describe in a moment, sexual relations then become the only way left, when older, to learn those intimacy skills never learned earlier. Such is the price we pay for prematurely developed awareness when we live in a society that still rejects part of its own humanness.

Just as we humans are not built to contain our emotions and be cool, so we are not built to be neither touched nor touching. We are not built to be lonely, isolated individualists, despite the philosophy of some youth today who deny their own humanness to boast of being a law unto themselves. To feel rootless, adrift, isolated, and lonely is excruciatingly painful for adolescents. How are they trying to cope with the pain associated with their growing alienation?

As I mentioned when discussing boredom, many pressures influence a youth to act, particularly if he acts in a deviant or illegal way. Certainly, some of the drug activity fulfills the needs of adolescents to belong, to be socially "in." The rapidity with which pot and speed have been accepted into the peer culture is a fascinating phenomenon. How could a small group, easily less than ten percent of the students of a school, give the impression to the remaining students that they could not be socially "in" unless they had smoked pot? Compounding the problem are the unreasonable laws that aggravate the spread of drugs by forcing students to join together in small conspiratorial groups, bound together not only by the ritual associated with sharing the drugs, but also by the fear of a bust. Some young people, for the first time, feel that they belong.

A confrontation also binds students together. Observers of the Paris, Columbia, and Harvard riots noted that they brought students into comradely relationship with each other that was exciting and deeply moving. Speaking of the Columbia fracas, a faculty observer noted,

> An intense communal life emerged, in which students at least enjoyed the shared commitment and purpose that the "normal" functioning of the University denied them. This enjoyment became one of the chief purposes of the uprising, something that could not easily be bargained or negotiated away (Silver 1969).

And an undergraduate at Harvard wrote of its riot in the *Harvard Crimson,*

> What was most euphoric, however, was us and what we were to each other. For those few hours we *were* brothers and sisters . . . You had to realize, whatever your politics and whatever your tactics, that we were very beautiful in University Hall, we were very human, and we were very together.

We might well ask what has happened to a society when young people must fulfill their need to be "very human . . . very together" by participating in violence and destruction that fracture, ironically the few fragile ties that keep the community together.

There is a strong student interest in all forms of sensitivity groups. They help a youth become not only alive to his own feelings, but also open in his relationships with others. One fifteen-year-old boy told me after a six-hour session, "It helped us to open up and be more comfortable with each other. I found out others felt the way I do. Before how could I go up to a guy ['guy' refers, for some, to either a boy or a girl] and say

I liked her? Now I'm not so scared."

This generation is exploring other ways to cope with its loneliness. The life style it wants is crystallized in four words: trust, openness, love, and community. And these four values find their realization in the commune movement. We would be startled by the number of students who daydream about dropping out of school and forming a commune in the Rockies or Southwest. In the commune, so a youth believes, he will be accepted for what he is and is prompted to do. There he will experience the trust, openness, and love of a sharing community. The rock festival at Woodstock, where several hundred thousand youths came together, celebrated with folk rock and drugs their liberation from society. As Simon and Garfunkel said, its significance was that it was their "thing" to which they belonged. At the Chicago Seven trial in 1970, Abbie Hoffman was right. He answered Judge Hoffman's question, "Of what country are you a citizen?" by replying, "Woodstock Nation." Woodstock Nation is that ideal way of life our children want and which they feel they belong to. No matter that they might not even know the full name of the person they slept, smoked grass, or swam in the nude with. No matter that they might never meet again. They belonged together because they both were part of the Movement, the vision of the society in which there is trust, openness, love, and a sharing community. Unfortunately, such communities are notoriously unstable, particularly when no transcendent religious belief, social ideology, or common work preempt the jealousies and hostile feelings that inevitably occur in any group of strongly narcissistic individuals. If Woodstock had lasted more than a week. I doubt that it would have been as beautiful an experience. The anonymity of three days protected many from the intimacy a longer festival would have demanded. Certainly, the subsequent Altamont free festival of the Rolling Stones and 300,000 people was not so beautiful: "four dead, hundreds injured, thousands freaked out and the counter-culture riven to its base" (*The New York Times,* January 3, 1971, Section D, p. 9).

Not many youths will find their way to a commune for part of their life. But most will find their way to some other person. Increasingly, the value of intimacy is eclipsing the traditional American values of achievement, success, security, and status. Our young people encounter a severe dilemma. Many of them have few deep emotional ties to other groups that satisfy their dependency and belongingness needs. The decrease in the extent and intensity of their social ties increases their need for a close one-to-one relationship; it doesn't make much difference with whom. What is important is that one *has* an intimate relationship. The Beatles said it in their classic *Sgt. Pepper's Lonely Hearts Club Band,*

What do I do when my love is away. (Does it worry you to be alone?)
Do you need anybody.
I need somebody to love.
Could it be anybody?
I want somebody to love.

Yet, to commit one's self unreservedly to another is to become vulnerable.
You can be shot down for good, for you have few personal sources of support. A way out of the dilemma is to become involved with another, but
without full commitment. I call it the intimacy game. I ive like a married
couple without the formal contract. When the going gets rough, you can
always split without a hassle. Increasingly, the protective barriers of our
adolescents will become more permeable, but there will be a tighter wall
around their inner cores. It will be harder for them to "fall in love."

What does intimacy mean to this generation? It means more than
just sexual relations or erotic pleasure. Actually, the prior question should
be, what does sexuality mean to this generation? Adults mistake the meaning of the increasing frequency of premarital sexual relations. There is at
least a 25 percent increase in the number of youths who have had premarital relations in the past two decades. The youth culture is rapidly
moving toward the Swedish pattern in which 85 percent will have had
premarital relations and almost 50 percent of the women will be pregnant
at the time of marriage. Mutual sexual exploration is becoming the accepted route for testing whether or not two people can become more intimate,
that is, open and trusting, with each other. No wonder young people in
some sections of the country say that the invitation to go to bed is replacing
the kiss on the second or third date. If sex is good, then let's have another
date, not just for sex, but to discover if we can now love each other. At
least we've gotten our sexual compatibility settled! Sexuality becomes
the way to learn those intimacy skills never learned earlier.

But when the social and moral barriers that have both prevented too
ready indulgence of one's sexual needs and heightened the anticipated
pleasure of sexual release fall, sexuality begins to lose its value and excitement. The sexual activities of this generation, as increasingly free as they
have become within just the past several years, may not be as joyful an
abandonment to sensuousness as *Playboy,* the mass media, and our imaginations make them seem. For many, their sexual activities seem to be compulsive, driven by a need to be close to another to learn how to communicate more openly with each other. Rollo May also has noted that sex is
losing its passion; it, like the indiscriminate use of the word "love," is,
ironically, becoming used in an alienated way (1969). Gagnon, formerly

of the Kinsey Institute for Sexual Research, has noted the same phenomenon, "Sex means less and less to this generation. There's a kind of cooling off of sex as an important organizing tendency in life, part of a generally cool attitude that comes from affluence." Students have been telling me this past year that sex is boring.

The danger of the intimacy game is that when sexuality becomes so commanding in late adolescence, genuine intimacy may not be learned. It can become rationalized sexual license. That almost half of our current teenagers who get married are divorced within two years may be due to many factors, like the difficulty of securing an abortion. But such a divorce rate suggests that intimacy and sexuality are readily confused with each other.

The pursuit after intimacy is taking a new form. The demand for coed dormitories expresses the desire to live more fully with the opposite sex, the logical outcome of which is cohabitation. Within the past two years there has been a remarkable acceptance as well as outburst of cohabitation in some colleges. Even seventeen- and eighteen-year-olds are beginning to play the intimacy game. By the time they are twenty-one they will have lived through a series of cohabitating relationships, each of which may have lasted from several weeks to several months. Already, one college I know of assigns women and men to the same floor of a dormitory, but then lets them redistribute themselves any way they see fit. *The Harrad Experiment,* seemingly so revolutionary and remote but a few years ago, has already arrived. As the drug thrill begins to crest, as it is in our more avant-garde schools and colleges, indiscriminate sexuality in all its forms as well as serial cohabitation may well become the next thrill. Within five years, if not earlier, we'll see the flowering of communal cohabitation in the dormitories. Perhaps by 1980, our youth may be ready to return to a more ascetic way of life for their kicks and begin the cycle all over again.

Drugs, confrontations, communes, and cohabitations deeply trouble many adults — and so they should. But not just because we believe them to be destructive to our children and society. More importantly, we should understand their deeper significance for all of us. Bob Dylan was right when he titled a song, "The Times They Are A-Changing." Could our youth be trying to warn us that the times they live in are not the times we believe them to be? Could they be trying to tell us that they find it increasingly difficult to grow as whole and healthy persons in these times? In seeking to create a life style that heals their inner divisions and reunites them with other persons, they risk, it is true, excess, danger, even destruction. Within their Woodstocks are their Altamonts — a fact those who over-idealize the counter-culture conveniently ignore (Reich 1970). But of one thing we can be certain. Woodstock is a criticism of our society. Our youth are telling us that they feel increasingly lost in a society whose traditions no longer offer the life style and cultural ethos they need in order to become whole persons.

Chapter 3

Meaninglessness

A teacher from California wrote to the editor of the *Saturday Review,*

> Not all the romantic wishful thinking in the world from intellectuals is going to mold this "sensual revolution," or stop this generation from abolishing intellectuality . . . Like Winston Smith in Orwell's *1984,* I can remember, I can read. My students can neither remember nor read, nor do they wish to. Living in a perpetual Disneyland society, with fresh stimuli to twitch eroded nerve endings, they have abolished history—not just the formal chronicling of the past, but the past itself (Cummins 1969).

A twenty-four-year-old graduate student expressed for many students this reaction to Nixon's Cambodia adventure,

> Few of us have faith in any kind of future, and even if we did, the future is so uncertain and ambiguous, how can we commit ourselves to anything? Who knew two weeks ago that the nation would be submerged into its present crisis? What will Super-Reality submerge us into next week? Everything is so fluid and transient, what occupation, what program is worth subscribing to? And what kind of personal response can one make in reality that is appropriate to our involvement in Super-Reality?

The Now generation is here. So each says. Why? What happens to a youth whose sense of time becomes so foreshortened that his and his species' past become irrelevant and his and his children's future improbable? When time is only the imperative of the moment, what meaning do life and death have? What becomes of tradition and myth, mystery and tragedy, faith and hope, meaning and purpose? These questions are too apocalyptic, of course. For this generation does not live just in the Now. It is too hyperconscious of itself to forget its past or to be that uncurious about its own future. Yet, the questions are being asked in one form or another. Students ask, "Why is this relevant? Why is the curriculum so oriented toward the past when we are faced by the terrible problems of the present? What's the purpose of it all, anyway?"

I will examine briefly some sources of the feeling of "imminence" and then in more detail how students are coping with the despair that the threat of a purposeless existence always poses to an overly conscious human being.

Before Hiroshima, man confronted only his own death and that of his loved ones. Now, he must face the possibility, some say the increasing probability, of the death of his species as well. The imminence of the overpopulation and pollution specters only aggravates an agonizing uncertainty about his existence.[1] Uncertainty is the principal cause of anxiety. Adolescents have always been anxious about the loss of self-confidence they experience when they first confront themselves self-consciously. Now, they must also endure the dread that comes from sensing that there may be no future for them. We whose consciousness was nurtured on pre-Hiroshima assumptions and myths don't bear that anxiety as weightily. The reality of the destruction of our species remains but an intellectually remote and very small black cloud to most of us. But the consciousness of our youngsters has been shaped by that cloud during the years of the Cold War, the Cuban crisis, and the Vietnam catastrophe. The terror that such a possibility excites in a youngster was expressed in the Vacuum Man in the Beatles' movie, *Yellow Submarine.* Remember him? He has a long funnel-like snout and compulsively sucks up everything in sight. Seeing his own tail, he sucks that up and himself as well. How do young people find inner certainty and centeredness in a world they expect to suck itself into oblivion? The invasion of Cambodia was a symbol of the Vacuum Man. Any eye-ball to eye-ball international confrontation risks the instantaneous death of the world.

Most adults deny the possibility of such a death. They see it as a possibility, but don't *really* see it. But our youth live in the world we don't see. Youth cannot deny such a possibility as readily, just because they are adolescents. It is characteristic of young people to struggle with their own destructive, sadistic, and impassioned impulses by projecting them onto

[1] Some youth are aware of predictions that unless the problem of nuclear control is solved, the probabilities are that the world will be totally annihilated within fifty years, and that five to twenty years from now, famine and ecological catastrophes may well bring great destruction (Platt 1969).

external reality which then becomes magnified beyond proportion. A person close to his own destructive impulses is predisposed to anticipate a cataclysmic event and then react to that expectation. The agonizingly slow political response to the horror of the catastrophes some of our youth project predisposes them to apocalyptic, violent revolutionary efforts to forestall doom. Given this view of the world, what do concepts like the future, immortality, faith, and hope mean? To plan thirty, ten, or even five years ahead is an empty gesture. The problems are now.

A second source of a sense of imminence is the confusion and disorganization that inevitably accompany the dissolution of formerly stable patterns of living and values. The rate of technological change in our society has been impressive. Think of Sputnik and then the Apollo moon landing twelve years later. The rate of some social and psychological changes has been even more impressive. Think of the drug scene and what has happened to it in less than five years. These changes are so obvious that they don't require documentation. But what is not so obvious is that a principal spur to the sensitization of a person's consciousness is confrontation with the necessity to make decisions for which there are no societally provided guidelines. When there is no longer a cultural consensus about the limits of sexual behavior, the stability of a marriage relation, the sanctity of one's own mind, the right to dissent, or the purpose of the society itself, decisions inevitably become more self-conscious. Energy becomes redirected to the present. A youth doesn't necessarily face each of these decisions, of course. But he does live in a society that struggles from one crisis to the next, as he can vicariously experience every night with the seven o'clock news. Consciousness can become so focused in such times of personal and social disorganization that the past cannot be recalled nor the future anticipated. The person who probably lives most consistently in the Now is the President of the United States. That is the danger of Super-Reality.

A third reason for the emergence of the belief that it is this world we must be concerned with is that man's thought is being rapidly secularized. The effect of Freud has been to make it harder to hide our wishes and fears in "out there" mythical constructions and concepts. Both God and the Devil are being brought back inside the human skin, where it is much more difficult to ignore them. The demythologizing of many of our long-cherished truths is in full swing. More and more youth refuse to accept the truths we know to be truths, even those we *know* from our own expertise to be true! Increasingly, young people view some of our truths as only illusions.

Certainly, fewer students now accept our belief that there is a divine purpose to this universe or that there is a God's will to be discerned and then followed. What do they think of other traditional religious beliefs and practices that shaped our consciousness? Studies since 1914 indicate that there has been a gradual decline in religious orthodoxy for over fifty years (Hoge 1969). Since the late fifties, however, the decline in commitment to traditional religious beliefs among seventeen-year-olds has increased sharply (Heath 1969a). Young people are less inclined to interpret their experience in religious terms. Cause is not interpreted in terms of a "first mover" or God. The Bible and sermons are less useful as sources of revelation and insight. More youths nowadays believe that the church should encourage altruistic activities rather that spiritual worship and a sense of communion with the highest, that mathematics rather than theology will ultimately prove to be more important for mankind, and that a spouse should be chosen for qualities other than his or her spiritual attitudes toward life. Clearly, the traditional religious way of life is no longer a source of meaning for increasing numbers of youth.

Another truth now viewed as an illusion is that we live in a democracy in which there is equality and justice for all. Fifty-eight percent of college students said in 1970 that they see the United States as a highly repressive society, intolerant of dissent. Sixty-seven percent agreed with the President of Yale's statement that it is questionable that a Black Panther could secure a fair trial in any American court (Harris 1970). Nevertheless, there is a fierce commitment to our traditional democratic ideals on the part of many activists. It is the discrepancy between our ideals of liberty, equality, and justice, and the devastating realities of our society that move them to call for a second American Revolution.

A truth on which I was bred, but which is now questioned, is that more and more knowledge is desirable, that disciplined intellect at work in science and technology produces progress and progress is always good. The deepening distrust of the "truth" science produces is seen in the growing criticism and rejection of science itself. I expect declining enrollments in mathematics and the sciences in the next few years due, in part, to the defection of some of our brighter students, who don't want to be identified with what they consider to be an immoral enterprise. Increasingly, the assumption that a scholar should be free to pursue knowledge for its own sake, regardless of where such knowledge may lead, is being rejected as inappropriate for the times in which we live.

There is also the growing repudiation by some of our more intellectually acute activists and others of the assumption that man by means of his own rationality and understanding can guide and control his own irrationality and destructiveness. The value of man's rationality itself is under attack. Increasingly, the belief of the liberals that man by enlightened reason can secure his own salvation is being rejected. There is a deep skepticism among our most well educated youth about the assumption that man will be able to adapt his social institutions to his technology by democratic, peaceful means—in time. The members of the Greenwich Village bomb factory that exploded included a graduate of Swarthmore College, a graduate student of Bryn Mawr College, and a former student of Columbia University. They are the visible tip of the iceberg. Eleven percent of college students identify themselves as members of the far left. Including the radicals, 52 percent of the country's students identify themselves to be left of center (Harris 1970). In a different survey of 275 colleges, only 18.1 percent of the freshmen identified themselves as conservatives or members of the Far Right — a decline of almost five percent since 1969 (Astin 1970). When 23 percent of a national sample of students indicated that it would support the use of violence to induce social change, then one must ask what is happening to our faith in the use of man's rationality as the principal instrument for social betterment. They say their models of violence are our use of violence in Vietnam and police busts. They insist that at least they don't kill people; they only destroy property. They become bewildered, and furious, when we protest their breaking windows, but condone our own murdering of women and children in Vietnam. Is it any wonder that 76 percent of students say we must make basic changes in our system of values to make this a better America (Harris 1970)?

Thought has indeed become more relativistic. Increasingly, our more sensitive youth know there is no absolute principle or certainty to be found. It is the first generation to know there can be no hiding place from uncertainty, that we do live in an absurd world.

What happens, then, to a youth whose thought has become secularized and relativized and who must now live contingently in a confusing and sometimes chaotic society whose future existence is increasingly problematical? Hopelessness and despair. I don't believe that those over thirty can understand the depths of despair that some youth feel these days when they think of their society and its future. We adults continue to live out blindly the destiny for which we were programmed earlier. Our consciousness was formed when God was alive, when our children were our guarantee to immortality, when there was consensual agreement about the value of the Puritan way of life: achieve, work hard, be responsible, save, postpone pleasure now for a greater future reward, like more money, more material goods, more security. We adults do have a program to follow—even though it may not bring us much joy or be very relevant to the emerging world our youngsters perceive. But at least we have a program.

But for our youth? Seventy-eight percent surveyed in 1970 reject our programs. They believe America lacks moral values and is only conformist and materialistic. They feel our country's first priority should be to change its values (Harris 1970).

I asked a healthy and involved senior, "What are you going to do next year?" He said,

> Well, I'm getting married next Saturday and then I'm off to four years of med school. I'm fortunate. I don't have any real financial problems. We'll work them out. But . . . I don't know . . but I wonder what's the purpose of it all. I don't really know why I'm getting married and going to medical school. Life seems so empty, somehow.

He's programmed too, but his program no longer provides meaning for him. Adolescence is the time to question one's purpose in life. In the past, such questions were based on an implicit hope about the future. No longer. For more and more of our youth such questions now grow out of despair.

Just as man is not built to be bored and emotionally constrained, nor built to be lonely and touchless, so he is not built to live without a purpose. Man is a meaning-creating animal who needs both order and purpose to survive psychologically. How are young people trying to find some meaning for their lives? What are the emerging values around which they are forming their identities in a contingent and uncertain world?

The traditional societal roles that served in the past to organize a person's identity are becoming peripheral to the lives of contemporary youth. The roles of homemaker and mother for a woman either leave little for a woman to do or are being devalued by a society that doesn't want the children she nurtures. The work-vocational role for a man is losing its power to attract the commitment of the young. The traditional economic, managerial way of life is scarcely very tempting to many youth for whom IBM and Dow Chemical are symbols of the dehumanization of their society. A student at Whittier College summed up a pervasive attitude this way:

> The things I was told I was supposed to want to do I find boring and mundane. The business world type with his 40-hour-a-week job, the whole middle-class thing—I know someone has to do it, but it doesn't offer any appeal for a satisfactory life (*New York Times,* June 7, 1970, p. 75).

The meaning of "work" is changing, partially in response to the waning of the Puritan tradition. Furthermore, the vocations of the future are

becoming less predictable. Increased specialization provokes decreased
personal fulfillment and increased boredom. Increased bureaucratization
limits individuality.

Many youth are not going to accept the suppression of their individuality or boredom as the price of job stability and security. Nor will they
be held by the traditional values and incentives that make us prisoners of
our jobs. Money, prestige, appearance, and even power are not values they
honor. In a recent national survey of youths between 14 and 25, only 47
percent said making money was a main goal; among college youth 44 percent said that to better mankind was their primary goal (*Philadelphia Inquirer,* September 9, 1970). Studies of college freshmen concluded that
both Christian and Jewish youth no longer valued as highly the "leading
achievement values of former generations," whether they be intellectual,
economic, or political (Hoffman 1970). So they will increasingly shift to
other jobs more readily when bored and restless or drop out of the job
market for varying periods of time. Only 31 percent of college students
thought it good to stick at a job (Harris 1971). A man's identity in the
future will no longer be tied as tightly to his work or achievement.

If achievement through work is not likely to capture their devotion
and provide that centering experience that defines a person's identity, will
some form of religious-philosophical-mystical quest do so? I ignore those
few enamored of astrology, witchcraft, and the Tarot cards. They are playing a rebellious game simply to assert their independence of the rationality
of our scientific age. But the religio-philosophical route, though not that
of the institutionalized church, still appeals to a considerable proportion
of our more sensitive youth. My studies show no consistent decline in the
number of youth who call themselves very religious in comparison to the
declines in their adherence to traditional religious beliefs (Heath 1969*a*).
To find some meaning for their more secular lives, increasing numbers in
colleges have been taking courses in religion within the past five years.
Under the guidance of men like Allan Watts they are searching Zen Buddhism and other Far Eastern religions. How persistent these interests will
be is questionable. As a member of our Religion Department said, "What
will happen when these kids find we don't have the answers either?" And
I would ask, "What happens when they find that Zen, Yoga, and other
meditative ways of life demand severe forms of personal discipline for a
lifetime, not just for the weekend visit of the Maharishi?"

I believe the current religious searching can be described this way.
Contemporary young people devalue spiritual communion, reverence, worship, and revelatory experiences, though not the intellectual understanding
of religious history and ideas. The value placed on maintaining one's con-

trol puts down any form of worship or prayer that requires a youth to submit, become dependent, or bend *his* will. So he separates the safer academic intellectualized pursuit from the experiential. He remains consciously unmoved and detached, but unconsciously hungers to be moved and devoted. The current religious search is more in the service of fulfilling the self than in the pursuit of losing the self—the traditional route to satori, inner peace, and God (Heath 1971*a*).

The center of a youth's identity in the future may well be a deep commitment to self-fulfillment. Self-realization, self-actualization, freedom to be one's self, do your own thing, the appeal of Neill's *Summerhill* and of John Holt's philosophy, the Free School movement, even the integrated school day, Esalen, and the human potential movement are the symbols of this new identity. If you no longer have faith in the "system" out there, its myths and traditions, at least you can have faith in your own potential. (In Chapter Seven I discuss self-actualization as an educational goal.)

To live in the imminent present, to collapse time to this moment, to live above history and outside of eternity is to risk never encountering one's humanity. This is not to say that a person cannot discover much of his own humanness in a weekend encounter group that focuses on his feelings now. But failure to identify with what one has been (one's ancestors, traditions, and homeland) or with what one could be (one's grandchildren, hopes realized, and the Kingdom) must truncate one's perspective, aggravate arrogance and diminish understanding of the potential of the human procession and thereby of one's self.

The risk in psychological terms is that man becomes the supreme narcissist. Or in the words of Janis Ian, the folk-pop-rock singer, "We have no need of a God: each of us is his own." It is a thin line between narcissism and its pride and humanness and its humility.

Two related trends suggest a growing self-centeredness in the young. For example, two decades ago 25 percent, but now 56 percent believe they are important persons; 45 percent then but 66 percent now say they could work great benefit to the world if they were only allowed to do so; 20 percent then but 38 percent now say they know more than experts do. In the words of a reporter, "Increasingly, students at Harvard are displaying an unnerving self-confidence in their own ability to do anything . . ." (*Time,* March 14, 1969, p. 57). Students increasingly distrust the competence of their teachers. The headmaster of a secondary boarding school in Appalachia, while driving me from the airport to his school, said,

> I don't know if I could take another month like this one. . . . It's the students. . . . they seem to be more totalitarian. A group of

them got together and told the teachers they didn't trust them.
They said what right does a teacher have to tell them what to
learn. You can't discuss with them. They won't listen.

Students also wish to shape their own curriculum. A philosophy major
approached a member of the English Department and requested that he
be allowed to make a film for credit. The faculty member agreed, but then
the student replied, "Under two conditions." "Well, that's interesting.
What are they?" asked the surprised faculty member. "First, that I never
have to consult with you during the semester and second, that you not
see the film I produce."

And then there are those students who insist they should be on all
of the committees of the school, including its finance committee, though
they may not know what a capital gain or loss is. These assertions of autonomy provide rare opportunities for us to help them to become maturely autonomous—if we could find ways to keep such self-assertions alive.

The second related trend is an increased emphasis on the aesthetic
or subjective way of life, as revealed in the psychedelic color our youngsters have brought to our rather drab lives, in their folk rock, dress, and
make-up. The traits associated with a commitment to the aesthetic have
been described this way,

> Each single experience is judged from the standpoint of grace,
> symmetry, or fitness. He regards life as a procession of events;
> each single impression is enjoyed for its own sake. He need not
> be a creative artist nor need he be effete . . . In social affairs
> he may be said to be interested in persons, but not in the welfare
> of persons; he tends toward individualism and self-sufficiency.
> Aesthetic people . . . oppose political activity when it makes
> for the repression of individuality (Allport et al. 1960, p. 4).

While perhaps a more formal statement than that of the teacher who talked of the "sensual revolution" about to abolish intellectuality, it does
describe the growing subjectivity of many youngsters. The significance of
the psychedelic or aesthetic emphasis is that the criterion of what is good,
right, or true is no longer what parent, teacher, minister, or tradition defines. Rather, the criterion of good, right, and true is beauty as *I* experience it. If I freak out, have hallucinations, and land in a hospital, but the
trip is beautiful, then, that was good. My subjective experience becomes
my authority. The authority of competence, tradition, age, or position
is no longer legitimate to me. Any social, political, or academic rule that
makes me uptight, that restricts my freedom or my self-development is

bad and wrong. The ultimate consequence of this aesthetic criterion of truth is, of course, nihilism or anarchy, which one sociologist has perceptively noted,

> . . . has begun to attack the very core of culture and to proclaim a way of life that is really a withdrawal from society, a retreat into the "interior distance," a new gnostic mode which beats against all the historic, psychological taboos of civilization . . . The postmodern sensibility seeks to abolish constraint by substituting experience for art, sensation for judgment. And it wants to impose that sensibility of undifferentiated experience upon all realms of culture (Bell 1966, pp. 308-309).

What keeps the aesthetic way of life from being only narcissistic self-indulgence is its integration with other values. The effect of a liberal education is just that. It liberates a young adult from many of his inhibitions, but such a release does not result in the dissolution of his conscience. Rather, a youth becomes more sensitive to his own humanness. His knowledge and values are maturely integrated and stabilized and provide his freed impulses with more differentiated aesthetic, social, and political outlets.

But when the aesthetic way of life is valued to the exclusion of other values, like social, economic, political, or religious concerns, then aestheticism readily becomes narcissism. Energy is withdrawn from the practical demands of the external world and is focused on an internal world of bodily sensations, vague and fleeting mystical feelings, and abortive preoccupations about being creative. Too frequently the aesthetic experience becomes a substitute for direct emotional and social experiences with others. For some, of course, their dominant aesthetic interest can be integrated with their talents and can lead to a genuine and not just dilettantish creativity. Others identify with rock heroes like the Rolling Stones who may or may not lead them into greater maturity. But too often, such a way of life for a teenager leads only to increased self-sufficiency, a profound passivity in emotional expression, and retreat from the real problems of the world. In an inhibited person, buffered by the cool philosophy and lacking skills to reach others, the aesthetic orientation most likely will lead him further into the "interior distance" and the hallucinatory world of pot and acid.

Although the psychedelic life is romantically attractive, my hunch is that most young people are aware that they have neither the skill nor the discipline to make it the core of their identity. As John Lennon said, "The dream is over." Instead, the impulse of the psychedelic life is being translated into self-actualization. Whether the goal of realizing one's potentials is a fancy rationalization of one's narcissism remains problematical. I expect that a commitment to self-actualization will encourage more and more youth to reject any societal expectation that limits their right to explore any way of life that might fit them. Their search will also free many of us of hang-ups we didn't know we had. They will deliberately explore every deviant and perverse mode of behavior—drugs, sexual activities, communal "families," and so on. It is understandable why Genet's semiautobiographical forays into every kind of evil appeal to many. Educators and psychologists will have to redefine what is deviant and pathological because what will look like traditionally defined pathological symptoms will be under their control to "turn on and off" when they wish.

I have said nothing about other possible organizing values for this generation. The polls indicate that the large majority of students identify themselves as political liberals and are less prejudiced than we adults. But I doubt that either political or social man is going to rise up out of this generation as the modal person. Our society would have to become much more responsive and provide the opportunities for effective and sustained political and social activity than it is ready to do now or in the next few years. If we could find ways to help our youth actualize themselves in genuine political movements or social concerns, then they might escape the seductiveness of their own narcissism and experience the transcendence of commitment to a cause or to others. However, I fear most will remain caught in their own selves—just like most of us over thirty—only more so.

Such is the deepening alienation of youth: boredom, belonginglessness, and meaninglessness. This is where I think we have to begin to educate. But we don't educate on a desert island. We educate in a society. Until we understand how our institutions, particularly schools, contribute to this deepening alienation, we will not know how to change them to create a healthier society for all of us.

Part II

The
Changing Times

Think of the past two decades: television, computers, mass air travel, sex in the movies, man walking on the moon, paper clothes, New York City, transistor radios, air and water pollution, riots in the universities, black sheriffs in the South, nuclear power plants, *Playboy*, seven million students in college, heart transplants, the Pill, and the death of God. And what of the future?: choice of the sex of one's children, even more powerful drugs that affect our moods and consciousness, men digging around on Mars, postponement of aging, automatic grocery stores, direct home connection to central information retrieval centers, genetic manipulation of physical traits, purchase of embyos from babytoriums, mechanized housekeeping systems, and, so it has been predicted, "nonharmful" methods of "overindulging" and even programmed dreams (Bell 1967)! What more could our children possibly want?

The very rapidity of technological and social change threatens our survival   not just physically, but also psychologically. We have not learned how to control and direct such change to make a healthier society. We have learned only recently how our technology destroys our environment and physical health *before* we know such effects have been occurring. Mercury in the fish we eat. DDT in our vegetables. Cigarette-induced cancer of our lungs. We have yet to learn how to determine if our societal changes are destroying our psychological health and spirits *before* such effects have become irreversible. Too few of us concern ourselves with the full range of effects of potential change. For example, few "experts" predicting the economic, technological, and political changes in the year 2000 considered their effects on human beings. Nor did they even question the value of the changes they predicted (Bell 1967). Few educators consider how their innovations affect the healthy growth of their students — so evident among those predicting what the colleges will be like in 1980

(Eurich 1968). Psychologists preoccupied with developing gadgets to accelerate the acquisition of information don't ask what such acceleration may do to the educability and health of children. Administrators obsessed with the economics (and prestige) of large schools ignore even the documented alienating effects such schools have on their students.

Man must learn how to use more effectively his most powerful adaptive skill, thought, to consider the human consequences of his innovations. Thought enables us to understand, imperfectly to be sure, the effects of past change. Thought could help us anticipate, even more imperfectly, the potential consequences of future change. Then we could create new ways to modify the anticipated consequences to be more appropriate to our ideal of what our lives should be — if we have such an ideal.

Part I describes the deepening alienation of increasing numbers of youth. Their estrangement could be a harbinger of what our society is doing to the rest of us, *before* we adults are aware of its effects. It is imperative that we know what causes this alienation. We might then be able to change our institutions, like the schools, to moderate their alienating effects. Chapter Four explores how changes in institutions such as family and church in the past two decades have aggravated the alienation of youth. By concentrating on those institutions that *directly* affect young people, I don't imply that there aren't more profound changes occurring, like increasing technology, urbanization, and secularization that in turn are changing the character of our institutions. The following chapter should be read in the context of historical analyses of religious (Cox 1966) and political-economic trends (Reich 1970). In this book, I can only highlight the principal *psychological* effects of our changing society, which have been insufficiently studied.

Furthermore, if we are to educate our youth now for their future, we must think ahead to the kind of world we will have in ten or fifteen years. Chapter Five identifies those underlying trends now in process likely to shape the world of 1984 and suggests what their effects might be on the healthy growth of youth. I rely on studies where I know of their existence. But since remarkably little objective information is available about, for example, the effects of television on the peer culture, I must often speculate.

Chapter 4

Our Changing Society

A large number of social changes are alienating many young people. To be brief, I must be arbitrary. I don't believe that the Vietnam war, the draft, the Johnson and Nixon administrations, or the pollution, racial, and center city problems are the critical causes. They obviously have affected our expectations and values. For example, the Vietnam war increased feelings of depression and anger in two thirds of a random survey of college students in 1970. It decreased interest in education for one third and accentuated disenchantment with the Republican and Democratic parties in about a third (Gergen and Geigen, *Time,* July 6, 1970). But the deepening alienation is not confined to America. It is occurring in many countries not affected by our social problems or wars.

A few general principles about the institutional determinants of personality development are relevant here (Heath 1968*b*). First, no specific institutional change is likely to produce the same effect in every youth nor is a particular personality effect, like increased loneliness, likely to be the consequence of only one type of change. To attribute the current violence of some youth, for example, to an unresolved and unconscious oedipal hatred by sons of their fathers is too simplistic an explanation (Feur 1969).

Second, a particular societal change is likely to have a greater impact if its effects are similar to those of other types of changes. It is the consistency of the psychological climate generated by many different, but related, changes that creates powerful and enduring effects on us. We must look to those changes in our society whose effects strengthen each other. Take, for instance, the increased size of our consolidated schools. The evidence, which I summarize later, is clear that they have profound alienating effects on many students. We have had large schools in our cities for years. Few people have been particularly disturbed about their unhealthy

43

effects—which, of course, don't mean they didn't have any. But their alienating effects are now more pronounced because of other societal changes that produce similar effects. For example, about twenty percent of our population moves each year to a different location, Mobility produces children who feel more isolated from other children. At the same time, teachers now require students to spend more time on academic work, schools are more competitive, television usurps thousands of hours of time from play, and families are less cohesive. The net effect of these changes is to accentuate the estrangement of children from each other by robbing them of opportunities to form stable personal relationships. To build larger and larger schools exacerbates the impersonalizing trends in our society.

Third, the more of a child's time an institution appropriates, the more opportunity it has to have enduring effects on the child. The implications of this obvious principle have been too often ignored in educational planning. The longer the bus ride to school, the longer the homework assignments, and the more years a youth stays in school, the greater is the opportunity for the school to have a greater impact on the child—and for the family to have a lesser one.

We are in the midst of an historic transition in the power of different societal institutions to affect young people. The family, church, and neighborhood are rapidly losing *their* power to nurture emotional spontaneity, rootedness, cooperative, intimate, and caring attitudes and skills, and stable integrative values. The mass media, peer culture, and the school which increasingly dominate the lives of young people, induce passivity and inhibition, conformity and impersonalization, and conflicting and unstable values.

The Erosion of the Family

There is much debate about the American family and its changing character. Much of the alienation of youth is attributed to the decline of parental authority and the rise of permissiveness. Certainly, few young people believe that they have been brought up too permissively. Eighty-one percent say that they have been brought up neither too strictly nor too permissively (Harris 1971). Unfortunately, there is very little good evidence that documents the widely held opinion that today's families, *in contrast to those of two decades ago,* are more permissive, less cohesive, more mother-dominated, and less central to the development of children. They may well be. Where there is so much agreement, there may be fact. There is just very little good evidence. These trends were also in process in the forties and early fifties. Even then, the typical American family was becoming increasingly permissive "in such diverse areas as oral behavior, toilet accidents, dependency, sex, aggressiveness, and freedom of movement outside the house" (Bronfenbrenner 1958, p. 424). But since the early fifties the rate of change has slowed.

I have some evidence from seventeen-year-old males for each year since the end of World War II who answered questions about their own families and upbringing. The results showed no major changes in permissiveness for more than twenty-five years. For example, there was *no* noticeable increase in the proportion of young people who said they were more independent and free of family rule (about 55 percent). A constant 15 percent claimed that their parents objected to their friends. Only 8 percent a year said that their parents found more fault with them than they should. A constant 60 percent said that their parents often made them obey even when they thought it was unreasonable. There was a slight decline from 65 to 55 percent in the proportion who said that they had quarrels with their parents.

Furthermore, there was no detectable change in the atmosphere or affective tone of familes. A constant 85 percent reported that the members of their family got along quite well with each other and that their home life was as pleasant as that of most. Only about 35 percent said that they occasionally had wished they could leave home. About 5 percent said that there was very little love and companionship in their homes compared to those of their friends. Although a constant 95 percent of the young men said that they loved their mothers and 85 percent their fathers, only 65 percent felt that their relatives were in sympathy with them. Over the years about 50 percent of the men said that the person they admired most as a child and still felt most attached to was a woman. There was a small increase in the number of young men (now over 90 percent) who said that they had never had an older male be strict with them. Many young males lack a strong affectionate father to identify with. Studies on the effects of physically absent fathers indicate that such "orphaned" boys, in particular, do not develop strong needs to achieve, are less able to postpone satisfaction, think less highly of themselves, and are more susceptible to group influence and delinquency (Bronfenbrenner 1968). A present but weak father may well have similar though not as decisive effects.

In interpreting these figures, we must not forget that they come primarily from middle-class white suburban seventeen-year-old males. Unfortunately, no comparable data exist for other groups. Nor do we know about changes in other types of child-rearing practices for the past several decades. But certainly on the basis of these very limited data we could scarcely attribute much of the personality change described in Part I to any *marked change* in the affectional, supportive, authority, and discipline patterns of middle-class families. Young men agree that their families were nonauthoritarian, nonrestrictive, affectively close, and strongly mother-centered.

Despite pronouncements by the mass media and some youth, the generation gap may not be the chasm it has been publicized as being. Most studies indicate that about 80 percent of the students feel close to their parents and believe that their parents understand them most of the time (Adelson 1970; Astin 1970; Birren and Bengston 1969). However, a more recent study of youth suggests about 30 percent have difficulty communicating with their parents (Harris 1971). Again, in contrast to popular folklore, the radical left-wing students are not revolting against their parents. Instead, their basic political and social values are similar to those of their parents—except that they are a little more radical. They, as their parents, are politically liberal and humanitarian, and they value self-actualization more than personal achievement and conventional moral positions (Flacks 1967; Keniston 1967). However, when studies press deeply into generation differences, much larger discrepancies appear between the feelings of today's youth and their parents *about certain critical issues.* Forty percent believe there is a gap between themselves and their parents on some issues. Of these students, more than half disagree with their parents' "way of doing things" (*Philadelphia Inquirer,* September 9, 1970). Seventy-eight percent say America lacks appropriate moral values, but 50 percent of them say their parents would disagree with this statement. Eighty-one percent believe that there is going to be serious conflict between them and adults until the latter try to understand their changing life style, but only 50 percent of the students believe that their parents would agree with them. And on a core Cold War issue, 69 percent of the students don't see Communism as a big threat, but a whopping 71 percent of them believe that their parents think it is. Of course, the limitation of this survey, as of most in this area, is that it measures only what the students believe their parents would say and not what the parents may actually believe.

There is more strain between many kids and their parents than these formal surveys suggest, if I am to believe what students and guidance people have been telling me in most parts of the country in the past few years. The emergence of drugs and liberal sexual attitudes has created considerable strain. I don't know how valid the observations are, but guidance counselors have been mentioning that they have noted a small but increasing number of parents who seem no longer to know what to do about their children and are leaving them alone. An observer of hippies in the East Village of New York, a director of a project on alienated youth, said, "There's a notable absence of conflict with parents, but also a lack of affectionate deep relationships in the home . . . The parents are very permissive and tolerant." Such permissiveness could be interpreted by an affection-starved youngster to be indifference.

But why then is the family becoming a less powerful socializing influence? My hunch is that one of the more significant changes occurring in families is their declining guardedness against other social influences. American middle-class parents are scarcely authoritarian, dogmatic, or punitive. They seem, rather, to be increasingly confused and doubtful about their own values and beliefs and about how to raise their children. Such parental indecision not only affects the child directly, but makes it possible for other forces in society to have direct effects upon him. Television, for example, brings into the center of the family thousands of hours of "out there" experiences that reflect values frequently opposed to those of parents. Children see more alternative ways of living than we ever did when we were young. They watch how other people fight, kill each other, decide what to buy, live in excessive splendor, make love, disobey their parents, and get what they want. They become aware very early of every adult secret, our perversities and weaknesses, our conflicting ways of life. They see every disaster, relive the assassinations of their heroes, and suffer their funeral marches along Pennsylvania Avenue. Since we adults are less certain about what we believe, our children no longer encounter within the shelter of a guarded home many stable, convincing models.

Another reason the American family is having less influence on its children is that they are increasingly less absorbed in parental or home activities. Increasingly, families do not eat, work, play or worship together. No longer is a baby born, or does a grandparent die, at home. No longer do we have relatives in for Sunday dinner. The advent of television has reduced the amount of time parents read to their children, participate in mutual activities, or exercise direct guidance of their growth. We have no information about the number of hours a week a child was in direct contact with his parents two decades ago and the number he is now. But it probably is less, and probably less than in many other societies. American families are apparently not as child-centered as we have believed (Bronfenbrenner 1970).

The family's greater openness to contradictory influences, its increased confusion and bewilderment about its own values, its lack of clarity about how to raise children, and its decreased amount of time spent with its children in mutual activities increasingly make it a less powerful determinant of maturing. What might the effects of these changes be? Have our youth received less experience in learning how to express privately shared feelings like sorrow, anger, affection, and joy? Have they had less opportunity to learn cooperative and intimacy skills? Have they developed less caring attitudes as well as failed to secure a stable core of values? By 1980 when we will have day care centers for all infants, required educational television programs for two-to-five-year-olds, and even smaller families than we have now, what will our youth then be like?

The Declining Influence of the Church

The centrality of the church to the personality and moral growth of young people is also visibly on the wane. Institutional religion is being pushed to the periphery of a young person's experience. Most Sunday schools, educationally bankrupt for decades, serve primarily as baby sitters while parents are in church. How much influence can an institution have on youth in this highly seductive culture when they are under its care for no more than one or two hours a week? Or, increasingly, not under its care at all? To understand how religious practices are dying, note the trend in one college's entering seventeen-year-olds since the late forties (Heath 1969*a*).

Percentage Agreeing in:

	'48	50	52	54	56	58	60	62	64	66	68	70
I go to church almost every week	48	46	51	37	49	38	40	31	26	24	20	20
I pray several times every week	36	42	51	35	54	34	29	24	31	28	19	12

Like the family, the church is being deeply affected by persuasive secular forces that blunt its power to shape a youth's values (Callahan 1966; Cox 1966). Cox has described how the erosion of our beliefs has been due to a change in our mode of thinking. Secular man no longer believes that the natural world, including his own behavior, is determined by other-worldly or mythic forces. Nor is he as concerned about the religious symbols that once provided "personal and cosmic values and explanations" and served to integrate his culture. Traditional religious mysteries that turn man's attention away from pressing problems of his immediate existence are no longer of interest. "Ultimate" questions that are not answerable by pragmatic intelligence no longer preoccupy him. Instead, secular man has become his own determiner and oracle. Aware that "his own point of view is relative and conditioned," (Cox 1966, p. 27) believing that he is the creator of his own myths and values, knowing that "the world has become . . . [his] task and . . . [his] responsibility," (Cox 1966, p. 12) secular man defines the world solely in terms of himself. Whatever meaning his life is to have he must create.

Such dramatic changes in man's stance toward his world result from the rationalization of man's thought processes that science and technology have wrought. The psychoanalytic revolution has also made man aware of his ways of dealing with his anxieties. So rather than create gods to blame or to emulate, or form obsessive metaphysical systems to hide behind, he is now aware that he uses mechanisms like projection and rationalization, denial and repression. He knows that his beliefs may be merely his own unacceptable wishes and fears unconsciously externalized and elaborately disguised (Heath 1969*a*).

It is not only young people who are becoming secularized in the way I described in Chapter Three. Increasingly, the religious, including priests, ministers, and nuns, are beset by doubt and confusion – just as parents are. They too question the value of the institutional church, its potency to minister to the needs of its parishioners, and its readiness to adapt to the type of society that is developing. The defection from the established ministry and religious houses of ministers in many denominations and, most dramatically, members of the orders in the Catholic tradition, has reached crisis proportions within the past five years.

The current decline in the presence of the church within our cities and suburbs is accentuating youths' sense of meaninglessness in two ways. First, the church, though not some of its ministers, is increasingly perceived as floundering morally. It remains caught in the archaic world of the typical prejudiced adult (and studies clearly show that prejudice is more characteristic of church goers than non-church-goers) and so acts hypocritically—as on the black issue. To more youth these days, the church has lost its moral authority and so its soul. And second, ministers themselves are isolated and lonely, suffer their own identity crises, question their own faith, and despair about the effectiveness of their own ministry. The community, and particularly its youth, then lose psychologically the adult model whose life and commitment, rightly or wrongly, form the ideal of meaningful living. The consistency of the atmosphere of value that the family-church-community formerly radiated and from which a youth could not escape exists no longer. As the context of our experience becomes fractured and less coherent, the moral authority of the family is no longer supported by that of the church or vice versa. Both then lose some of their power to offer the integrative and stable values that provide meaning to young lives.

The Death of the Neighborhood Community

Within the past two decades, the American neighborhood has changed dramatically. As of 1970, more people lived in suburbs than in cities and rural towns in this country (*Time,* July 6, 1970). Modern suburbia fractures the nexus between the family, church, and the local neighborhood-community. It breaks up the sense of community in which persons other than just your family or pastor know and care about you as a person. Bronfenbrenner contrasts the life of many young people several decades ago with that of many more today.

> Then, . . . people used to live in neighborhoods. A neighborhood was a place where everybody knew each other. And everybody in the neighborhood knew the children . . . If you walked on the railroad trestle, the phone would ring at your house . . . People on the street would . . . ask why weren't you in church last Sunday? But you also had the run of the neighborhood. In those days you were allowed to play in the park. You could go into any store whether you bought anything or not. They would let you out back where you watched them unpack the cartons . . . (And as researchers have shown) children in a small town get to know well a substantially greater number of adults in different walks of life, and, in contrast to their urban and suburban age-mates, are more likely to be active participants in the adult setting which they enter.
>
> Now, . . . for millions of American children the neighborhood is nothing but row upon row of buildings where 'other people' live . . . In many new urban and suburban developments experiences available to children are extremely limited. To do anything at all . . . you have to travel by car or bus. You don't see people working at their trades . . . Nor can you listen to the gossip at the post office or the park bench. And there are no abandoned houses, no barns, no attics to break into. It's a pretty dull world. It doesn't matter really, for you're not home much anyway. You leave early on the school bus, and it's almost supper time when you get back to the house . . . If you are not with your parents or other adults, with whom do you spend your time? With other kids . . . the passing of the neighborhood school in favor of "educational" advantages made possible by consolidation, homogeneous grouping by age . . . has set the pattern for other activities, so that, from pre-school onward a child's contacts with other children are restricted to those of his own age and social background (1968, p. 8-9).

Although this description of the neighborhood of several decades ago is romanticized to make a point, the experience of belonging to a local

community is certainly less frequent and embracing. The structure of the
contemporary suburb, in particular, and some sectors of our cities dominated by apartment house buildings diminishes the number of personal
relationships we have with others during the day. We travel several miles
to the shopping center that boasts parking space for five thousand cars.
We work outside the neighborhood, travel miles for recreation, and send
our children to a consolidated school in a bus or car. At PTA meetings we
know few of the parents. We don't need our neighbors and they don't need
us—except to borrow that posthole digger or fertilizer spreader. In fact, we
may not even know the names of most of our immediate neighbors. Studies
show that in a highly mobile society like ours, people don't expect to remain long in a community, don't make an effort to know the neighbors,
and don't participate in local affairs. Because our lives are so scattered and
segmented, we know each other primarily in terms of only one role, typically an instrumental or commercial one.

What happens to a youth growing up in such an environment? He
learns that his relations are to be tentative, impersonal, and role-deter-
mined. He knows few people, if any, all the way around, nor is he known
by anyone else all the way around. He encounters few adults who work in
the community or who are deeply identified and involved in communal
affairs. He learns how to be rootless.

The family, church, and local neighborhood have traditionally nurtured intimate face-to-face relationships. The decline in the number of
hours as well as in the number of roles and activities in which a youth
directly interacts with the adults of his immediate environment dilutes
their influence upon him. Insofar as our emotionality and its modes of
expression are shaped by our close relationships, the dilution of such
relationships and the development of impersonal roles encourage the
suppression of emotional expression and attachments. The increased
vulnerability of the family to competing values, the secularization of
traditional religious myths, and the break-up of the self-contained community mean that the socialization of a child is less consistent. He encounters fewer adults whose lives are stable and organized around values
he wants to make his own. The meaning of the generation gap to today's
youth is that they know too few adults whose lives are relevant to the
world they live in. As a consequence, contemporary youngsters are less
stably formed and more open to the influence of other social forces.

The Rising Influence of the Peer Culture

Increasingly, young people have few relationships with any adults,
including their parents. No wonder gaps occur between different age

groups. Our society has become severely age-graded. A ten-year-old spends most of his time with other nine-, ten-, and eleven-year-olds. The exclusion of grandparents and maiden aunts from the home, the smaller families that constrict the age range of one's brothers and sisters, and the strict age-grading in schools have immaturing effects. Such exclusion reduces the number of hours of experience a youth has with persons who are at different stages of maturity in emotional expression, social skills, and values. A youth nowadays can easily forget that he once was an infant and that he will become a grandparent. His sense of time is foreshortened. The decrease in contact with his parents thrusts his own age group dominantly into his consciousness, heightening his narcissistic potential as well as his dependence on others his own age.

I distinguish between the peer group and the peer culture. The peer culture increasingly determines a youth's alienation. I don't thereby devalue the power of the peer group, particularly from puberty on, to socialize a youth. All the research evidence demonstrates its importance. But if growing numbers of young people are loners these days, are less able to initiate and sustain mutually cooperative, playful, and intimate relationships, and are more self-sufficient and narcissistic, then increasingly it will be by means of the mutual ties each has to his peer culture that he will be influenced by others and will develop any sense of belongingness.

What do I mean by *peer culture?* It is that ethos, that mystique, those shifting, frequently amorphous, expectations, "ideas in the air," that define what an adolescent should be like in this society. The culture is transmitted by television, the popular magazines, the underground newspapers and comic books, films, books, psychedelic posters and symbols, folk rock, festivals, electric circuses, and the intricate underground network of Johnny Appleseeds transporting drugs, visiting friends, moving from one commune to another, or just bumming around, sharing a pad in New Haven one week, Boston the next, Buffalo and points west thereafter. So when the Beatles take LSD and smoke pot, live with women outside of marriage, seek out a guru, live chaotically as they did in *A Hard Day's Night,* engage in hedonistic and self- but not service or other-centered activities and proclaim that music and love will chase the Blue Meanies away, then millions of young people around the world take notice, and some do likewise. When Bob Dylan sings, "Everybody must get stoned," insists that the older generation is in the way, and tells us, "Your sons and daughters are no longer under your command," millions listen, and some follow the call. When Mick Jagger thrusts his sexuality at his rock audiences, is prevented from performing because of lewdness, and gets a girl pregnant, the consciousness of millions of young people is titillated, and a few may act like him. As one student told me, "When guys in California start wearing their shirttails out and headbands, you can bet that in two weeks we'll be doing the same thing here in Baltimore."

We have a truly national, homogenized, and conforming culture among our age-segregated youth. Researchers of adolescents have not caught up with this fact. The real educators of the young are increasingly our Dylans. Their persistent attacks on convention, tradition, and the authority of those over thirty, who, as we have seen, no longer have much functional contact with those under thirty anyway, leave a vacuum of moral authority. There is no Communist plot or organized effort to undermine our traditional values. Many different bubbling springs contribute to the swelling river. Gradually, a distinctive ethos, a mood, a youth culture is developing that provides models of behavior and powerful emotional supports for values frequently opposed to those of the adult culture. A youth culture only minimally connected to the adult world may well become increasingly closed to adult influence, but open to manipulation through the mass media by its heroes.

So despite the isolation of increasing numbers of youths from each other, they are united in their common identification with their peer culture. Hence, the powerful hold that the ideal of Woodstock Nation has for some. The culture provides the myths, shapes the expectancies, and creates the self-fulfilling prophecies which give meaning to many of this generation.

The concept of the generation gap, the spread of drugs, and changes in sexual behavior illustrate the power of the peer culture. Its attack on adult authority, compounded by the mass media's exposé-of-the-month of the generation gap, created the idea that there is a gulf of unbridgeable proportions. Some adolescents have started to act as if there were such a gulf. They have magnified typical parent-child disagreements into major misunderstandings that only confirm their expectation that they are not understood. Remember that about 80 percent of middle-class college youth report that their parents are understanding and close to them. But when asked if they thought there was an inevitable and real generation gap in the country, 80 percent answered that there was (Birren and Bengston 1969). All of us, and particularly our youth, are prisoners of our sources of information. We respond to our expectancies about a situation rather than to its realities.

Drugs spread very rapidly throughout the peer culture for many reasons. One was the illusion that everybody else was on drugs. In many schools it took only a small group of proselytizers to create very quickly the impression that drugs were rampant in their school and that a guy was square if he hadn't turned on. If there hadn't been a supporting peer culture ethic that valued turning on or taking a trip, drugs would have spread much less rapidly.

A similar self-fulfilling prophecy about sexual behavior is now at work. "What's wrong with having a girl live with you for several months in order to find out if you groove together? Everyone else is doing it. What's wrong with you? Are you queer?" It takes considerable maturity to resist such persuasion, particularly when the peer culture not only sanctions, but encourages, such behavior.

Prolongation of the entrance of a youth into meaningful and responsible relationships with adults accentuates his sense of alienation from their world. Consequently, the peer culture increasingly provides the emotional support youth need in their frenetic search for novel ways of actualizing themselves, escaping boredom, finding roots, and creating meaning.

The Growing Tyranny of the Mass Media

Movies, records, posters, radio, magazines, paperback books, and television surround us, particularly television. Our seventeen-year-olds grew up with it. Unfortunately, social scientists have not studied the full range of its cumulative effects on those who have been glued to it for thousands of hours. Psychologists have been primarily preoccupied with the effects of its violent and sadistic program content rather than with other more significant, long-term effects.

Just how many hours children look at television is not known with certainty. Studies done in the late fifties suggested that the average five-year-old looked at television about two hours a day or about seven hundred hours a year, and the average twelve- to-fourteen-year-old about three hours a day or about twelve hundred hours a year (Bronfenbrenner 1968). Estimates are that the average seventeen-year-old has seen some seventeen thousand hours of television. A recent Presidential Commission said that there are youngsters who have spent more than half of their waking lives looking at the tube. Let's be very conservative and agree that most seventeen-year-olds have probably watched television for about the same amount of time that they have been in school—twelve thousand hours.

For me, this fact is the most significant and important social statistic of the past two decades. If twelve thousand hours of school probably have some major effects on our children (certainly unsympathetic critics think they do), is it not reasonable to believe that at least as many hours of television must also have some profound effects on them? Certainly, hard-headed advertisers believe that TV has persuasive effects. And politicians do. Why don't we educators think so? Why don't we demand that as much research be done on its effects as is now being done on the effects of many minor educational projects?

How does television affect our children—and us? Some of its more important effects are indirect ones. How does a youth spend his time? Since Sputnik, our schools have demanded more work. Homework assignments have moved down into second grade. Consolidated schools require children to travel an hour or an hour and a half everyday to and from school. And now, in addition, our children have seen twelve thousand hours of television by the time they are seventeen. Where do all those hours come from? They come from learning how to cope actively with boredom, how to play, how to relate to adults and, more importantly, to other children.

Before television, when a child was bored he learned to do something about it. He was spurred to develop some hobbies, to get the gang together for a monopoly or baseball game, to explore his environment, and even to work. Now, when a child is bored he has learned to turn on the television set. When he's older and he's bored, he has learned to turn on his stereo or with pot.

We have little information about the change in children's recreational patterns since the advent of television. Television has been found to reduce the amount of reading that children do. The marginal reader, which includes boys more than girls and the less rather than the more intelligent, spends more hours looking at TV and reads much less (Himmelweit, Oppenhiem, and Vince 1958). Fewer adults now read paperback books, which may support McLuhan's prediction that reading books is declining (*New York Times Book Review*, February 16, 1969, p. 1).

The more enduring indirect effect of television may be that the time spent is taken away from the opportunity to learn how to initiate and sustain a relationship with another person. We educators don't have the remotest idea how many thousands of hours it takes to learn basic human skills like playfulness, empathy, consideration, sympathy, and cooperative accommodation to another's needs to achieve some mutual goal. How many hours does it take to learn to argue without getting angry and walking away? How many hours does it take to learn to negotiate compromises or come to a consensus? How many hours does it take to learn to understand and take another person's point of view? In other words, how many hours of social experience do we need to nurture and stabilize our potential for caring, understanding, and cooperativeness?

Psychologists know that there are certain periods in development when a person is more ready to grow in some ways than others. If he doesn't have the appropriate experiences at that time, he finds it more difficult to learn such skills later. One such critical period for the development of intimacy and peer group skills is early adolescence. But these are the years that television is most frequently watched. Television provides an escape for many adolescents from the frustrations involved in learning how to form enduring attachments to others.

Television has a second immeasurably important effect. It greatly expands a youth's consciousness. He absorbs thousands of hours of miscellaneous information about all kinds of natural and human situations. He becomes much more knowledgeable. He sees different ways of expressing impulses, settling conflicts, relating to others, and dealing with one's parents. He becomes much more psychologically minded. He also acquires words and concepts earlier. To be able to identify and label things about the environment and ourselves increases awareness. But what happens to a youth who acquires words and ideas too far in advance of directly experiencing for himself their meanings and emotional connotations? Does subsequent learning in the classroom become increasingly only a meaningless verbal game? Does the classroom become dull and boring, particularly when most teachers cannot compete very successfully with the expressive, exciting, and entertaining puppets of *Sesame Street* or the intense actors of *Mission Impossible?*

Television may have a third related effect. It can accentuate the discrepancy between a youth's expectations and the possibility of fulfilling them. In twelve thousand hours of television, he accumulates a vast store of images of what the good life is in the world of the upper middle class, which dominates the screen. In that world, for instance, people are seldom shown working for more than a few moments to secure the money to pay for that apartment overlooking San Francisco Bay. He learns to value the product of hard work, but not the process of work itself. And if the images he has formed are not integrated with the discipline of work in his affluent home, what happens in consciousness between his images of the good life and the means to achieve that good life? Wish becomes instantaneous reality. Skill, tedious work, patience, saving, and other prosaic means and values don't become integrated with his expectations. The consequence, of course, is a deeply embedded expectation of being able to have what one wants now, which brings further consequences: a decreased willingness to tolerate frustration, a disdain for the arguments that it takes years to make significant institutional change, the quick despair that comes when a March on Washington does not stop the Vietnam War, and recourse to the non-negotiable demand.

A fourth effect of television is that it teaches a person to receive information passively and impressionistically. Reading is a more active process. When you read, not only must you identify your interests, learn how to select what to read from a wide variety of books, concentrate for extended periods of time, but you must also learn how to weave what you read into an imaginary context. Television provides only limited and stereotyped choices and makes few demands on the viewer's imagination. I fail to understand how these thousands of hours of viewing can possibly stimulate initiative and self-generated effort. Are teachers correct in noting an increasing impoverishment of imagination and decreasing attention span in their children? A kindergarten teacher told me last year,

> I'm returning to teaching after fifteen years. I thought I'd begin
> class the way I always used to. I asked my children to imagine
> a picture and then share it with the group. The children just stared
> at me. You know, they didn't know how to think up a picture?

We desperately need sound studies about how the mode of information transmission affects the development of such skills.

Another important psychological effect that television may create is more complex. To sustain interest, television must induce some tension, usually by introducing novelty. Human experience is not infinite. Nor is there an unlimited number of countries in Africa to build an hour documentary around. Nor does the moon seem worth fifty or more inviting television programs. A space flight soon becomes very tedious. To keep us from becoming jaded, television must compulsively and insatiably depict more and more bizarre, way-out, fantastic, and perverse human experiences. The increase in sadistic and sexual themes in the past few years was psychologically inevitable.

The portrayal of some emotion on the screen triggers in the viewer a corresponding, but less intense feeling, as every pornographer knows and as current studies on the effects of violence in film demonstrate. What happens at this point in the viewing sequence? Those studies that demonstrate that more aggressive children have seen more hours of violence are difficult to interpret. Aggressive children may be attracted to such shows in the first place. Laboratory studies show that an aggression-arousing film induces aggressive behavior (Bandura et al. 1963; Berkowitz 1962; Hicks 1965). But what happens in a home, particularly a reasonably loving middle-class one in which batting one's little sister results in mild punishment from parents? My hunch is that the vast majority of young people find that their impulses to aggress, for example, are intensified by television. However, because of past punishments for expressing violence, they learn to inhibit their feelings. And just what do youths do who are erotically aroused by TV? They suppress their feelings. After thousands of hours of this inhibitory conditioning, they unconsciously have learned how to "cool" their impulses. They begin to react similarly in other emotional situations. It becomes more and more difficult to let one's self be spontaneous and expressive. Some evidence suggests that viewing intense emotional situations on television begins to desensitize a youth to passion, horror, and grief. Eventually, he can watch a Vietcong peasant being killed without anger or remorse. More intense stimulation is needed to "turn one on."

Television, then, may place considerable strain on young people by heightening tension for which society provides fewer acceptable outlets. What happens when such inhibition is accompanied by hours of boring academic work that also requires the suppression of impulse? Eventually that tension is defended against by a profound apathy or is expressed in erratic, irrational, extreme emotional outbursts. No wonder folk-rock festivals or riots make a youth feel alive or that pot makes him feel that life is indeed beautiful. They release youth from the thousands of hours of inhibitory conditioning they have received.

I am not condemning television as *the* culprit for the deepening alienation of young people. It is only one of many complex determinants of personality development. Its potency is, as I said at the beginning of the chapter, affected by the similarity of the effects that other types of nontelevision activities create. The Vietnam War, urban riots, assassinations, and some of our educational practices provide supporting models for expressing hostility. They contribute to a cultural ethos that strengthens the predisposition to use violence, for which TV provides the more obvious models. The purpose of my analysis is to bring into awareness some of the probable psychological effects of television in order to illustrate how the effects of our changing society need to be analyzed for more judicious planning in the future.

The Emerging "System" in our Schools

What has happened in our schools in the past two decades that has accentuated the deepening boredom, the sense of rootlessness, and meaninglessness of our students? Critics have identified many things about our schools that could be improved (Silberman 1970). That dismal litany need not be repeated here. Much of it, however, has ignored the two most important changes that have occurred in our schools in the recent past: the accelerated narrowing of our educational goals and the Conant recommendations that we create large consolidated schools.

Although the trend began piror to 1958, it was Sputnik and the recriminations of critics like Rickover that climaxed the move to abandon the principal goal of every major educational philosopher since Socrates, as well as the one educational goal most appropriate for a democracy. We substituted academic excellence for human excellence. We set as our criteria of excellence verbal and mathematical abstract ability instead of the educability and maturity of a child. The price we have paid for that substitution is deplorably high: the wounded self-esteem and damaged self-confidence of millions of youth who are not gifted in handling abstractions; the increased tensions and competitiveness resulting from severe academic pressures; wide-spread boredom and joylessness; and the increased alienation and reduced educability of large numbers of young people.

The "academicizing" of the school has taken many forms. We have placed a premium on refining too narrow a range of academic, particularly verbal, skills. The university specialists who plan a school where each youth will have his own cubicle with a TV screen, computer terminal, and programmed materials scarcely understand how this generation needs to grow (Paschal 1968). Faculty meetings preoccupied with curricular changes and administrative problems rather than with the climate of the school or the needs of individual children betray our commitment to academic excellence alone. Why have so many schools kowtowed to the battery of tests syndrome and failed to assert their independence of college admission requirements (Tiedeman 1970)? What is signified by the deep resistance of many principals and teachers (and parents too) to the idea that more meaningful growth may occur for some children outside the classroom, even outside the walls of the school? It reflects their belief that becoming educated means mastering the information called for in the lesson plan for the day, the grudging acceptance that school time should be available for athletics and extra-curricular activities, the overvaluation of the high school teacher who teaches history and the undervaluation of the nursery school teacher who educates children, the psychological and prestige separation we make between vocational *training* and academic *learning,* the gasps of shocked surprise and incredulity that a principal would build into his modular schedule time for students to do just "nothing," the terrifyingly rigid curricular plans that make a teacher only an automaton in the service of protecting academic standards, the boast of mathematics teachers they can teach third graders complex algebraic operations, the identification of English and social studies as "major" and art and music as "minor," the adulation of *Sesame Street* because it accelerates the acquisition of numbers and letters, and . . . .

One of the pernicious effects of the obsessive pursuit of academic excellence has been the dogged efforts to accelerate the intellectual development of children. Too many university professors, committed to an academic specialty, but ignorant of a child's need to grow wholly, have intruded themselves into the curriculum of the schools. So now we teach calculus in eleventh grade in some schools even though it is much too abstract—a verbal game as some say—for most students at their stage of maturing and is not necessary—even for future mathematics majors—to take in high school. We revise our physics curriculum (and I don't imply it shouldn't have been revised) to encourage more youth to consider physics as a career. Eight years later there is a decline in the number of students receiving BA's in physics. Both teachers and students complain that the physics curriculum is too abstract and advanced. We justify the inclusion of television in the classroom because children learn information more quickly from it. We ignore its other effects. In fact, our criterion of the success of a program is only a narrowly academic one: does the child learn more information? We pressure our nursery and kindergarten teachers to begin to *teach* their children instead of letting them just play and socialize much of the day, as if playing is not learning. We seek to find ways to accelerate letter and word recognition, whether by means of *Sesame Street* or more directive instruction in our nursery schools (Bereiter and Engelmann 1966). Might not the academic satiation and anti-intellectualism seen in some of the most qualified students nowadays in the colleges be due in part to the too intensive academic work in our schools? Students say they need to grow in other ways too—and they are right.

The development of healthy, educable, and mature children should be our goal. Academic excellence is one component of human excellence, but the test of our academic programs should never be just the amount of information ingested or class results as measured against national norms. The success of *Sesame Street* should not be measured only by the increased rate of letter recognition or advance in a child's reading. It should be judged by its effects on a child's subsequent attention span, his threshold of boredom, his independence of exciting sensory stimulation as the spur to motivation, his image of himself, and the maturity of his values.

Central to the academic improvement of the schools, so university consultants like Conant maintained, was the consolidation of small schools into larger ones. To provide quality comprehensive education that included specialized courses, adequate science and language laboratory facilities, effective guidance programs, better libraries, and more professional teachers and pupil personnel services, many states mandated that small school districts be merged to form larger ones, frequently into ones of ten to fifteen thousand students. To illustrate the absurdity of defining academic quality in terms of the size of the school district and hence the size of the junior and senior high schools, let me cite some examples from my own experience. The Pennsylvania legislature picked four thousand students to be the minimum-sized school district. In the mountainous area of the state some elementary school children now board the school bus at 7:30 in the morning and don't reach home again until 5:30. In fact, one principal told me that the bus-school-bus day is so long for his very young children he has them come to school only every other day so they can rest on the days in between

In the Philadelphia suburbs, school districts of one to two thousand students, known throughout the state for their exceptional quality, are being forced by the courts to break up their high schools of four to six hundred and create high schools of several thousand. The school districts are resisting consolidation in the courts. The court cases in which I have participated have given me the feeling of being a participant in a Gilbert and Sullivan operetta. I would laugh except that the entire process and results have been so tragic. Judges are now the current educational experts, for they must interpret the exceptions to the legislature's mandate, which has been a proscrustean bed in some courts. I testified for a defendant school district fighting a neighboring district that wanted to incorporate it. There was no question that the defendant district offered a high quality program that met the spirit of the legislative act. Yet, the district was forced to prove in court that its consolidation with the appellant district would result in *poorer* quality education for its children than what it was providing. Now, just how do you cite legal proof in a strict constructionist's court that consolidation that has not occurred will definitely result in poorer quality education?

Just as the psychiatric profession almost a decade ago discovered that mental hospitals of several thousand patients induced further regression, dehumanized their patients, and handicapped the treatment process, so is the education profession now awakening to similar conclusions about its large schools. I have met a number of progressive school superintendents who feel saddled by their beautifully tiled buildings. They are trying to break up such large schools into smaller "houses" of four to five hundred students each. The irony we educators face, now that we are stuck with our mammoth structures for sixty more years, is that our communication and computer revolutions will make it possible for even small schools in the future to have access to the same educational materials that only a large school allegedly can provide.

What does a large high school do to students? I know of few other educational topics about which so much research has been done with so few contradictory results. First, there is remarkably little research that supports the Conant thesis that the alleged benefits of a large school make any noticeable contribution to any educational outcome. Neither the school's holding power, the students' scholastic achievement, their subsequent performance in college or satisfaction with their school experience, nor their self-esteem and competence have been improved significantly by any of the reasons for which large schools were proposed (Coleman 1966; Tamminen and Miller 1968). Given the billions spent to consolidate our schools, these findings are devastating. But school boards continue to build large schools under the illusion that they will make a significant difference.

From many visits to schools of all sizes I know that high quality education is not dependent upon a new chemical sink, a beautiful auditorium, or a language laboratory. I have been in powerfully educating schools of fity to seventy students where the classrooms are still heated by wood stoves. Follow-up studies show that their students have no difficulty academically in college, if we still want to use such a traditional criterion.

Second, the evidence from several studies of the past five years suggests that the crucial educational determinants of a student's development are the humanistic climate or atmosphere of the school, the student's sense of involvement in its programs and his identification with the purpose of the faculty (Coleman 1966; Tamminen and Miller 1968; Heath 1968b). In our preoccupation with structure, we have ignored the critical element of atmosphere. An extensive study of the Minnesota public schools found the humanistic atmosphere and breadth of courses available to be the most telling educational predictors of every outcome variable used in the study, whether they were measures of academic achievement, student satisfaction, or self-image (Tamminen and Miller 1968).

Third, increasing evidence reveals an inverse relation between the size of the school and any of the indices of a school's humanistic climate (Barker and Gump 1964; Chickering 1969; Heath 1968b). That is, the larger the school, particularly schools of more than five hundred students, the more impersonal and bureaucratic its atmosphere. No adult in the school knows all of the students, if even just by name. Discipline of such large numbers of students must be regulated impersonally by rules. The source of decisions becomes obscured. Only in small high schools did the statistical analysis demonstrate a humanistic atmosphere (Tamminen and Miller 1968).

Fourth, evidence from studies done in all parts of the country overwhelmingly shows a direct relation between the increase in a school's size and the decrease in student involvement in the activities of the school. The research is clear that as a school gets larger there is no proportionate increase in the number of its extracurricular organizations. Students in large schools consistently participate in fewer activities and hold fewer positions of leadership and responsibility compared to students in smaller schools. The school's football team does not double as the school's size doubles. There is still only one president of the Student Council. Students in large schools encounter their friends in fewer activities and spend fewer hours with them or with the adults in the school, particularly the guidance and administrative personnel (D. D. Heath 1971). There is a direct relation between the size of the school and the frequency of cheating by its students. Interestingly, students in large schools take more specialized and advanced courses and so do not have the same intellectual breadth as do students in smaller schools. Their self-esteem is less broadly based than that of students in small schools. Students in large schools tend to be more competitive and develop a narrower conception of their own worth. The larger the school, the more alienated its youth are likely to be from the school and its activities.

Large schools not only rob students of a sense of belongingness, they also adversely affect teachers. Although I am aware of no studies of the effect of the size of a school upon a teacher's identification with the school and his sense of belongingness, in my work with thousands of teachers in the past few years, no teacher has yet approached me to say he prefers teaching in a large rather than a small school. In fact, increasing numbers of principals and superintendents, as well as teachers, have been commenting negatively about the impersonal factory-like atmosphere of their schools and their wish that they could return to the days of the smaller educational community. The evidence is again clear. Teachers in large schools seldom talk with each other about students, they know few of the same students, and they are more impersonal in their relationships with students (Tyson 1957). Their faculty meetings are concerned primarily with administrative rather than educational policies (Monahan 1965).

What is the effect of a large school on the effectiveness of guidance personnel? Recall one argument for a large school — that it would improve the effectiveness of the guidance departments. The evidence is again very clear that the claim is false (Tamminen and Miller 1968). The Minnesota study of its guidance personnel unequivocally concluded that the most effective counselling was found in the one-man counselor school of four to five hundred students. Why? In the larger schools, the guidance personnel stayed in their offices and did not become involved in the activities of the school. In the one-counselor school, much of the guidance took place in other parts of the school where the counselor saw his students within a fuller context of their lives over a longer period of time. In a large school, a youth is frequently passed from one counselor to the next as he progresses from ninth to twelfth grade.

We have misidentified the crucial determinants of a student's growth. Our pursuit of academic excellence has improved the academic preparation of some students, but has also narrowed their sense of competence, limited their self-esteem, and made increasing numbers of them resistant to subsequent intellectual growth (Heath 1970a). Our large, impersonal, rigid, bureaucratic, and frequently authoritarian schools are, indeed, "systems." They are *the* models of the Establishment against which to develop antisystems and, perhaps, by extension, antisocial attitudes as well. *The large school is the one sysetm young people do know well.*

Obviously, many other characteristics of a school also contribute to the student's increasing estrangement from his own emotions, from other students, and from traditional democratic values: authoritarian attitudes of principals, classroom domination by teachers, the lecture-information format, the constriction of the teacher to a specialty, accelerated courses (particularly in the sciences), and the failure of the schools to deal with value conflicts.

The family, church, and communal neighborhood have been the traditional conservators of values. As transmitters of tradition and accepted "truths," they provided stable expectations and values which, when internalized by the young, gave them a sense of rootedness and historical perspective. But an adolescent peer group is more erratic—even tyrannical. It restlessly experiments with and indulges in new styles and insistently tests its vitality and emerging passions against the existing order and establishment. It is easily influenced by its models, whose opinions and tastes are now instantaneously known by means of the mass media. The school is both a conservator of cultural tradition and a source of innovation and change. The progressive decline of the family, church, and community combined with the rise of a mercurial peer culture and kaleidoscopic mass media will make the school in 1980 society's principal means for guiding with consistency the development of a youth into maturity.

The extent of the discrepancy between expectations and achievements defines success and failure. In the past two decades, our expectations, like those of youth, have increased dramatically, thus heightening the probability of failure. The critics of the schools may be too severe; they sometimes forget that schools are only one, and not a very autonomous, part of a complicated and intrusive society. Looking backwards to the transformation of our schools since 1900, and using *conventional* academic criteria of effectiveness, the decade of the sixties will probably stand out as an unparalleled one of improvement. But looking at the needs of youth today and forward to those of society tomorrow, our schools may indeed verge on failing if they continue to adhere to the traditional notions of education. I have talked of our youth and some of the causes of their alienation. It is now time to turn to their future and that of our society for which schools must educate.

Chapter 5

The Emerging Society of the Eighties

Should we educate for a society that is and is likely to be, or for a society that should be? What if the evolving character of a society is destructive to the health and humanity of increasing numbers of its members, particularly its youth? Do we continue to educate a student to adjust to a society that may be increasingly less hospitable to his spirit and health? Do we mindlessly continue to build monstrously large, impersonal, anonymous, IBM card schools — for supposed economy, efficiency, prestige, and academic excellence — even though such schools will lock our youth into a dehumanizing system for years and years?

The question is no longer academic. It is urgent. Increasingly, our children tell us that our society is "sick," even "insane." They say they cannot grow healthily as whole persons in our schools and affluent suburbs. Is their deepening alienation a warning to all of us that to grow healthily in our society now requires becoming estranged from it? I confess that for too long I reacted to their polemical slogan of "sick society" as just that — only another angry but empty phrase of empty minds. But I reread Orwell's *1984* recently. Their cry became a warning. Why? Because Orwell told me that by ignoring an assumption about human nature I have long held I may have been misinterpreting the cause of their cries.

I assume man does more than just react to his environment. He has a genetic-bio-psychological core that resists excessive environmental manipulation. He needs to be active, to belong, to feel in control of his own destiny; he needs to have purpose. He is not infinitely malleable, manipulable, and controllable (Trilling 1965). He is more than just the product of his particular history of learnings. The significance of Orwell's brilliant analysis of our emerging society was the fact of Winston Smith's abortive rebellion against Big Brother. It isn't important that Big Brother was able to crush Winston. Each of us can squash another's life if we are

66

strong enough. Some teachers do it every day. But it *is* important that Winston asserted *his* will—even though he knew the inescapable consequences. Man does have a backbone and a will. The "sick society" polemic then provokes these questions: Are the societal trends that define the emerging society of 1984 beginning to suppress and distort man, as Winston's humanness was suppressed and eventually destroyed by his? Are the increasingly more violent and suicidal rebellions of our more sensitive youth similar in kind to Winston's struggle to survive humanly? From the perspective of 1984, we may look back to the youthful storms of the sixties with gratitude. Such rebellions may have warned us that our future sanity was being threatened by the societal changes in process.

The emerging society of the 1980's will be more affluent, complex, interdependent, unstable, incoherent, and pragmatically rational than today's. What are the psychological effects of such a society likely to be? How *should* we educate a youth to develop wholly for such a society? How should we change our institutions, like our schools, through which such trends are expressed, in order to moderate their potentially destructive effects?

Toward Increasing Affluence[1]

The hazards of predicting future trends have become very clear in forecasts about our economy and those of other countries. On the one hand, economists predict startling gains in real income for the typical American family in the next decade. Yet, others say that the earth may not have the natural resources to sustain the current standard of living of the United States and other technological societies. Just how much longer can the American economy continue to consume more than 50% of the natural resources used in the world each year—or possibly 75 to 80 percent of such resources by 1980 (Lyle 1967)? Not many years ago population experts predicted that there would be mass starvation in India and Pakistan in the early seventies. President Ayub Khan of Pakistan predicted in 1964, "In ten years' time, human beings will eat human beings in Pakistan." However, the development by the Ford Foundation of new strains of wheat in the past few years may make it possible, according to other experts, for India and Pakistan to become increasingly self-supporting in grain. Social commentators have been predicting for years that automation was displacing labor more quickly than new jobs were being

---

[1] I deal with the effect of affluence in only the most general terms. The issues are obviously much more complex. As is the case for each societal trend I identify, my purpose is to raise and not exhaust some issues that we educators should concern ourselves with.

created (Seligman 1966). Yet, despite a recession, the unemployment rate of highly automated 1971 America was still tolerable economically and, in fact, slightly lower than it was eight to ten years ago when automation was much less developed.[2] So what is an economically naive person to believe?

I assume that our scientific and technological resourcefulness will find ways to maintain the affluence of our society, that automation will continue to alter drastically the pattern of our job market, and that such an economy will provide increasingly more leisure time for many workers, though probably not for the more highly educated and skilled professional groups like educators, doctors, and lawyers.

Our children will know that government will provide for their physical and health needs as long as they live. They will have access to as much education as their talents can handle. Large numbers will study and travel abroad to meet formal educational requirements. To keep them occupied and out of the labor market, we will require them to stay in school longer. As adults, they will work fewer hours than we had to in order to purchase the comforts we now have. Within several decades, the average laborer may work less than a thousand hours and have a thirteen-week vacation a year. Even now, electrical workers in New York City have a contract for a 32-hour work week. One seemingly fanciful estimate is that by 2000, only 30 years away, only 2 percent of the population will need to manage our means of production (Suhm 1964). If this work were equally shared by the labor force, each worker would work 48 minutes a week. Clearly it will become necessary to require some men not to work. All of us will be guaranteed a minimal income whether we work or not. Sabbatical leaves for workers will be introduced to more occupations. Retirement by 50 may be mandatory in some fields within several decades. To have the opportunity to work may become more desirable than to be paid not to work.

The character of work will continue to change. It will demand less physical strength, exertion, and endurance. There may well be so little physical work for youngsters to do in the society of the eighties that few

---

[2] The issue of automation and its future effects on the economy, unemployment rate, patterns of employment, psychology of workers, and standards of living is much too complex to be discussed here. Seligman presents a provocative analysis that predicts radical changes in employment rates and patterns. He also suggests that. "The overall effect of automation . . . appears to be an intensification of the sense of alienation" (1965, p. 22). I interpret his discussion to suggest that automation produces boredom because of the automation of decision-making and the down-grading of the monitoring skills involved; loneliness because of the impersonalization of relationships and reorientation of one's interactions with machines; and meaninglessness because of the felt loss of power by the worker over the work process and of pride in his own skill (pp. 219-223).

will ever know what it means to work hard physically for more than several hours at a time. Women will be freed from most routine housekeeping chores. With the anticipated decrease in the size of families, more women will seek work, particularly in fields with the largest number of openings like nursing, teaching, and office work. The Bureau of Labor Statistics predicts that by 1980 more than half of the employed will be in white collar jobs, primarily because of the vast expansion of service-related jobs since the mid-fifties. The fastest growing occupations will be the professional and technical fields which may include 50 percent more workers by 1980 than in 1968. The number of semiskilled workers will increase by about only 10 percent and farm workers will account for less than 3 percent of our total work force (1970). Obviously, greater demands will be made upon the more intelligent and mature members of society to care for both machines and those increasing numbers who will have little to contribute to a technical and affluent society. The schools may well be training the less educable person to learn how to play and enjoy his free time while educating the more educable to enjoy working long hours serving others or programming and monitoring automated factories and computerized offices.

Some Psychological Consequences of Affluence

When large numbers of people, and not just the rich, have most of their basic wants satisfied, what happens to them? No one knows. Psychologists know little about the consequences for healthy growth of living in an affluent society. For centuries most men have been driven to work by hunger and the fear of insecurity. But in the affluent society of the 80's, youth will no longer feel compelled to work to save for the future. They will certainly not need to protect themselves financially from the insecurity of old age and catastrophic medical problems or save for the future education of their children. Young people know now that they need not deny themselves pleasures for some long term future pleasure, as their emerging hedonism indicates. To save for the future will be a disvalue in a society that depends upon high consumption to maintain its economy.

If enjoyment and happiness are found as much in the anticipation and pursuit of some goal as in its consummation, what happens to the quality of life if both anticipation and the pursuit are foreshortened? As clever people have known for centuries, the value or worth of a pleasure is directly related to how difficult it is to secure. We overvalue what we don't possess. It's always greener on the other side of the fence. Meaning and contentment, even happiness, come from putting a great deal of ourselves into what we want. What is the consequence of too effortless gratification of our desires? My guess is that we begin to devalue our wishes and hence ourselves. If I can purchase my wishes instantaneously, my wishes don't have much value. My possessions become too readily replaceable. Does affluence fill our lives with possessions, but empty them of meaning? Apparently, a twelve-cycle washing machine, a frost-free freezer, a self-cleaning swimming pool, and two air-conditioned cars don't bring much meaning and happiness to many discontented Americans. Furthermore, when we devalue what we work for, don't we also question the worth of work and achievement themselves? Some of our young people, nurtured in the cradle of affluence, question the value of work. The hippies are anti-bank account (in principle), anti-achievement, and anti-sustained work. Increasing numbers of young people do not want to work primarily to generate more profits for *the* company. Some economists predict that maximizing profits may become less important even to the businessman of the future (Crozier 1969).

The principal psychological effect of affluence may be to make our lives less meaningful and accentuate our feelings of emptiness and boredom. The ultimate irony for our affluent society may be its rejection by its beneficiaries as a false road to happiness. Maybe the affluent youths who prefer ragged levis, third-hand jalopies, and bare apartments are harbingers of the coming maturity of our society. Money may become a less potent manipulator of men. Maybe nobler motives will rise to the surface. Law firm recruiters from Wall Street have encountered more young idealists who ask about the social contribution the firm is making to those in the black areas of our cities. Maybe a college education will no longer have to be justified by the extra hundred thousand dollars it allegedly makes possible. Maybe our psychologically bankrupt affluence will force us to forge a more mature and humane vision of what life should be.

If man's survival, health, and educational needs are guaranteed, why will he work in 1980? To answer this we must examine the relation between work and healthy growth. Hard work itself has never driven a person into mental illness, nor has idleness fostered emotional health. Freud said that a mature person can love and work. I would add that a mature person can and *does* love and work. A person must have something to do that ties him to reality and that organizes his time and effort for some long-term purpose. Work can be an act of transcendence through which we externalize our hopes, talents, and knowledge in something outside ourselves. Much work, of course, can be repetitive, routine, and destructive to some people if it doesn't provide them with ways of expressing their individuality. For others, however, even ritualistic, monotonous, "machine-like" work may direct the time and energy that they haven't the skill or maturity to organize otherwise. Through work—whether in rearing a child, writing a poem, or lumbering Maine firs—we become more integrated and stable. One knows a man through his work. For an immature youth tied up in himself, work can be neither joyful nor freeing. He does not have a stable enough identity to be able to lose himself in sustained work. I question the judgment of the cast of The Living Theater who scream at their audience derisively, "Who enjoys work? Give up your work to live."

Man needs work, though not all types of work are fulfilling or maturing. As the affluent society replaces work with nothingness, we risk producing even more bored and ill people. Increasing numbers will object to enforced idleness. Fifty-four percent of labor union members, according to one Gallup poll, opposed a shorter work week even if they got the same income for the reduced hours (Suhm 1964). The danger of affluence is ennui and aimlessness. If there is no work to do in the affluent society, men will have to create work to preserve their sanity.

Part I describes the changing attitudes of middle-class youth toward work and achievement. It may be that the replacement of the value of work by self-actualization as the core organizing value of a youth's identity is the most adaptive way to respond to the dilemmas of the 80's: rapid job obsolescence, probability of several different jobs during one's lifetime, more specialized and technical vocations that are nonintegrative of one's social and emotional needs, and months, if not years, of enforced leisure. Those youth who will enter the business world will increasingly expect more opportunities for continued personal growth—an expectation, incidentally, that more and more business managers are aware of and are trying to meet (Bennis and Slater 1968). But some of our most highly educated, professionally oriented youth may never have the leisure to pursue such a value. Ironically, it may be the increasing numbers of unemployable, unskilled, and less educated persons who will have more leisure time in our society to fulfill a wider range of their needs. Yet, it may be just such persons who need regular jobs to preserve their sanity.

How *should* we educate now so that our youth will be educable for the affluent eighties and nineties? The most powerful forces of our society, including our schools and the mass media, tend to produce passivity and apathy. Our challenge now is how to help a youth learn how to take an assertive attitude toward life, how to initiate and sustain activity over long periods of time. We need to help him develop interests and experience the confidence that comes from having control of his own destiny. Then he will be able to convert the boredom latent in the affluent moments of the 1980's into work that is both freeing and joyful—that is, playful.

Toward Greater Complexity

Our society will be more complex, specialized, professional, and technical in 1980. Research will continue to extend knowledge in existing fields and stimulate the development of new ones. Those of us who recall the thirties and forties scarcely need to be reminded of how much more complex our world is today. Some 85 percent of the drugs now in our drug stores were developed within the past decade. Today's grocery stores demand many more decisions than yesterday's did. Computers, artificial hearts, television, the interstate highway interchanges. Xerox machines, and the Apollo moon vehicle were scarcely more than dreams in the late forties. Compare a travel agent's book of airplane schedules and fares fifteen years ago with today's. The obvious scarcely needs to be detailed. But what are the educational implications of such complexity and specialization?

Certainly, to live and work in the society of the 80's will require more knowledge and training. Formal education will be extended further and further into the adult years, particularly in some specialties. Drugs will be used to facilitate a child's learning and recall. Societal pressures to teach more specialized knowledge earlier in school will become stronger. As knowledge accumulates, education will become more verbal and abstract. More and more students will not face until their late twenties any meaningful and direct test of how they can handle important problems. Learning will be oriented more toward the present. Students will have to know more about contemporary China, Russia, and Latin America, urban problems, human relations, and computer operations. Educators will have to be more selective about what of the past is to be taught. Just as scientists have criteria to judge what of the past is false or less useful, so social scientists and humanists will develop similar criteria to exercise more discrimination about what they teach.

In 1980, our schools will have some of the technology needed to help children learn to adjust to a more demanding and specialized society. A child will work at his own pace on materials different from those of the child next to him. He will have a schedule that takes him to different resource centers of the school throughout the day. He will have his own learning cubicle for his individualized television unit and computer terminal. He may have more hours of sustained contact with audio-visual gadgets than with people. Schools will no longer have the traditional "class" or grade level, for children will be progressing through sequences of material at their own rate. A youth may float from one group to the next and not be held back because of less rapid learners. He will be known all the way around only by the school's computer that programs his day for him, monitors his problem solving step by step, and keeps accurate accounts of his progress for his "teacher" to review at the end of each day. The college student will have his own individual bedroom, study independently of other persons at least 70 percent of the time, and participate only in those formal courses to the extent he needs particular types of information. Such is the students' world of the 1980's predicted by experts in the sixties (Eurich 1968).

Some Psychological Effects of Complexity

To respond to increasing complexity by demanding longer intellectual and technical preparation risks imbalancing a youth's growth. Young people—all of us, in fact—are not so built, yet, to grow only partially, that is, intellectually and informationally. Already our intellectual demands on our young are inducing symptoms of excessive strain. Increasing numbers of students, including many of our more sensitive future leaders, have become turned off, antagonistic toward the "system," less educable for more formal education. My own research results support Jung's assumpttion that a person develops as a whole person, and that too extended development of his critical, rational powers impoverishes his vitality and spontaneity. He writes,

> The predominantly rationalistic European finds much that is human alien to him, and he prides himself on this without realizing that his rationality is won at the expense of his vitality, and that the primitive part of his personality is consequently condemned to a more or less underground existence (Jung 1961, p. 245).

> The more the critical reason dominates, the more impoverished life becomes; but the more of the unconscious, and the more of myth we are capable of making conscious, the more of life we integrate. Overvalued reason has this in common with political absolutism: under its dominion the individual is pauperized (Jung 1961, p. 302).

Few of us can live only in a world of abstract symbols for any extended period of time. To play verbal games, to take only "as if" positions, to argue both the pro and con of an argument with equal force, to know more and more may make scholarly Fausts of young people who also will cry, as Gounod's Faust did as he contemplated suicide, "I see nothing! I know nothing! Nothing! Nothing!"

We know something when we test it in action. At some point we must learn how to choose, act, and test what we think we know. An education whose *only* test is verbal recall and subtle symbolic manipulation eventually becomes an unreal education. Students now say that their education is irrelevant because what they learn is too distant from the time it is to be tested in action. Real education, for some youths, now comes only from the issues they provoke with their administrators and faculties. For them confrontation and conflict are the tests of one's self.

Societal pressures to force earlier and earlier specialization may well violate the natural rhythm of the growth process and create unhealthy resistances to further growth. Increasing numbers of seventeen-year-olds arrive at college with their interests so preformed that they fail to explore the richness and variety of the liberal arts curriculum (Heath 1968*b*). Whether such prematurely differentiated interests help or hinder a person's educability for the complex society we are developing is another one of those crucial questions not being studied. My own experience with youths struggling to free themselves from prematurely formed interests and vocational choices does not make me sympathetic with trends toward early collegiate specialization and vocational commitment—particularly in many natural science students. Sanford wisely comments that,

> . . . students who are relaxed about their future vocation are likely to be open to the genuine educational influence of their college, and thus to be "shaken up," to be made aware of many possibilities, and to take the time they need to settle upon an identity (1968, p. 195-196).

In a simpler society a child knew from personal experience its principal occupations and could early develop some reasonable preferences. Our society has over twenty thousand different and shifting vocations, only a handful of which young people may know reasonably well. It is unrealistic to expect most of them to make mature decisions about their futures until they have more experience. Actually, recent evidence suggests that more of our better students are postponing vocational commitments until several years after college (Katz and Associates 1968).

We educators face a deepening dilemma as we prepare a youth for the complex, specialized world of the 1980's. We need to help him want to get more education, to go more deeply into some limited area, and yet also grow more wholly as a human being. We need to discover how to help him stay vitally alive and educable day in and day out, year in and year out, for fifteen, twenty, and twenty-five years in our schools. He will come alive when he must act responsibly. Our schools must disrupt the relentless, but immaturing march to graduate school to require guided apprenticeships in different adult activities at several points in a student's development so that he can experience concretely the complexity of real problems.

Toward Increased Interdependence

Another inevitable social trend accompanying complexity and specialization that also has profound psychological effects is our increasing dependence upon each other and on our machines. The society of the 80's is not for rugged individualists. The sheer increase in numbers of human beings and the consequent morass of problems we produce for ourselves, as well as the amount of technical knowledge required to solve them, demand even greater interdependence and more restraints on "freedom." Our dependence on others becomes dramatically galling when only a few thousand subway and bus operators or garbage collectors go on strike and disrupt the lives of millions. Recall what happened when the electrical power failure in New York stalled elevators, stopped home freezers, and imprisoned hundreds in subways. In 2000, when our current kindergartners will be in their mid-thirties, our country may have 320 million people, 120 million more than now crowd each other (Kahn and Wiener 1967). Those of us who recall the 1930's may have forgotten that at that time the *total* population of our country was only 120 million. Just think how much carbon dioxide 320 million of us will be exhaling—and reinhaling—then. More people will aggravate already serious air, water, and noise pollution, air and ground transportation, and other urban problems which will require highly organized regional administrative solutions, thereby curtailing our freedom even more.

We educators will become more dependent on each other and on complex educational technology to educate children. By 1980, there will be seven to eight million more five-to-eighteen-year-olds than there were in the mid-sixties. In 1970 there were seven million students in college; in 1980, there may be twelve million (Tickton 1968). Consolidation of students into large-scale educational factories, introduction of team teaching, and the specialization of a teacher's role, even in the elementary school, are but other rational, though not necessarily healthy, ways to take advantage of the efficiency of interdependence.

Some Psychological Effects of Interdependence

But what happens when we become so dependent upon each other for our physical and psychological survival? Certainly, the type of interdependent society we are creating does not develop intimate I-thou relationships, but instead task-oriented, impersonal ones of I-you. The specialization of a task narrows the personality requirements necessary for its successful completion. A youth will have to learn to relate increasingly to others in narrower and narrower roles. A child now plays at home with children he doesn't see in his school. He plays in the band or on the school's football team with other children he never sees at home, store, movie, church, or in class. He is shuffled from one teacher to the next. Within the past decade, the elementary child has become less of a whole person to his teacher. His reading teacher knows his reading; his mathematics teacher knows his arithmetic. But no teacher is responsible for his growth as a person. Some studies of the effect of team teaching suggest that children do not develop strong ties to their team teachers nor have as many friends in the school—predictable consequences of a task-centered rather than a person-centered school (Almy). Increasingly, children may never develop a sense of wholeness, of being wholly knowable and known.

Large institutions are necessary for the dubious benefits of interdependence to be maximized, though a person as a person becomes less important to other members of such institutions. Dependence upon many other persons to accomplish a task increases the potential for becoming frustrated by them. I anticipate that increasing numbers of young people will feel under more tension in their I-you relationships. To preserve the efficiency of their common but interdependent efforts, they will have to learn how to "cool" or suppress their frustrations and other potentially disruptive feelings even more by the 1980's.

Increased interdependence also affects our sense of individuality and control of our lives. Decision-making becomes increasingly a corporate effort, as is true in many large-scale organizations now. It becomes difficult to identify who is accountable for specific decisions. Individual effort loses its prominence and impact, as has been happening, for example, in scientific and technological research. The complexities of such problems are so great that highly organized teams of specialists, heavily dependent upon computer and systems procedures, are necessary to accomplish a project. I marvel at the organization and interdependence required to allocate two billion dollars to five hundred subcontractors in order to produce and then coordinate the million parts for a moon-landing vehicle.

To become educable for the more interdependent world of the 1980's, a young person needs *now* more cooperative-learning and decision-making experiences. He needs the opportunity to learn how to create new social forms. Our problem is how to provide such experiences in a way that does not intensify a youth's anonymity. Each of us needs to be known not as an IBM punch-card number or one of thousands of cogs of a system, but as a person. Rebellious students from Berkeley to Boston have been telling us that now for many years. Somehow we must enhance a student's sense of individuality and worth without reinforcing his latent egocentricism. We need to learn how to listen to a student and to really care for him as a person, and not merely measure him by the amount of information he knows. We need to provide an educational community in which he can be known and respected, but at the same time a community which he feels part of.

Toward More Rapid Change

Almost certainly, the world by the 1980's will be changing more rapidly than the world of the past decade. Many forces will accelerate the rate of change. The predicted doubling of the world's population in the next three decades may lead to catastrophic changes that few of us have the imagination to anticipate. Just our own country's modest population increase will produce severe strains.

New knowledge and technology will also produce profound changes. Over the long run, the federal government's budget for research, not to mention the Research and Development budgets of business or the expectations of research within the universities, will probably expand as the magnitude of our social problems requires increasingly more knowledge. To maintain full employment, our economy requires high rates of obsolescence and ceaseless innovation. It is the "growth" companies that attract the investment community's favor and capital. In its 1969 annual report to its stockholders, RCA handsomely pictured its hundreds of products and then summarily, almost boastingly, said that few of the products would be on the market ten years from now.

The invention of powerful tools for generating even more information accelerates change many times over. What will be the high altitude cameras, the radioactive isotopes, electron microscopes, Skinner boxes, lasers, and IBM 360's between now and the 1980's? Computers immeasurably magnify the amount of information we can secure from our data. In the fifties, I drearily punched a Marchant calculating machine for two years; in the early sixties, an IBM 1620 reanalyzed (and to my chagrin, much more accurately) the same data in less than two hours. How depressed but exhilarated I was when in fifteen more hours I reaped more findings from my data than I could have calculated in my lifetime.

Our knowledge revolution raises deeply troubling questions for educators. How do we keep from being drowned by the amount of information being generated nowadays? How do we prepare a youth for a world in which knowledge is changing so rapidly that the alleged facts of 1970 may no longer be facts, but biases or at least not relevant to the 1980's? How do we help a youth remain educable who believes that what we require him to memorize today will not be useful in 1980? Certainly by then schools will be packaging knowledge more efficiently and will have simplified some of its basic structure, as has been done in our mathematics and science curricula. We will know more about how to organize the process of mastering information itself, as programmed learning materials now seek to do. Hopefully, we will be more careful about using up scarce cerebral synaptic connections when we require memorization. No longer can we blithely assume that a child is able to store infinite amounts of information (Miller 1967). In the 1980's, schools will not seek to make a youth self-sufficient in his information. They will teach him how to attach himself to a computer retrieval system to get the information he needs. His problem will be how to know what questions to ask the computer. Our dilemma is how to get him to want to ask the questions. How do we help a youth become educable, more open toward change, and desirous of questing after the unknown?

Some Psychological Effects of Rapid Change

Although the species *homo sapiens* has been marvelously adaptable for thousands of years, individual members differ markedly in their capacity and desire to make continuous adaptations in their own lifetimes. It takes great maturity to remain educable to continuous change as one becomes older. It will take even greater maturity to be able to adapt to the more rapidly changing world ahead. I am not as apprehensive about our willingness and capacity to adapt to most technological innovations, if only because they may increase our comfort and enrich our opportunities for play and pleasure. I am more concerned about our psychological readiness to modify rigid social prejudices and encrusted political institutions. Growing numbers of persons will feel out of phase with the society of the future. Inevitably, we will witness much more conflict and disturbance. Younger persons are no longer subdued by fears of authority. They will impatiently seek to make our archaic social institutions more appropriate to the world they perceive. Violence may become even more prevalent as a way of reacting to the severe frustrations rapid change will induce.

Just how are we educators now helping youth to respond maturely to rapid change (Heath 1970d)? The growing amount of knowledge necessary to understand and respond to the complex problems emerging in the future may induce informational and intellectual backlashes. Already some of our brighter youths disclaim the necessity to make carefully reasoned analyses of even the presently available information. They extol simplistic ideologies, like law and order, non-negotiability, participatory democracy, imperialism, and revolution, that close them to other possibilities, deny relevant information, and ignore larger contexts and other people's viewpoints. Such thinking avoids the effort and patience necessary to make sense out of confusing patterns of change.

A rapidly changing society produces other effects that, as Bennis and Slater (1968) have so clearly analyzed, create an increasingly temporary society: increased mobility, fewer identifications with stable groups, increased interchangeability of persons for a given occupational role, dilution of stable personal relationships, increased numbers of unstable marriages, and so on. To counter the incipient rootlessness that such effects bring, they suggest that man will have to learn how to form intense and intimate relationships very quickly and then how to leave such relationships without nostalgia and regret.

Man is not built, however, to be so free-floating in his commitments and attachments and still remain healthy and satisfied. Although Winston's job was to re-edit the records of the past to make them consistent with the prescribed interpretation of the present, his memories kept returning to his own past. Fromm is right. Man needs a sense of rootedness, stability, continuity, tradition, and kinship with his past. A human being is never thoroughly contemporary. He is accumulative. He cannot escape, for example, his memories unless he develops amnesia. His memories may block out his vision and limit his ability to change. They may also bring perspective and enrich his life. How barren life would be if our daily moments were not occasionally warmed by nostalgia and sentiment, fused into daydreams of lingering adolescent delights and worries, and mellowed by the wisdom that as sharp and troublesome as today's moment may be there have been sharper and more troublesome moments in our lives and those of others. Too rapid change may cut people off from the power of their own tradition—religious, ethnic, familial, or geographic. A person is much more than what he thinks himself to be. His roots—character, values, modes of thought—go deeply into his history and into his native soil. From such rootedness comes the possibility of wisdom and strength. I think of Jane, a perceptive twenty-year-old, who said of the death of her grandfather,

> Although not observant by Rabbinical standards, he lived a truly Jewish life, and from him more than anyone else, I gained a sense of the tradition of my people. His death reinforced my feelings of kinship with the past—feelings which like many others, I had once dimly felt, but had never acknowledged with proper emphasis.

To be educable for the rapidly changing world of the 1980's, young people need to learn how to learn, to want to learn continuously, to teach themselves the skills they will need, and to want to solve problems without resorting to simplistic solutions out of frustration and impatience. They also need to learn now how to discover a kinship with their own past. They need the skill to recover the wisdom contained in their own traditions. They need to know that they are but one member of a long continuous procession of people who also have had to adapt to ceaseless change.

Toward Greater Incoherence

Although a more complex, specialized, and interdependent society provides greater diversity and choice, it does not necessarily become thereby more unified or integrated. Rapid change breaks up age-old patterns and fractures the ties to tradition that give continuity and integration to life. I have not been able to find the precise word I need to describe a trend toward growing complicatedness, disunity, divisiveness, discontinuity, fragmentation, and confusion. Incoherence seems less pejorative.

Some might question whether there is such a trend. They would claim, and rightly so, that we are developing a more homogenized national and partially international society. Regional, religious, ethnic, social, and economic differences are becoming less salient and are creating fewer and fewer distinctive personality differences. Despite the material diversity our affluence brings us, we are becoming more standardized in our customs. We drive cars on interstate highways through cities that are scarcely distinguishable from each other. Many Americans read the same few national magazines. Most see the same television programs. A traveler to Europe buys his gas at British Shell stations, washes his clothes in Belgium laundromats, and shops in Italian supermarkets. In studying both Italian and Turkish young men, I was struck by the similarity of their aspirations and values to those of American students. Even the Fiji islands are getting Hilton Hotels and Hertz agencies. In Texas recently I saw more hippies than I did cowboys. I have been impressed by how similar our public schools are from one region to the next. Our religious beliefs, spurred by the ecumenical movement, are losing their sharp and distinctive edges. It is becoming easier for members of the same generation to communicate across national borders.

But increasing similarity or sameness does not necessarily bring greater integration or coherence to one's life. The sheer size, complexity, and interdependence of our society complicates rather than simplifies every decision. Establishing any priority will become inordinately more challenging. We will have to digest, organize, and judge more and more information about each problem we confront. Several decades ago, a college student chose from a hundred different courses; now he must choose from a thousand. Few students outside the sciences have any integrated curricular experience. Efforts to insure some core educational experience have withered away. A student's vocational choices have become impressively enriched but more difficult to make. In the forties, a person identified himself as a psychologist. In the sixties, he identified himself as one of twenty different types of psychologists. Increasing complexity and specialization have brought greater complicatedness and fragmentation—not simplicity and coherence.

Our society now provides fewer convincing myths or consensually agreed upon values, coherent styles, or ways of life that can bind together the lives of young people. Our faith that conflict should be resolved by reasoned discussion has been shaken. Our belief in a representative, democratic society is not so vigorous either. Many of us over thirty found our pattern in the Puritan ethic of frugality, orderliness, sobriety, responsibility, hard work, achievement, and competition. When we applied these values to our scientific knowledge we produced a remarkable technological, materialistic, and affluent society. For the reasons I've mentioned earlier, this style of life increasingly does not appeal to young people steeped in our affluence. The Puritan threads that wove our lives together in a simpler age are beginning to unravel. So although a homogenized national (and European-Japanese as well) culture is on the verge of appearing, many young people find its historic ethic and way of life nonintegrative for them. Our society in the 80's will be too complex to be comprehended by any simplistic unifying religious, social, political ideology, or faith—unless it be an imposed one.

Some Psychological Effects of Incoherence

An increasingly complex, fragmented, and rapidly changing society risks inducing discontinuities in the growth process. It already is more difficult for young people to develop a meaningfully integrative life. They are experiencing more discontinuities in their growth than we felt at their age. Probably no society has ever approached, or should approach, a smooth and serene cogwheeling of its expectations and values with the readiness of its young to adjust to them. Psychocultural discontinuities have always been with us, but some of them are becoming too exaggerated for the healthy growth of children.

Young people are maturing sexually earlier and earlier. They are also sexually more sophisticated that we were at their age though they may well know less about genuine intimacy. They have been ceaselessly titillated by the mass media. They can purchase John Lennon nude on the cover of a record album or watch intercourse in *I Am Curious (Yellow)* or dozens of other commerical films. But our society and many state laws still sanction only one acceptable form of sexual expression. Only in marriage can a youth secure sexual pleasure without bumping up against some taboo that may induce guilt. Few young people can yet masturbate with enjoyment without some twinge of shame. It is too much to expect a youth who is coming into his adult sexuality earlier and earlier, ceaselessly stimulated during his teens, most sexually alive at eighteen, to postpone acceptable gratification of his sexual desires for six more years until he finishes his education and marries. Of course, young people don't wait. Increasingly, as they now are doing, they will defy a culture that stimulates and inhibits them simultaneously. Some parents already openly sanction premarital sexual liaisons of their children, rationalized as trial marriages. Attitudes toward other forms of sexual expression, including homosexuality, are becoming less suffused by repugnance and rejection. Increasingly, sexuality is being taken out of the realm of the ethical.

Another discontinuity of our society exists between our stereotype of what a man and woman should be and the needs of our emerging society. For example, because we insist that a boy be aggressive and competitive, we do not value those interpersonal attitudes and skills necessary for him to be able to form cooperative, intimate, and enduring personal relationships. But our more interdependent society will not need physical strength, aggressiveness, and competitiveness. To respond healthily to the loneliness a rapidly changing society produces, boys need to learn how to become more sensitive, open, and trusting of others. Our concept of a male also insists that he be a "success," particularly financially. His wealth is the key to power and power is a male virtue. But in a more affluent society, such driving achievement and symbols of power may become grotesque, particularly if such achievement occurs at the expense of living a more humane and fulfilled life. Or to insist that a boy be cool, squelch his feelings, and not cry or express tenderness or affection is to rob him of feeling alive in an increasingly detached and dehumanized world whose complexity and rationalism overvalue his intellectual control at the expense of his potential vitality. Our traditional concept of masculinity is destructive of today's males and psychologically dysfunctional for the world of 1980 (Heath 1970*b*).

A more insidious discontinuity is the intellectual prematuring of young people beyond their ability to integrate their knowledge into their emotional and social experiences. The mass media revolution of the past decade and our cultural expectations have forced them to learn more information earlier and earlier in the absence of much practical experience at all. Our society will continue to accelerate such early intellectual development as it finds ways to educate economically even one- and two-year-olds. The government may move to regulate television content more stringently by the 1980's, in response to growing public concern about its effects on youth. If so, it may not just be proscribing but also prescribing certain "educational" TV experiences for prenursery school children to prepare them for the increased demands of the schools. But such mental prematuring may already be developing at the expense of learning how to form enduring and affectionate friendships, to cooperate, communicate, and share emotionally with others as well as initiate one's own play. As young people themselves now say, they feel unable to integrate their emotions with their intellectual awareness. Some have skipped much of their childhood; more most of their adolescence. This discontinuity may well become even more pronounced by the 1980's.

Other discontinuities, like the so-called generation gap or the discrepancy between their expectations and skills, I have discussed earlier. One, however, may prove to be particularly troublesome. That is the discrepancy between society's growing need for people who can fit themselves into large bureaucratic organizations and the increasing resistance of young people to do just that. I have suggested that the black flag of anarchy, the slogan of "doing one's own thing," the condemnation of the "system," and the espousal of revolution are in part rationalizations for an inability to cooperate, to work closely with other persons, and to accommodate one's needs to organized group efforts. If this hunch is correct, then many of our brightest potential leaders may become actively subversive of the economic and political complexes of the 80's. For some, the path of subversion may be integrative and maturing. For others, this path may deepen their estrangement from others and themselves and so be immaturing.

As I've suggested earlier, too great discontinuity in the growth process induces resistances to further growth in the already overdeveloped sector of the personality. Psychological imbalances accentuate restlessness and rebelliousness, particularly in adolescents. If society suppresses discontent instead of modifying its expectations, then disenchantment and apathy are more likely to occur. Too-early-educed sexual impulses preoccupy consciousness and lead either to compulsive sexual behavior or, more frequently, larger suppression and replacement by a cool, or listless ennui that interferes with educability. Too exclusive an intellectual diet produces less educable students for more intellectual nourishment.

If a student is to remain educable for a more incoherent world in 1980, we must help him learn how to find his own integrative solutions to the discontinuities of his experiences. No longer will he find preformed cultural patterns and myths that serve as integrative models for him to emulate. He needs to learn more healthy ways to express his feelings than to suppress them under the guise of maintaining his cool. We need to help him enjoy his sensuousness responsibly. We have to be open to his efforts to develop sanctioned modes of sexual expression other than marriage. If Orwell is right, it is passion that will be difficult to keep alive in the complicated, rationalistic, incoherent world of the 80's. If a young person is not to become a disembowelled, desexed, walking head, he must learn how to integrate his feelings with his intellectual talents. We need to find ways to help young people become deeply passionate and committed, but intellectually disciplined. We need to test not just their academic competence, but their human effectiveness. Our task is not just to adjust them to the society of the eighties and nineties. Our task is to give them the skills they will need to modify that world constructively. They are learning few of these things in most classrooms today.

Toward Greater Pragmatic Rationality

Other societal trends are also in process. Certainly, our society of the 1980's will be more urbanized, impersonal, crowded, and probably hedonistic. But there is one trend that I sense has had, and will have, increasingly significant effects on the maturing of our youth, though I have had difficulty clearly identifying it and its likely psychological effects. Trends toward increasing secularization, meritocracy, egalitarianism, and intellectualism seem to be different though related manifestations of a growing pragmatic rationality in our society. By that I refer to the increased reliance on the pragmatic test of rational alternatives rather than upon the judgment of authorities. The ethic and mode of science are becoming *the* criterion of value in our society. Neither tradition, the Pope, the Bible, common sense, nor age, status and wealth are sufficient "authorities" for these days. Pragmatic rationality means taking a "sciencing" attitude toward a problem—that is, looking at the real world in objective, critical, empirical and probabilistic ways. Time and motion studies, simulation models, flow charts, management analyses, and war "games" manifest the increasingly rational temper of our time. Increased technological efficiency is, for example, one practical test of the rationality of an operation.

Pragmatic rationality is also reflected in man's changing attitudes and values about his relation to the world. Chapters Three and Four described how our religious beliefs have become demythologized of gods, fate, and demonic powers. Man increasingly solves his practical problems without reference to some other-wordly, mythic force. His attention is directed to the problems of this world that can be pragmatically dealt with.

In contrast to most other societies, ours is moving rapidly to adopt rationalistic criteria for determining a person's worth. Increasingly, a person's race, color, ancestry, sex, and age are less useful keys to privilege, status, and superiority. They are also less acceptable indices of wisdom, maturity, and authority. In 1984, more people will have to *earn* their value and respect, which will not be as readily ascribed because of some nonrational or nonfunctional attribute like whiteness, age, or wealth. From a larger perspective, the turmoil of society today (the demands of the blacks for justice and equality of opportunity, or the claims by the young that age cannot be equated with wisdom or maturity) reflects the confusion of moving away from such privileged and nonrational indices of worth to more openly meritocratic and rational ones.

For example, I expect that by 1980 we will have demonstrated the irrationality of many stereotypes associated with sexual differences that have been used in the past to justify the suppression of women. Women will no longer be occupationally and economically discriminated against. Husbands will give up their jobs to follow wives who get more attractive job offers. The double standard will be but a memory of those over thirty. Women will also be liberated from some of the limitations their physiology has imposed on them. New contraceptives and drugs that regulate their biological rhythms will further help to obscure the differences that now distinguish men from women. The ready availability of abortion will free women from unwanted constrictions on their freedom.

I anticipate that the sciencing attitude will infiltrate the humanities curricula in various guises. It will be thoroughly entrenched in the social sciences in the seventies and eighties. The magnitude and complexity of the ecological, social, political, and human problems we will have created for ourselves by 1980 will alter our educational priorities. The fifties and sixties belonged to the physical and biological sciences. The late seventies and eighties will "belong" to the social sciences. We may not survive otherwise. We will see radical changes in the way the social sciences are taught. By 1980 few social science courses will be taught at the secondary and college level that do not immerse students in meaningful fieldwork in complex community and national issues. The school's walls will no longer keep students from learning about the community's problems.

Some Psychological Consequences of Greater Pragmatic Rationality

An increasingly rationalistic temper heralds radical changes in all types of authority relationships, as we are now seeing for instance in the Third World, in the Catholic Church, schools, and businesses. No longer are the commands of the priest, the old man, the white man, the politician, the teacher, the boss, or any person for that matter, accepted without critical question and test. No attitude of papal infallability on our part is appropriate for the days ahead. Even those allegedly bureaucratic and authoritarian worlds of the army and business are feeling the effects of this societal trend. A recent article was titled "West Point Cadets Now Say, 'Why, Sir?'" (Fleming 1970). Business leaders speak of the managerial revolution,

> We are passing from the time when it was expected that the few would direct the actions and efforts of the many to a time when men demand to make decisions for themselves, to determine according to their own perceptions what is good or not good for them (Management Newsletter, 1968, p. 110).

The pragmatically rationalistic attitude will be applied to all areas of life. And where it is less applicable, say with respect to matters of taste style, and values, the young will reject the authoritative standards of some "expert" as only his opinion and bias. The dissolution of the legitimacy and hence power of authority and tradition threatens the annihilation of historically evolved aesthetic standards and communal values. It could create moral anarchy. It also enhances the conditions for the emergence of a "strong" man who by force or charisma imposes his vision and order. But the dissolution of authority *also* provides us with the opportunity to create more mature values for ourselves.

The destruction of our traditional masculine shibboleths about women and their emergence into full psychological equality portends some profound changes in the relations between the sexes. For a boy to become a boy and a girl a girl may not be as psychologically important in a society in which one's competence as a person, not his status as a male or female, produces the important consequences in his life. Not only will our concepts of masculinity and femininity become more similar, but our perceptions of each other will change. For men, women will lose much of the mystery that has puzzled and attracted them since women appeared. For women, men may not be as necessary to their psychological and economic survival, as the members of Women's Liberation are now proclaiming. There will be less novelty, surprise, and passion in marital relationships, in which the roles of husband and wife will become increasingly blurred. Increasing similarity and longevity mean more marriages will become boring. It will become the norm for our youth to have several marriages in their lifetime. Already the growing experimentation with serial cohabitations is predisposing them to expect to have only temporary marriages. They will abandon an ideological "til death do us part" attitude and become more pragmatic about their relationships.

But as the off-Broadway plays, like *Dionysius 69*, tell us, or more dramatically, as Orwell was trying to tell us when he described the romantic revolt of Winston Smith, a pragmatic rationalism cannot become the sole criterion of value in a human world. Humans are much more than persons who just rationally calculate and test anticipated consequences. Men need to be irrational as well as rational, graceful and charming as well as efficient and impersonal, intuitive and redundant as well as logical and economical. The tribalistic revolt of the hippies, the irrationality of some off-Broadway plays and contemporary art, the regressive experience of drugs, and the appeal of Eastern mysticism express deep resistances to the restraint and order, the impersonality and efficiency of rationality. An increasingly rational society may well provoke more intense irrational outbursts among its members. More than primitive societies it may need its Saturnalia and Roman circuses.

There will be no certainty in the world of the 1980's. As I've suggested earlier, young persons will have to learn to live contingently with uncertainty. No absolute imperatives will be intellectually convincing to them. What will for them be right and wrong will depend upon their emotional reactions to the personal relationships they have at the moment. Yet, young people will not be satisfied with relativistic and contingent beliefs. Their greatest unfulfilled need may well be their hunger for some integrative purpose and meaning, some ordained law or way of life that will order their days and bring peace out of stridency. Only a few youths seeking to find some belief that "explains" their existence will find such an explanation. Fewer will ever "achieve" a stable identity in the future. Instead, they will have to learn to live provisionally. They will live through a series of partial identities as they continue to search, but futilely, for some absolutes that give meaning to their lives.

Those who make self-actualization the regulating principle of their lives may be able to create a stable identity. But they risk regressing into narcissism or illness unless self-actualization becomes integrated with some transcendent cause. Many of our pragmatic and rationalistic youth may be unable to make that kind of commitment. Most humans need the certainty that faith brings. But we live in a society that increasingly rejects faith in things unseen and untested. So I expect either an enduring and aggravated sense of insecurity and restlessness or, paradoxically, temporary impulsive flights into religious fads (for example, astrology, witchcraft, alchemy, ESP, and voodoo) or submission to a charismatic leader, maybe even Orwell's Big Brother, who promises salvation.

How do we prepare students to deal with an increasingly rationalistic society? We need educational forms that encourage the expression and integration of impulse, feeling, fantasy, and rational thought with adaptive action. Our humanities courses must become more involving and action-oriented. Too many of our humanists are much too stuffy. Because they deal most directly with human values and experience, they could provide moving, reverent witnesses to the full measure of man's being and to his eternal search for new, more satisfying models of living. We must engage our students more directly in such a search by confronting them more self-consciously with their values. We have ignored too long the problem of *how* to help students learn to develop mature values. The world of the 80's will require young people to make provocative choices on their own. They will have to decide not only about the Pill and their sexual practices, but also about other drugs that affect their minds and moods, about organ substitution, the postponement of death, and about thought control, privacy, and Big Brother.

The sciencing process is a powerful model of how to solve problems. We educators have failed to realize its potential for teaching youth *how* to approach complex social and human and not just physical and biological problems. As we help a youth learn how to identify a problem, seek alternative modes of solution, create new integrations, test and then select the more appropriate ones, we also further his maturing. That is, to learn the process of sciencing human and social problems is to learn how to become more mature.

The emerging society of the 1980's will look quite different from that of 1970 in ways we cannot yet foresee. But it is highly probable that it will be more affluent, complex, interdependent, changing, incoherent, and pragmatically rational. Each of these trends runs afoul of man's nature in some way or other. Each has the potential of destroying man's sanity. We must educate our youth now to be more mature so that they will be able to respond healthily to such a society.

Part III

What
Should We
Educate For?

"Heath, you're a cop out. You're justifying what the school is already doing—adjusting its kids to this evil society and destroying them. You say nothing about revolutionizing society, like getting rid of our schools. And what've you done? Throw the same old jargon. Teachers have always said they developed initiative. They say they already teach responsibility and form values. Besides, you've said nothing specific that helps me in my classroom. Words—just words! The cop out of a typical educator."

"I'm not copping out. What do you mean, 'cop out'? You're the cop out. Turn society upside down? What do you mean get rid of the schools? Turn the kids loose, free them? How? Lock the doors of your school for a year? Turn them into Red Guards? Return the schools to the people? Slogans—just slogans to keep you from feeling less guilty about not doing anything except complain."

"Come off it. You know what I mean. You'll never change the system by *your* words. Nobody can loosen up the fossils in my school. The School Board is running so scared it fired Harry last year because he grew a beard and challenged the kids' ideas about Vietnam. 'Unprofessional,' those dinosaurs said."

"OK! Sure they're scared. Who isn't these days? But you don't change people by threatening them—unless you've got power to back it up. Do you want a Kent State in . . . "

"Cut it out. You're shooting the same old crap. What do we do? Sit and fiddle while Rome burns? Power. Sure. I've got power. I've got the power of frustrated, bored kids and a lot of disillusioned young teachers. We know how to shut this school down in an hour."

"What then? Split the faculty even more. Burn up the parents. Have police patrolling the cafeteria the rest of the year? Look—"

89

"Don't 'look' me. We're not getting anywhere. What's your line? Are you or aren't you trying to adjust my kids to the 1980's?"

"Stop being dense. Real power comes from trying to understand — our students, our society, their future. If our understanding is near the truth and we can get it across to those who call the tunes, maybe they'll drop some old prejudices and fears. Who knows what might happen then? Who has the power anyway to make a revolution? Each of us. The thousands who teach. But we need to free ourselves from our hang-ups as teachers . . . "

"There you go again. Another sermon."

"Don't interrupt . . . to be more full human beings ourselves. The only way our kids are going to grow into 1980 as full human beings is to live in a more human environment now. And that includes us and other adults. Stop smirking. I know what you're thinking. 'Get on with it.' OK. What about the cop outs you accuse me of."

Cop Out No. 1:

No, I'm not advocating adjusting students to this society or to that of the 80's. We need to help our students become *healthily maladjusted* to this society and more able to create a healthier one for the 80's. Just because our society is likely to become more complex, interdependent, and so on doesn't mean we can't change its institutional forms. It's through them that underlying trends are revealed. We have to eliminate their potential unhealthy effects on all of us. Do I have a specific vision of that healthier society of the 1980's? Yes and no. I have some ideas about how our schools need to be changed in the next decade to help youngsters grow more healthily. I also have some notions about what it means to be a healthy person, which may be helpful in judging the effects of the specific institutional changes we should make. But I do not have a specific program for a revolutionary society that I plan to unveil in the last chapter.

The critical question is what do I mean by "healthy maladjustment?" To continue to educate only for academic excellence, when our children need to grow in the ways I've suggested, is to educate for potential disaster. The psychological survival of society is at stake. To survive humanly in the future will require greater maturity and educability. The next two chapters explore the meaning of growing healthily and maturely and thereby more humanly.

Cop Out No. 2:

I agree that we educators talk a good game. Every curricular plan begins with imposing objectives: tolerance for different viewpoints, understanding of one's self, responsibility for one's self and others. But reality is different. I spoke recently to a group of teachers about the theme of Part I. After I had discussed boredom and emotional inhibition, the group broke itself into smaller groups to examine if what they do in their classrooms may be emotionally suppressive and boring. Most of the groups talked about details of curriculum but not about their own courses and relations with students. The mind-set of teachers is toward the content of what has always been taught rather than toward the needs of students. Recently I tried to free my own teaching to encourage self-initiative, self-exploration, emotional spontaneity, and other "humanistic" qualities by using a variety of new teaching and experiential procedures. Four weeks into the semester I became anxious. We weren't moving through the course outline very rapidly. The students were not learning as much of the content of psychology as I had planned.

It's true. We talk one way outside of class and act another way in class. One reason is that we don't really understand what does help a youth become more educable. We don't know how to implement high-sounding goals like developing tolerance and responsibility. Most of us act as if it is our lesson plan that is *the* principal cause of any growth our students may show. Many of us believe that it is what we say that is important. But our daily sermons aren't important for most of our students. There are other more powerful determinants of educability (Heath, 1968b). Part IV highlights them.

Cop Out No. 3:

"You've said nothing specific that helps me in my classroom." You're right. But I'm trying to explain *why* certain kinds of radical changes must be made in our schools. We teachers are too easily upset by critics and the trauma of the times. We are easily seduced by the advance men of educational technology and any other passing messiah who promises that his new curricular innovation or textbook will be our salvation. We react in a frenzy, American-style, and pour money into fad, fad, and fad—but the school never seems to change. I'm trying to discover ways of introducing the right changes so that adults will respond judiciously and effectively. Part V describes the types of changes necessary to humanize our schools now to prepare our students for tomorrow. And don't expect miracles. Most have been proposed or tried before. But maybe the mix needs to be altered.

Chapter 6

Healthy
Maladjustment

To be frank, most of us get bored when we must read about educational goals. We've read innumerable books and wrangled in dozens of meetings about "goals." Who does not educate the "whole child?" Who does not believe in educating for human excellence? Who cannot in five minutes cite twenty-five goals he is trying to achieve? And if pushed, who couldn't add eight more to his list? But who of us actually has a carefully thought-out program to implement each goal and then determines if our students have approached our expectations by the end of the year? Our failure to be clear about our goals and then to implement them contribute to the deepening alienation of youth.

What should we be doing in our classrooms? Easy. Creating healthily maladjusted students. What are they? Let me describe my experience with one boy whom I'll call Rusty and his maladjustment and then, using criteria drawn from research on the maturing process, assess how healthy his maladjustment was. Once we are clear about what healthy development is, I will evaluate in the next chapter the maturity of our increasingly alienated youth. The model will help to determine how they need to grow more healthily. Then we will be prepared to talk about the specific goals of education in these times.

One night the telephone woke me at 11:30. An excited freshman, whom I didn't know, insisted that I immediately talk with a confused friend of his who was depressed and ready to "crack up." When I reached my office twenty minutes later, there was Rusty, a towering gangly young man, slouched by my door. He immediately blurted out that he had just run away from a midwestern university. Ever since he was thirteen, when he began to spurt physically ahead of the other boys in his class, everyone, including himself, expected him to be a basketball player. Urged by his friends and his father, he worked night after night at the gym and eventually became the star attraction of the state. The university was on the make for a reputation and offered him a full athletic scholarship and other inducements. Rusty literally was escorted to the train by a brass band and his proud father. During his first six weeks at the university, he was rushed by every frat, junior class coeds pursued him, and the basketball coach who dreamed of a team that would bring glory to the university, gave him the royal treatment. But something began to work inside Rusty. He confessed to a friend that he didn't want to play basketball. He wanted to live differently. In fact, he had always wanted to write poetry and live "that life." Rusty became more and more miserable, split between living up to the image of a prospective university hero and fulfilling a growing need to deepen his own inner life.

One night everything became clear. He and his body had been used. It wasn't he, Rusty, who was looked up to. It was his 6'8" body. He'd always sensed that, but this night he really knew it for the first time. He fled east, pursued by his erstwhile friends, his coach, and then his father. Torn apart, tearfully distraught, and confused about what to do, he didn't want to let everyone down. He wanted anonymity and quiet to find his own way. I spoke later to his father who accusingly replied to my plea that he support his son's struggle to assert himself and create a life fit for him, "He's nuts. You're only making him worse. Stop interfering. He's to go back to school and play basketball. He'll be okay there. That's where he belongs." Perhaps, Rusty returned to the university. But what is he now? I don't know. Maybe his revolt gave him the courage to begin quietly and less dramatically to carve out a more integrative and autonomous life that didn't snuff out his growing awareness that he could be, in his words, "much more a person that just a star basketball player and frat man." Only time held the answer to the question, "Was Rusty's flight a symptom of a profound disturbance or did it lead to healthy growth?"

What clues might tell us if Rusty's sudden flight was basically a healthy reaction? Did his experience help him learn how to create a more satisfying way of life that reconciled the expectations of his friends and coach with his private needs to develop aesthetically? What criteria define an optimal adaptation for him? The growth process itself is the only practicable guideline we have. That is, if Rusty's flight and return furthered his maturing, then his flight was a healthy adaptation to a difficult situation. If he returned only to conform to the life of BMOC and suppress his need for more autonomy or only to live out, say, a hippie way of life, and fail to fulfill the responsibility implied in accepting an athletic scholarship (as masterful a riposte as such defiance would be), I doubt that he would have been open to further maturing. Both conformity and defiance expose a person to profound guilt that usually constricts rather than expands life. However, sometimes either, and frequently a *protective* defiance for adolescents, may indeed be temporarily necessary while a person searches behind the scenes, so to speak, for a more integrative way of life.

How does a person grow healthily? He grows in five interrelated ways. He becomes increasingly able to *symbolize* his experience, and more *allocentric* (roughly, other-centered), *integrated, stable,* and *autonomous.* Increasing maturity produces freedom and joy.

Some critics will object immediately that these are just my values, which I am masquerading as a factual description of healthy development. This objection is critical for I will later use these criteria in Part V as the rationale for suggesting change in our schools. In reply, I reject the prevalent view, even among psychologists, that statements about healthy development are only assertions of idiosyncratic or societal values. There is now more research evidence supporting this formulation of the growth process than exists for any alternative comprehensive model of maturing.[1]

Growing Healthily

Learning to Symbolize Experience

Confusion and uncertainty incite action to eliminate the anxiety that accompanies not knowing what to do when faced with a problem. As Dewey graphically portrayed, such action leads to new ideas and an expansion of awareness.

> Abruptly he is pulled up, arrested. Something is going wrong in his activity. From the standpoint of an onlooker, he has met an obstacle which must be overcome before his behavior can be unified into a successful ongoing. From his own standpoint, there is shock, confusion, perturbation, uncertainty. For the moment he doesn't know what hit him, as we say, nor where he is going. But a new impulse

[1] I do not intend to imply that the model is complete or is as sharply described as is desirable. Many issues, both theoretical and methodological, have not yet been resolved. The model is consistent, however, with psychoanalytic ego psychology (Hartmann 1939; 1960), Piaget's conception of growth (1947), Rogers's research on the fully functioning person (1959), Lois Murphy's description of developing children (1962), and studies of the development of students in college (Chickering 1969; Heath 1968b). Finally, the model has been supported by fifteen years of research on mature and immature groups of youth in America, Italy, and Turkey (Heath 1965; 1970e) as well as on adults developing through their twenties (Heath 1971c). Analysis of theoretical issues, like the equation of health and maturing, can be found in *Explorations of Maturity* (1965), Chapters 1 and 14. The relevance of the model to the goals of philosophers of education is discussed in Appendix A, *Growing Up in College,* (1968b).

is stirred which becomes the starting point of an investigation, a looking into things, a trying to see them, to find out what is going on . . . " (1922, p. 181).

As a child matures he learns how to investigate, to look into things, to find out what is going on. In short, he learns how to inhibit his impulse to attack whatever blocks what he wants, to grab the toy away from another child, to burst into tears, to express his tension in restless and erratic behavior. A child becomes less of an "itch" to his teachers as he learns how to pause and substitute images for the action he is tempted to do. He recalls similar experiences, plans different strategies, and anticipates consequences. Action becomes internalized, so to speak. He becomes increasingly able to use symbols — words, numbers, pictures, art — to represent what he might do. A more mature person is a more reflective person. He is more aware of his values, of himself, and of others than is an immature person.

Our first criterion, then, of how healthy was Rusty's subsequent development is whether he was able to reflect about why he impetuously fled the university. Did he grow in understanding his possible fear that he might not be able to live up to the high expectations that everyone had of him? Did he become more conscious of other desires he had that must have been long suppressed by his exclusive attention to basketball? Remember that his flight was triggered by an awareness that there was more to him to be realized than just being a basketball player and frat man.

If students are to become healthy persons, then we educators must help them become skillful in reflecting about themselves and their world. How seriously have we thought about how to nurture the power to reflect? Do we encourage students to try to put into words their inchoate thoughts and feelings? Teachers are not therapists, but they risk producing uneducable students if they don't sensitively and lovingly help a youth develop the ability to understand his strengths and weaknesses when he is ready for such knowledge. I think of Joey, a very restless nonverbal third grader who ceaselessly wandered around the classroom, enjoying what he thought was helping ("bothering" according to his teacher) other children. With me, he sat quietly for an hour, fidgeting only occasionally, as he became engrossed in problems that challenged his analytic and mechanical mind. I said,

"Joey, it's hard to sit quietly for so long, isn't it?"
"Yeah," he grunted with a grin.
"You have trouble sitting for long periods in class?"
"Yeah, I do."

"Do you know you've been sitting here for an hour?"

"No. An hour! I thought it was only half an hour."

"You see, you can do it. Maybe you get restless when you're bored or things are too easy for you."

"Maybe."

His teacher could help Joey become aware of his beginning restlessness by having, for example, a secret understanding with him. She could casually say whenever he became restless, "Joey, how about going over to the tape recorder and telling me a story about what you'd like to be doing?" Doesn't Joey, to become more educable, need to learn to recognize oncoming restlessness, how to verbalize his feelings, how to begin to deal with them imaginatively, and then how to find engaging work to do? How would you have have helped a Joey learn to handle his restlessness? When our students become blocked by a problem and get impatient, give up, or refuse to do their homework, how do we help them learn to explore *why* they are having trouble with fractions or anything else? How many of us teach only the product of what we have learned instead of helping students understand the process we went through? To do otherwise is to rob them of the opportunity and joy of learning *how* to think about their experience.

How do we help students learn to symbolize their own beliefs and values? Do we talk (modestly and without proselytizing) about what we believe and why? Allowing ourselves to be drawn into this form of self-revelation may create just that powerful opening-up experience that adolescents need in order to learn how a mature and respected person has also struggled with his beliefs and values when he was younger.

I recall Joan's question of me. I was working in a seminar with a group of six college students who were living in a black section of Philadelphia and working in its elementary school. "Why are you working here with us?" Taken aback by the suddenness of this question, I impulsively said, "For justice." "Why?" Off we went into *me* and how angry I get when I encounter injustice. Joan may not have learned much of substance from me that night, but she saw me struggle trying to understand why I felt as strongly as I did. We adults tell our young people, "Be honest." "Don't have premarital relations." "Don't smoke pot." But how many of us relive with them what we went through to arrive at what we now pontifically tell them? If we teach reflectively, might not our students learn how to be more reflective as well?

Becoming More Allocentric

As we learn to reflect more deeply about problems and issues, if that reflection is to be adaptive, we must learn how to look at problems, including ourselves, from the vantage point of other people. A mature person entertains and shares a multiplicity of viewpoints and so is able to place his personal views within a larger social context when necessary. Reflection that does not become socialized can limit educability; it may lead to delusions.

So the next clue we have about the maturing process is that a child becomes more allocentric. He grows out of his egocentrism to become more other-centered. Through confronting the views of others and learning how to accommodate to others, a person becomes socialized. He internalizes the language and thought patterns of his culture and eventually learns to communicate clearly and logically. Increasingly able to take the role of another person while he thinks, he learns how to monitor the logicality and meaningfulness of his own thought. Through identification and empathy, he learns sympathy and care, love and devotion. He comes to think of and accept himself as a deeply human person and not as some rare or unique piece of God's—or the Devil's—handiwork. Research has confirmed that mature people are more altruistic, socially responsible, and tolerant (Heath 1965; 1968b).[2]

What about Rusty, whose dilemma was that he had conformed too well to the expectations and values of others? His flight itself tells us that he felt stretched too far by the social role he had been seduced by and yet also wanted to play. Development obviously can go awry and become unhealthy. A person may, for example, become a prisoner of his reflectiveness, like Hamlet. Obsessively caught in his own fantasies or in his need to know all the facts and alternatives before acting, he may never decide and never act. So may a youth become simply a social shell which, when cracked, reveals an inner hollowness and despair. Although Rusty clearly overconformed and needed to revolt, if he is to mature he will have to become a genuinely social, though not necessarily conforming, person. I would ask whether or not his flight and revolt led to genuine open re-

---

[2] The technical term "allocentric" connotes a more profound and complex process than just the development of more "other-centered" values. It describes the progressive objectification of thought, as both Freud and Piaget have described, the internalization of external reality, and the humanization of a person through identifications with other humans. Too-extended allocentric development, relative to growth in other sectors of the personality, produces conformity and excessive dependence on others. It is characteristic of mature people that they can allow themselves to abandon their allocentricism *under their own control.* That is, they can permit themselves to regress into their inner world of vague reverie and hunch to recapture the primitive subjectivity of the child. A mature person can tolerate the disorganization that comes from abandoning his ties to reality. To possess the strength to allow one's self to be confused is to be highly educable.

lations with other people from whom he learned that his dilemma was not unique and that others were also trying to develop a genuine identity? Was he able to move through what must have been a very deep resentment of his father by understanding paternal frustrated hopes and immaturities? As a result of the argument he provoked with authority, has his reasoning become more logical and acute? Or has he repressed his need to argue and retreated into a blandly vague and evasive way of thinking?

Much of our effort as educators is dedicated to socializing the thinking of students. Do we provide an atmosphere in class that provokes reasoned arguments and discussions so that students learn how to respond thoughtfully and objectively to the ideas of others? Many teachers who are not at home with aggressiveness inhibit spirited arguments and thereby shut off one way more assertive students can learn how to channel their energies. A good teacher knows how to ignite sparks and then use the heat to generate intellectual growth. It's easier and emotionally safer, however, to contain students by dominating the classroom. Most of us talk too much in the classroom. As a consequence, students don't learn how to communicate with each other and come to respect other points of view in an argument.

How do we encourage the development of more other-centered values and behavior? Students learn honesty, respect, and care from being taught honestly, from being respected, and from being loved. A teacher can't just talk about such values. He must live them. Do the principal and other teachers frown upon and subtly punish a teacher whose personal life is a vigorous witness to social justice? Too many of us have allowed ourselves to be conformed into people of insipid character and weak purpose ignoring the fact that young people need models of socialized and deeply passionate concern.

Do we assist students, particularly adolescents, to think of themselves as lovable and loving persons? I am always taken aback by the student who says in deep earnestness, "No one understands me," implying that no one *can* understand him because he is unique. Students need to feel that they are human—sins and all. They need to learn that most of their friends also have wished someone would take care of them for the rest of their lives, or are lonely and would like to drop their cool and just be themselves.

Becoming More Integrated

There are many different ways of looking at a problem and many different ways of solving it. At some point, we need to form different combinations of ideas, try out various alternatives, imaginatively or actively. As Dewey said, a person seeks to unify or integrate his behavior into "a successful ongoing." It is disturbing to feel, as one of my students reported, like a thousand pieces going in a thousand different directions. As a person grows he encounters progressively more complex problems that challenge him to make sense out of them for himself. A growing person is not afraid to confront the unknown and wrestle some consistency out of it. He is curious and alive to new ideas and ways of doing things. A person's beliefs are consistent with his acts. A mature person doesn't feel divided, say, as so many students nowadays complain, between his rational intellect and his irrational feelings. He isn't just a thinker; he is a passionate intellectual. He seeks solutions that harmonize his values, feelings, and knowledge. Because his ideas of himself are reasonably congruent with what he knows other people think of him, he does not feel compelled to play a role to live up to expectations that are not his own. He acts with integrity.

Obviously, Rusty is estranged from parts of himself. If the eruption of the insight that he was not being fully himself had maturing effects, then he will not suppress his emerging impulses nor deny his obvious athletic skill. One of the principal effects of an education is to humanize a youth's conscience. That is, he becomes more open, for example, to a wider range of aesthetic values. Fortunately, increasing numbers of men, no longer as hung-up by apprehensions about their masculinity, are now able to assimilate such values into their lives. Was Rusty able to abandon his stereotyped concept of himself as a jock? Was he able to come to terms with the expectations of others that he was to be a prestigious, gung-ho mindless athlete who made out with the girls? Was he able to accept himself as a sensitive, idealistic, intelligent young man who was adept at basketball but not yet ready to go to bed with a woman?

Philosophers have identified the ability to think relationally, to create meaningful syntheses, to shape a Weltanschauung to be an important goal of educators. But a youth must first have the desire and curiosity to want to form such connections or philosophy of life. How do we encourage the Rustys in our classrooms not to seal off parts of themselves because they can't figure out how to bring their lives into some central focus? What do we do to encourage curiosity, the desire to seek after meaning and reorganizations of experience? How do we help a youngster who comes across a word he doesn't know in his reading to *want* to search out the meaning? Do we pass off a student's questions or puzzled frown because we must complete the assignment today if we are to keep up with the lesson plan? Do we subtly turn off questions that may be disturbing to us because of our ignorance or prejudices? Does the teacher of history take examples from the work his students are having in physics and chemistry when describing the rise of science in order to help them see the inter-connectedness of knowledge?

Or what do we do to help our students open themselves to other experiences and learn how to integrate them with their values? Do we talk about our democratic society in social studies but have a powerless Student Council and a rubber-stamp faculty? How do we help youngsters value intellectual honesty and achievement? Too many students believe that intellectual accomplishment has no meaning. They know too many students who get high grades by cheating. Do we encourage the devalua-tion of intellectual achievement by the overvaluation of grades and so drive some students to cheat?

Not infrequently an elementary school teacher must suffer teaching a child who behaves in school the way he can't at home. Johnny picked on girls in class, fought constantly on the playground, and defiantly refused to work. His teacher sought a conference with Johnny's mother. "There's nothing wrong with Johnny at home. He's quiet and obedient. We have no problems with him. What's wrong at school? Be stern with him. He'll be OK then." But later, she learned that Johnny was fearful of his father who, in drunken outbursts, would take him by the hair and beat him if he didn't obey instantaneously. Terrified by recurrent nightmares of being "bait for a fish some guy tied some string to and which swam around and around me tying me to the bed," and petrified by the policeman at the school crossing, he came to school a seething volcano. How do you help such a divided child become more integrated so he will become more educable?

Becoming More Stable

Typically, the next phase in the adaptive process is to determine which of the provisional alternatives we have formed provides the most appropriate and satisfying solution to the problem. It is at this point that we must test the "goodness of fit" of our ideas. Actually, of course, this idealized version of how a person grows ignores that we are ceaselessly testing bits and pieces and then modifying what we imagine or learn. Each subsequent test results in some change in what we've just done. Eventually our knowledge, skills, and values do approach a "fit." An equilibrium be-tween our and others' expectations is reached, at which point stabilization begins to occur. We educators work hard to stabilize skills like reading and writing, which are so instrumental to learning other skills. Gradually, a child's relations with other children also become less mercurial. This morning, Betsy said, "I had Lorraine stay overnight with me last night." This afternoon, she said "I hate Lorraine. She's always showing off." But in a few years, Betsy's friendships will endure over longer periods of time and may not be so tumultuous. Similarly, one's motives and values eventually become persistent and predictable. As a youth moves into adulthood, his ideas about himself become more stable. Gradually, he finds a way of life that integrates his talents and values, that "fits" an option society provides. He centers down to an operable identity that, so Erikson says (1959), is recognized and valued by others. However, stability does not mean rigidity. A mature person remains open to new influences and the possibility of change.

So the fourth clue for assessing how mature were the consequences of Rusty's quarrel with the expectations of others is this: has he developed a way of life that permits him to become more of that person he dimly sensed he could be? Has he made a serious effort to test just what kind of poet he might be? What other activities has he tried and what other relationships has he formed that have persisted as sources of competence and enjoyment?

Because we have no curricular plans comparable to those for reading and arithmetic, teachers receive little assistance in developing and stabilizing other skills central to maturing. How systematically do we help children learn how to extract from their reading (and I don't mean a textbook) its internal order and then outline it? To know how to outline is to be able to think hierarchically, to learn how to identify a generalization and its subordinate parts. Do we require our students to write and rewrite and then rewrite again in order to learn how to winnow out the irrelevant and clarify the essential?

Is our identity as a teacher so stable that the ethic of truth is our ethic too—all the way through? Do we teach with integrity, humility, respect, and have the courage to stand up for what we believe to be the truth? If so, we provide the moral climate that nurtures the development of mature values. Do we really know our students well enough to help them form a genuine identity? Or do we, for example, believe that it is not feminine for girls to be mathematicians and so subtly direct a girl gifted in this area to other areas that fit our biases of what a girl should be?

How do we help six-year-old Jeannie who one day in class sobbed, "You hate me. My mother hates me. My sister hates me. Daddy hates me. I hate myself." How do we help her develop a core of self-worth out of which she will feel secure enough to reach out to others? How do we help her become more educable?

Becoming More Autonomous

The discovery of ways to resolve a problem and the stabilization of those ways lead to greater autonomy. To develop a stable habit or skill, for example, is to reach a new level in development. The continued growth of that habit no longer is a focal point of effort or concern; instead, stable skills become readily usable as means to grow in other ways. Our memories, skills, and values and our "selves" come increasingly under our conscious control. As reading skill increases, it can be used effortlessly and self-consciously to further maturing itself. Similarly, our memories and ideas become readily recallable when we need them. We can think about an idea, imaginatively reconstruct it, combine it with other ideas, break up that combination to form another more complex combination, determine its implications for our values, discuss it with others. We can do all of these things *without* ever limiting our ability to recover the original memory unshorn of all of the changes we have made. This is a remarkable fact about ourselves. We become free to think even of the unimaginable.

Obviously, increasing autonomy is contingent upon increasing stabilization. I have found it difficult to pull the two apart for research purposes. Could not a test of the stability of a value or skill be the extent of its resistance to disorganization under stress? Another test might be the capacity to recover, bounce back, if we do become disorganized. For example, we know that the multiplication table has become stabilized when a child can recall that 6 x 7 is 42 and vice versa under the usual stresses of oral recitation and written tests. A test of the autonomy of such skills is the degree to which they can be applied and used efficiently in situations different from those in which they were learned. For example, those who visit the human growth centers, like Esalen, report that their mode of relating to others is changed. But such a change may be primarily sustained by the unusual nature of the Esalen environment and not be really stabilized. The test of the autonomy of such interpersonal skills is whether the person can use them to modify his relationships in different situations.

As a person matures he becomes more independent of the control of others. He also becomes freer of his past. A mature person can selectively respond to the myriad demands made upon him. He can say no. He is less determined by earlier childhood conflicts or wishes. As he moves through the middle years of life, he reports that *he* feels increasingly in command. His self, his personality, becomes an instrument to further adaptation (Neugarten, 1967). A mature person then is more independent, less suggestible, more self-directing, able to defy the demands of his society for what he believes is right. But such courage, because it is an expression of a maturity that is deeply allocentric, will be considered and not blind. Because he can understand how other persons feel, he respects their views. His autonomy is moderated but strengthened by his allocentrism. I am not referring to those campus radicals who demand that the administration listen to them but who scream at and disrupt visiting speakers to the campus. They are immaturely and perversely defiant.

Our fifth clue then to the maturity of Rusty's subsequent adaptation is how autonomous he became. Did he return to the university to pout and sulk in his room or to continue, though sullenly, with basketball? Will he be mature enough to understand what his responsibility is for having accepted an athletic scholarship in the first place? Is he strong enough to decline the scholarship and independent enough to work to pay for his own education if his father refuses to help him, and *yet still* contribute his skill to the basketball team rather than deny this part of his own identity out of spite? Will he insist on exploring poetry and art even though his fraternity brothers may at first wonder what type of "brother" he is? Will he emerge out of his revolt his own man?

A person's growing autonomy is a test of his maturity. Do we provide opportunities for students to test their autonomy? Just how long do we keep them studying textbooks that don't ask them to ferret out and organize knowledge with some modicum of judgment? Have we found ways to help them extend their skill in sciencing to other areas of the curriculum? Can they phrase testable questions and then test them objectively and systematically in social science and humanities courses? Do we teach twelfth graders in the same way we teach ninth graders, thus not challenging them to develop intellectual independence?

What support do we bring to adolescents who resist caving in to the conforming expectations of their peers? Do we value an allocentrically rebellious youth or do we move, frequently unconsciously, to squelch him? Are we sensitive to the subtle and manifold rigidities of our large bureaucratic school systems? Do we find ways to keep their sheer mass from destroying any independence of thought and will? Do we let our affluence undermine our youths' need to meet adversity to test their competence?

I remember Jimmy who saw me after failing four of his five exams his first semester at college. His two roommates had paired up, leaving him alone to cry in his room at night. He used to escape the lonely college weekends in the new Mustang his parents gave him when he graduated from high school. When I asked him what he worried about most, he wrote, "I'd like to be able to know how to help solve my problems;" "It bothers me not to be able to get along with people the way I'd like to;"

and "I miss my girl and when I don't get letters from her for several days (or from anyone for that matter) I get depressed." His earliest dream was of "milk bottles . . . some . . . so many glass bottles, milk bottles . . . came from everywhere. Kept coming from nowhere, piling up around me but I could not grasp them for they were just like images. I was scared, frustrated because I could not do anything with them." I asked him what came to mind when he thought of milk bottles. He instantly replied, "Glass, water, drowning, drowning bugs." And finally, to a picture of a boy staring at a violin, he made up this story:

> Young Georgie about five years old was the son of one of the . . . a famous violinist. Ever since George can remember he wanted to learn how to play his father's violin . . . but his father said "No" because he felt his son was still too young. One day George was home by himself when he discovered that his father had left his most precious violin on top of the table. Knowing that his father was not around he sat down and stared at the violin. He wished someday too he would be able to play this violin. He had a risk [sic] to resist a great temptation to pick up the violin and play the instrument. Then his father came into the room and patted George on the head and praised the boy for not trying to play the instrument because it was his most expensive violin. Because George had been so obedient not to try and tamper with his father's instrument he got a reward of a violin of his own.

Could Jimmy be saying that he was a worthless bug that had drowned in the security of too much affluence (though obviously not genuine love)? As a youngster he had tried to "risk" (his unconsciously masterful slip of the tongue) asserting his own desire and independence. But whenever he tried to learn how to become a competent, autonomous male, he had been discouraged by a father who rewarded him for *not* trying to become independent. So although a brilliant and personable young man, his image of himself was of a five-year-old child dependent upon signs of love which never came or upon images which he could never grab. He had never learned how to determine his own life, to know "how to . . . solve my problems" and to form the close relations he wanted—not even with his girl. How ready was Jimmy to take charge of his own intellectual and personal growth in college?

Freedom and Joy

The "shock, confusion, perturbation, uncertainty" Dewey spoke of when growth is blocked can be painfully frustrating and disorganizing. In discovering how to remove the barriers to maturing, we develop the competence and attitudes that enhance growth. Energy is also released in forming autonomous habits. Where does the freedom that education allegedly produces come from? It grows out of the conviction that one is in control of one's destiny. Such control is the consequence of maturity. Too many students naively believe that freedom comes by escaping from or destroying their ties to others and to their society through anarchy. This type of freedom from the expectations of others may intensify a self-centered autonomy that is nonintegrative. Young people may repress their needs for others or, as with some who abandon their intellectual skills for psychedelic handicrafts, deny part of their own potential. Real freedom—as harsh as it sounds these days—comes from the pain and hard work of mastering the knowledge and skills that make a person more educable. It does not come from adjusting to a self-destructive conformity nor from impulsively fulfilling one's self to magnify one's self.

Our lives, of course, are often constricted by necessities we cannot change or by social conditions whose demands may seem inescapable. Many young people feel so caught. The violence of their resentment indicates how irresistibly seduced some feel by their own sticky affluence to sell out to society's way of life. A youth may respond to its demands by reorganizing and stabilizing himself at a new level of maturity. He then is more autonomous and able to adapt more selectively to others' expectations of him. Or he may have to regress, temporarily perhaps, to more primitive behavior, like that induced by drugs, until some change is worked in his society. Religion, psychotherapy, or even falling in love may impel some to reorganize their values and knowledge differently. Such periods of heightened disorganization and conflicts are periods of potential educability out of which more adaptive ways of living can be forged. If a person is not able to change the "system," he may be forced, as many before him, to seek a new environment more sympathetic to his needs. If reorganization of one's self, change in the society, or flight to another environment are not feasible, then a person may have to learn to accept suffering and adjust. He may, thereby, carve out of forced adjustment a new set of values. But in any case, the mature person tries to create appropriate alternatives. He has the courage to keep pressing and testing until he or others create a healthier society.

One test of the maturity of a person's freedom might be his ability (without the aid of acid or alcohol) to allow himself to regress. He can freely enter into primitive twilight states and nightmares. There he can re-experience the confusion and disorganization that frequently are the sources of creative insights into how to change one's self or society. My hunch is that a mature person has such inner freedom that he can give free rein to bizarre, illogical, and fanciful combinations of ideas usually only encountered in the safety of one's dreams. *But* a mature person, in contrast to the psychotic or the LSD user, can bring himself back (and his will to do so is not impaired) to his everyday world when he wishes. A mature person, then, is able to recreate the world of the primitive. He can experience the irrational and tap the power of his inner demons. Few of us have the inner freedom or self-trust of a St. Francis to allow ourselves to be "used" by the powerful forces within. Still fewer become joyful witnesses of the visions they encounter.

Perhaps the most distinguishing visible feature of maturity is an abundance of joyful energy. I do not mean the energy of the driven compulsive, who by being so busy protects himself from ungovernable impulses. Nor do I mean the energy of the manic who by fleeing into the world through outbursts of frantic activity protects himself from losing contact with it. But I mean that energy that enables a person to feel intensely, to bubble with good will, to be enthusiastic, to seek new difficulties to master, to be spontaneously expressive, to be humorous, to laugh, to play with the abandon of a child. A mature person is inwardly free to be a deeply joyful person despite life's frustrations and tensions, sadnesses, and tragedies. Freedom and joy are clues that a person is developing that knowledge and those skills and values that enable him to create a way of life that opens him further to life.

For me, the indication of a real teacher that last day of school in June is not the increase in his students' Stanford Achievement scores, but their increased educability. A youth may have markedly grown in, say, his knowledge or intellectual skills, but such development may not be healthy and may limit his future educability, Why? The answer lies in a very powerful assumption I make about maturing: a person needs to grow wholly if he is to grow maturely. Too extended development in one sector of the personality induces internal blocks to further development in that sector until some further growth occurs in the neglected sectors.

Rusty found that his absorption in basketball had been so consuming that he was growing only partially. His flight from basketball said he was ready to grow in other ways. Another illustration of the unhealthy consequences of unbalanced development is Howard, a brilliant mathematician who ever since eighth grade had been tapped by each successive teacher as a mathematical genius. In his senior year in college, he announced one day to his dumbfounded professor that he was abandoning mathematics for awhile. In reconstructing what happened, I learned that the night before he had this dream, which apparently illuminated for him his growing sense of self-alienation:

> Walking up and down in a skyscraper looking for where math class is held on the first day of the new semester, I was leading Bill (who impresses me as grinding in physics to show he can do it). Up at the very top is the math class. I begin walking into the clean, well-ordered room where someone is writing math on the blackboard. Then I am following Henry (he has done a lot of hitchhiking, traveling to South America and around) through a series of attics, filled with old furniture, interesting knick-knacks, exotic but dusty rugs. We are tunneling through the stuff, over junk and under tables.

He had interpreted his dream as telling him he had grown enough in rationality, logic, and order—now it was time to recover the more irrational, archaic, and disorderly cast-offs of his past. His dream was a warning that he was on the brink of severe internal division, which ultimately did demand professional help to heal. He never did return to mathematics.

I have quoted Jung earlier about the loss of primitive wholeness due to excessive rational development. One cannot escape the cost of overdevelopment of one part of the personality. Jung based his observations primarily on analyses of middle-aged people in crisis, whose very worldly success proved to be their psychological undoing. I find similar crises occurring increasingly in young people. Their flight into drugs, confrontations, and riots are, in part, only exaggerated compensatory pursuits after a sense of primitive wholeness. As I've said earlier, increasing numbers of young people feel empty. They sense that their excessively logical, rational, achievement-oriented and competitive middle-class expectations have suppressed their vitality and primitive wholeness too long. Many, like Howard, are no longer educable for the "clean, well-ordered room" where someone writes "math on the blackboard." They need to grow emotionally and socially before they are free to continue maturing intellectually.

Exaggerated behavior, like an opinion, an impulsive gesture, or a way of life, is frequently a clue to someone's suppressed need to believe, do, or become just the opposite. In the movie, *Bonnie and Clyde,* Clyde's murderous violence protected his image of himself as a male during the months he was sexually impotent with Bonnie. Once he and Bonnie were able to climax their love for the other, their violence no longer could be psychologically convincing. The movie had to end. The brilliance of its ending—Bonnie's erotically violent death—did not say that intimacy leads to death (the fear of so many young people nowadays) so much as it depicted

in the idiom of Bonnie's and Clyde's lives the intensity of their formerly
repressed passion.

Before concluding this chapter, I want to make a brief speculative
leap, which may help us set priorities about what changes we need to make
in schools if they are to become healthier places. John Dewey proposed
that there was an orderly sequence to the development of any habit or
skill (1922). I have described the criteria that define a healthy person in
terms of an orderly sequence also. The criteria describe the *process* by
which a healthy person adapts to a problem—like his own growth. I propose that this model describes Dewey's idea. The implication of this similarity is that the research demonstrating the validity of the model of maturity indirectly validates Dewey's insights into the nature of the ideal educational process.[3] To become educated then is to grow healthily as I've
described.

What is the process by which a person adapts to form new habits,
or more generally, becomes educated? He confronts a problem that provokes him to *symbolize* its elements. He reflects about what causes the
difficulty. He then searches for alternative answers *(allocentrism)* and
forms tentative *integrative* solutions, which he then tests. When he discovers the more adaptive one, he repeats it until it becomes *stable,* that
is, habitual. Once a habit has formed, it becomes *autonomous* and usable
in problems different from those for which it was learned. Automatization
releases energy to be used in developing other habits. Blocks may occur at
any point in this adaptive sequence. Because each stage is dependent on
the prior one, a diagnosis of where the block occurs provides the clues
about where to begin the principal remedial effort. If we look now at a
person as a whole instead of at specific habits, it is possible to secure some
insight into that phase in his development that may be blocking his subsequent growth. Clearly, then, that phase defines our highest priority about
where to institute change.

---

[3] I had not been aware of this similarity until I had studied how students grow
healthily in college. The results revealed a developmental sequence throughout the college years that paralleled Dewey's analysis of learning specific
habits (Heath 1968*b*, Chap. 6).

Chapter 7

What
Education Now
for the Eighties?

It is pointless to wonder whether this generation is more or less mature than earlier generations. The times are radically different and we have little information about past generations. What *is* important for us to know is how this generation needs to grow now for its future.

The leading edge of the maturity of young people is their heightened ability to symbolize their experience. From an evolutionary perspective, our youth may well be *the* transitional generation to a higher level of human consciousness (Reich 1970). The vast expansion of their information, their greater psychological perceptiveness, their increased mastery of tools like language, their more sensitized moral consciousness, and the greater value they put on honesty and integrity are impressive strengths on which our salvation as a species may ultimately depend.

The growing complexity and pragmatic rationalism of our society will only accentuate the need for more well-informed, highly conscious, deliberate persons. I have great respect for the potential of this generation of young people to provide such persons, since I believe another of its strengths is the allocentric maturity of its thought. It is a critical, insightful, argumentative, and intellectually sharp generation. These strengths fit the needs of our emerging society.

Another potential strength is that their values are other-centered ones. More youth are socially concerned, tolerant, and desirous of developing a just and healthy society. However, our societal failure to help them find ways to integrate and test such values and so stabilize them makes this only a potential strength.

At this point in the maturing process, a growing divergence is occurring between how some youth are developing, how they need to grow healthily, and the needs of our society. An overdeveloped self-consciousness and intellectual acuity distort growth of other personality dimensions and inhibit action, spontaneity, and joy. Premature sophistication robs a youth of vitality and playfulness. Boredom and despair result.

We confront a deepening dilemma. Man will continue to make much of this earth a rather joyless place. Our recurrent crises and emerging Orwellian society will demand greater awareness and intellectual skills to survive psychologically. How do we continue to develop such strengths and yet avoid so imbalancing a youth that he becomes less spontaneous and joyful as he becomes more sensitive to injustice and sorrow? How do we educate so he doesn't become less educable as he becomes more educated?

The answer, I believe is *not* to abandon academic excellence as a goal. The answer is to place greater effort at that point in the developmental sequence where our youth are failing to mature at the same pace as they are in their symbolization and logical skills. Their critical growth needs are for more allocentric relationships and more integrative learning experiences.

I have described interpersonal immaturity in terms of loneliness, inadequate development of intimacy and cooperative skills, and a growing narcissism. These immaturities limit maturing in other areas. For example, inability to acknowledge another person's viewpoint, so central to allocentric maturing, limits the use of one's logical and critical skills. A dogmatic, doctrinaire arrogance can result, as has occurred in some young people in the past few years.

Increasing contradictions are occurring between the emerging character of many youth and the needs of society. As society becomes more interdependent, more youth neither value nor have the skill of accommodating themselves to others and, particularly, to any "system." A rapidly changing society dilutes and impersonalizes relationships; yet, the critical growth need of youth is for more intimacy experiences. Educators are faced with a further dilemma. We need to develop a communal learning environment in which individuality is respected and encouraged, but where self-centeredness is discouraged.

Succeeding generations will have to struggle much more than we ever did to achieve a sense of inner consistency and integration. Those who are fighting society know that they cannot grow wholly until they bring some greater coherence to it. By fighting to change us, they fight not to destroy us, but to maintain their own sanity—and ours as well. Those who pursue drugs cop out. I don't know what will become of them. I fear that many may seek in suicide the ultimate reconciliation. But by far, the greatest number of young people blind themselves to the contradictions of their society, retreat into passivity, constrict their lives, and devote their energies to their own gain.

I don't fear as much for those who occupy buildings and raise hell as for the overwhelming silent majority who opt for security at a level of self-seeking and conforming that may well leave them discontented and unhappy. Passive resignation is more dangerous than emotional excess. I prefer vitality to the pall of premature death. Those who face the contradictions of society are educable. Those who are not open to being moved to indignation or tears are uneducable.

Again, we are faced by imposing dilemmas. Given the specialized, fragmented, and incoherent nature of our society and of our schools and curriculum, just how do we provide an integrating educational experience for students? How do we wake up more youth to the contradictions of their existence and help them endure the frustration and pain that will inevitably follow? How do we help them learn the skills for changing themselves and their institutions?

Just as it is becoming increasingly difficult to be an integrated person in a complicated and not very cohesive society, so it is difficult to become a stable person in a rapidly changing world. My hunch is that more young people have more stable intellectual skills than they do stable values, a sense of identity, or the capacity to form enduring relationships. How could it be otherwise, given a society whose basic values are in such disarray, whose future vocational roles are unpredictable, and whose personal relationships are so fragmented and transitory? If self actualization is becoming the central core value for youth, our dilemma as educators is how to help a youth fulfill his potentials without becoming narcissistic. How can we expose him to a wider range of tests of his values and ideas about himself? How do we help him learn how to be open to continued change and yet satisfy his needs for a sense of rootedness and continuity with his own past?

A mature autonomy is dependent on developing an integrative and stable personality. In some ways, our youth seem to be very autonomous. But neither coolness nor defiance necessarily indicates a mature autonomy. A person's independence may be so self-sufficient that it limits development. It may even be compensatory for strongly tethered, unacceptable, dependency needs.

The following are *not* examples of a mature autonomy: to want to drive the family car, but not work to pay part of its costs; to smoke a pack of cigarettes a day, but punish one's son for smoking pot; to demand the podium to assert one's views, but deny others the opportunity to speak; to strike to be on a school's educational policy committee, but fail to appear after the second committee meeting; to ask to determine one's own course of study, but fail to work out a program; to want to be on the policy-making staff of a McCarthy, but not be willing to push doorbells for years to get there; to demand more police protection, but vote against the necessary taxes. It is easy in this day of affluence and uncertainty for someone (young or old) to believe he is more adult then he is.

One index of a person's autonomy is his ability to be like a child. Play is an index of wholeness. It requires self-trust to abandon one's restraints freely. It uses surplus energy not tied up in defenses against conflicts and anxieties that in turn limit one's autonomy. My impression is that many young people don't know how to abandon themselves spontaneously to child-like play.

As our society becomes more complex and controlling how are we going to help a youth learn to develop intrinsic interests and become autonomous in initiating and directing his own activity? How can we help him become more playful? In an increasingly rational world that no longer provides acceptable preformed styles of life, how can we help him develop his own values and style? How can we help him live with uncertainty in a world that no longer believes in any transcendent myth or traditional authority?

Healthy Maladjustment

"But you've not said whether Rusty was maladjusted when he fled the university? You've not even said if the deepening alienation of youth is a maladjustment."

Both Rusty and our alienated youth are maladjusted: Rusty to his university; youth to their society. The real issue is whether they are *healthily* maladjusted.

To adjust or be adjusted is not necessarily healthy. To adjust is to come into harmony with and fulfill the expectations of other persons or the demands of a situation. Such expectations may or may not be compatible with how we need to grow. To be healthily adjusted is to adjust to expectations that further growth. To be unhealthily adjusted is to conform to the expectations of others that block growth. We teachers frequently fail to distinguish between these two types. For example, some youths who conscientiously adjust to our expectations and secure very high grades may be too allocentrically developed. They may never develop a mature identity or autonomy. I recall several seniors with exceptional grade averages who were examined orally by a faculty committee to determine if they should be awarded honors at graduation. Despite their high achievement, the committee consensus was that their education had not "taken." They had not questioned what they had learned nor formed any independent positions. We praise the very studious achieving girl in our class. She always completes all of her homework. We always call on her in class. But she never has an idea of her own or argues with us on issues. Conversely, we squelch the more volatile, rebellious girl. She is erratically prepared. She has many opinions and is always arguing. Her maladjustment to our expectations may be healthier.

We have even more difficulty distinguishing between healthily and unhealthily maladjusted behavior. Too often, a youth who does not meet our expectations, frustrates and offends us personally. We become impatient and carping. We assume that our expectations are wise and his resistance is stupid or perverse.

We cannot assess the healthiness of some kinds of behavior until we know their impact on subsequent growth. This is the error many psychiatrists make who have had limited contact with healthy youngsters. They overdiagnose the presence of pathology. I felt Rusty's flight was a healthy, though desperate, attempt to make a radical break with a way of life that was snuffing out his vitality. I detected no underlying pathology driving him. If we react hastily to disruptive behavior, as when we ship every unruly kid to a counselor, or to a violation of our expectations, as Rusty's father did, or to an infraction of our laws, as when we jail an adolescent pot user, we risk slamming shut what may be an opening to new growth. The real test of the healthiness of Rusty's flight was how he matured subsequently.

The deepening alienation of many young adults is a serious form of maladjustment. But perhaps its pervasiveness and depth indicate that our expectations and society's demands may be blocking their growth. In other words, some aspects of their alienation may not be unhealthy. We won't know until our youth become adults and their maturity is tested in other ways. For example, I've been asked many times in the past five years about the growing use of pot. I've refrained from judging it to be an *unhealthy* maladjustment. I don't know. Many young people may have become so hung-up that they need drugs to de-inhibit themselves. If pot helps someone express his tender feelings, enables him to form intimate relationships, and deepens his inner life, then what looks like pathological behavior may actually be a healthily maladjusted reaction to the stresses of society. However, my hunch now is that frequent and extended use of pot is an unhealthy form of maladjustment for too many youths. It accentuates passivity and does not foster the ability to cope with pressures.

"*You* can afford the luxury of waiting for years to decide if the crazy behavior of a student is healthy or not. You don't have him in your class, plus twenty-eight others."

Fair enough. I don't mean to suggest that we can't make some reasonable hunches about a student's maladjustment at the time it occurs, particularly if we know him well. Let's look at a few examples.

Peter, a bright eleventh grader, was referred to me by his teacher, who said he argued incessantly in class. Peter greeted me with, "How close do you think we are to a revolution?" Our hour discussion wove in and around one slogan after another, like, "America is the most imperialistic country on this earth. The only way it's going to change is by revolution. Revolution is coming." He indignantly rejected my suggestion that he might study the political effects of American overseas investments in the Common Market. "What's that going to prove? You can prove anything you want by statistics. Why study that? Imperialism is immoral and we're going to overthrow it." Peter's ideology is closing him off to any detailed, disciplined analysis, even of a topic that might provide some substance to his slogans. His values have become prematurely stabilized. They are rigid and unopen to change.

Debbie was driving her teacher frantic. She was a warm, outgoing, petite eight-year-old, flitting like a butterfly from one table to the next, ceaselessly seeking out her teacher, impulsively reaching beyond her grasp, skipping erratically across the words of her reader. When asked to draw a person, she drew a half-inch stick figure in the corner of a large piece of white paper. Working on a puzzle, she placed a horse's leg on it's head. She made up stories whose sentences were unrelated to each other. Clearly, she was a terribly insecure child unable to inhibit and then integrate experiences. Uneducable in the complex and distracting world of the ordinary classroom, Debbie needs a simpler environment and may require medication to counteract the unhealthy effects of a possible neurological impairment.

Henry was a bright eleven-year-old boy who was called an underachiever by his teacher (though he was on the ninetieth percentile on all his achievement tests except spelling), a troublemaker in the classroom, and sullenly resistant to her demands. He needed therapy, so I was told. Henry came from a distinguished family. His older brother was *the* athlete of the tenth grade; his sister *the* intellect of the eighth grade. Henry was *the* warmest and friendliest child of the fourth grade as well as its elected representative to the school's council. His family lived in an isolated part of the country. His only playmates were his brother and sister, who, he told me, always beat him in every game they played. He loved school. There he could be with his friends. It was the only time he had to play and talk. "How would you change the school?" "Cut out study hall. No one works anyway. Let me talk with my friends." Henry was maladjusted to the demands of that teacher, but he was scarcely unhealthily so. Happily, his teacher was educable. She set up informal conversation groups in class. Henry became more educable to her expectations. The point is that our expectations and the school's demands induce resistance to growth even in a healthy child like Henry if they are not individualized to fit his needs.

Susie is an eighth grader angry that the principal won't let the girls wear what they please. She wants to change the regulation, but feels the Student Council is powerless. She's about ready to begin a guerrilla war.

"The principal would never let the Council decide anything important."

"How do you know?"

"I know. That's the way he is. He's that way about everything."

"You're taking science, aren't you?"

"Yeah. What's that got to do with the price of eggs?"

"Well, is it a fact or a hypothesis that the principal won't let the Council decide anything important?"

Pause. "I guess it's a hypothesis."

"How do you know if a hypothesis is so."

"You test it."

"Well? But don't try to reach for the moon too soon."

Two days later, Susie said she had talked with the Council. It decided to propose to the principal that students be represented on the faculty committee that chooses the films for assemblies. A healthily maladjusted person brings what he's learned from one experience to bear on another and has the initiative and independence to test its relevance.

"But wait a minute. Haven't you been a little devious to emphasize the importance of educating for healthy *maladjustment*? Actually, your controlling term is "healthy" if you're also accepting healthy adjustment as a goal. To glorify healthy *maladjustment* betrays a choice among values you've not made explicit."

You are persistent! But the issues are still more complex. Let me try to be more precise about the goal I propose for educators before I get to the issue of values that you rightly question.

I've used the phrase "healthy maladjustment" as a rhetorical device to force us to think about the relation between the needs of a growing child and his society. It would have been too easy to talk just about the needs of a child, as some self-actualization theorists do, and ignore their relation to the expectations and demands of other people. The slogan is too simplistic. Let me restate my proposed goal: our goal should be to develop more educable students.

Educate for Educability

To educate a student may, but *not* necessarily, increase his educability. Neglect of this fundamental distinction punishes millions of students. We risk alienating students by only imparting information and cultivating academic skills, which is the actual meaning of "to educate" in most schools. Studies have shown that over 80 percent of our classroom tests test only the acquisition of information (Burns 1968).

To be educable is to be open to continued maturing. An educable person is able to fashion a healthy or mature adaptation that considers both the demands and expectations of his society and his own needs and talents. The crux of this definition is obviously the meaning of "healthy or mature adaptation," some signs of which are integration, autonomy, freedom, and joy.

To be educable is to be healthily maladjustable (a more accurate term than maladjusted). What initiates the process of adaptation that leads to maturing? Maladjustment. Disruption of habits and customary ways of doing things and encountering expectations which we don't immediately know how to handle stimulate efforts to adapt. They produce, as Dewey said, "shock, confusion, perturbation, uncertainty." Students found to be most educable at Stanford were those who had encountered personal crises and troubles (Katz and Associates 1968). A condition for educability is the ability to tolerate the confusion and perturbation of being maladjusted while seeking to adapt healthily to it. In fact, a mature youth may actively create maladjustments, hence anxieties, for himself as catalysts to his continuing development.

What is the proper role of the school? To individualize *and* socialize its students. It does this by helping a student *become an agent of his own growth*. It teaches him skills, provides information, and nurtures values that increase his power to create for himself a healthy way of life. I suggest ways of doing this in the following chapters.

Such is the choice we must make—to educate for educability. No longer do we know what knowledge our youth will need in their future. We must educate for skill and continuing interest in acquiring knowledge. No longer can we assume that there is some god-given healthy congruence between the needs of our youth and the needs of their future society. We must help youth develop the maturity to make their own decisions about what types of changes in their social institutions will be healthy for them.

Social institutions like the family and church, which formerly guarded our individuality and privacy, are no longer viable. Our conforming society is securing increasing power to be Big Brother. No longer can we blithely assume our survival, physically or psychologically. A free society requires healthily maladjustable people, adults who are *maturely* autonomous of societal pressures.

At the conclusion of Chapter Four, I said that society will increasingly expect schools to socialize our youth. If this is the case, then to meet the above-mentioned needs, we must begin now to individualize their development as well. For this reason, I've emphasized that our principal task is to produce healthily maladjustable rather than healthily adjusted youths.

The criteria that define the healthy development of youth are descriptive of how students become more educable (Heath 1968b). No value choice is involved in the description. But to choose to educate for educability is to make a value choice. Educability rather than adjustment or self-actualization is the only realistic choice we can make.

Those who propose that the educator's principal task is to socialize or adjust the individual to the expectations and needs of society find their justification in Locke's theory of knowledge, Watsonian behaviorism, and Skinner's *Walden Two* (1948). The child is assumed to be an undifferentiated, passive instrument of society who can be molded and shaped to fit its image through the wise operation of punishments and rewards. What man is and can become is what society wants and shapes him to become. Those who propose that man's first duty is to serve his country, who establish the priority of the nation's needs over those of its members, and who are enamored of Orwell's tidily controlled world (or by Chairman Mao's China or Franco's Spain) share similar assumptions about the nature of man. A youth's needs are either coterminus with the expectations of his society or irrelevant to the state. Adjustment becomes the end, whether it be healthy or not.

In a democratic society, the school's primary goal cannot be adjustment. A democracy values the "life, liberty, and pursuit of happiness" of each of its citizens. Their fulfillment requires a pluralistic society of diverse values, alternative life styles, and different types of schools. To educate primarily for adjustment is to indoctrinate a youth to one way of life which may not be right or healthy for him. It may limit his maturing and so his educability. To so educate undermines the vitality and strength of a democratic society. A school should expand a youth's awareness of alternative values and ways of life and provide him with the skills he needs to be able to select wisely and accommodate healthily to that style of life most suitable for him.

Those who say self-fulfillment or self-actualization should be the goal find their justification in Rousseau's *Emile* (1762), Fromm's (1947, 1955) and Maslow's (1962) writing, in much psychiatric thinking, and in the philosophy of teachers like Neill (1960) and Holt (1964). Those of this persuasion tend to assume that a child's potentials are preformed. Society and its demands only distort and contort the development of these potentials. Therefore, unless society is perfect, sane, or wise, it should leave the child alone, letting him grow, following his own direction. He will eventually find his destiny. Youthful advocates of "freedom," of the elimination of all restraints and regulations, and of unfettered individuality find their justification in the thoughts of such theorists and educators.

How can self-actualization be justified, particularly if, when taken as our primary or only goal, it could produce a destructively narcissistic person? The classical humanistic spirit or *paideia* of Greece could value self-fulfillment as its educational goal only because the pervasive identity that most Hellenes felt for their *polis* guaranteed that what was individual was also universal. This similarity of need and value, where whatever is expressed of the self is generally congruent with the expectations of the community, is a rare and precious experience for contemporary moderns. There are few persisting communities like the *polis* except some communes, perhaps, to give man that sense of wholeness or unity with others that comes from feeling little strain between his values and hopes and those of the group he belongs to. Contemporary man belongs to many groups with many conflicting values and expectations. In seeking to fulfill his needs, he more often than not creates conflicts with the legitimate needs of others.

A self-fulfillment thesis might be defended if one assumed that man was inherently and primarily social and cooperative. Such an assumption is patently false. The history of man's violence, greed, and jealousy indicates that these needs — not cooperation, altruism, and loving — are prepotent in many at different times in their lives. The only way to escape, therefore, the narcissistic consequence of a self-fulfillment thesis is to limit what is to be actualized, say, to those potentialities that would not harm others if developed. Man is of and in society. A person only becomes more fully human through give and take relations with others. A child deprived of social experiences that make demands of him becomes retarded in both his language and social development. No one can escape the shaping *and* restricting influence of others. Even hermits live with imaginations molded by and populated with people. Self-fulfillment is more a rallying slogan than a realistic prescription for educators.

"But," some might reply, "your ideas about healthy growth are fine for the average person. They aren't for the talented who have some leading and distinctive qualities. Maturity for you is a balanced blandness."

"That's not true. You're . . . "

"Let me finish. How many brilliant creative contributions to society would be still-born or snuffed out if we had encouraged our mathematicians, musicians, and writers to abandon, even temporarily, their highly developed talents to explore their personal exotic and dusty attics, as your mathematician Howard did? Besides, creativity emerges out of deep inner divisions. To meddle therapeutically or educationally with such private neuroses is to risk destroying creativity. The only reasonable goal is self-fulfillment, whether it emerges healthily or not. And to hell with adjustment. Society will take care of itself."

There may be some truth to the assertion that some creative work does emerge out of deep, even pathological suffering. Much contemporary research seems to suggest otherwise, however. Generally, highly creative persons are quite mature (MacKinnon 1960).

The heart of the issue is who has the right to decide which educational goal our schools should seek. Parents? The demands for decentralization, black self-determination, segregationist separatism have sensitized us to the issue. I also think of the fateful decision those famous mothers of musical prodigies made. They sensed early that their children could be geniuses. So they drove them to practice the violin or piano hour after hour, year after year, dominated their social and emotional lives, and pushed them through every door of opportunity regardless of the consequences to the children. The consequences? Perhaps suffering and suicide and/or great achievement and a deep sense of fulfilling one's destiny. Educators are perhaps more fortunate than mothers. Mothers must live with the consequences of their decisions. We educators don't even know what the consequences of ours are.

Educators? As an educator I believe my proper goal is to help a Howard or a Peter become free to continue his growth. Is it my right to encourage an unusual talent if I believe he will become less educable? Is that *my* decision to make?

Society? In many different ways, society shapes our educational goals. Just by providing certain types of equipment for the schools, it affects what we do. I think of the New York City high school senior who won a national science award. When asked how he did it, he said, "I spent six hours a day working on the school's computer for the last six months." At what cost to his future educability and maturing? What is our responsibility if we had been his teachers and had noted that those hundreds of hours pulled him away from other activities, isolated him from other students, produced a growing inhibition of his emotional life, narrowed his judgment about social and human problems—in short, inhibited his maturing?

Obviously, it is the future lives of our students that are the tests of how educable they have become in our schools. Since most of us never know (and, tragically, seldom care) what becomes of our students, we remain blind to what we may really be doing to them. It's true that by objective indicators contemporary students are better educated, that is, better informed (Jencks and Riesman 1968). But perhaps their stridency, riots, revolutionary slogans, epithets and obscenities, malaise, and hopelessness are other measures of our efforts. What's the good of producing better educated people if in the process they become less educable?

Parents, educators, and society each have responsibility. But within humane and constitutional safeguards, I believe the final responsibility should remain with the parents and the child.

Whereas a person sells his soul if he only adjusts, he risks distorting it if he seeks only to fulfill it. Neither brings maturity, both may bring eventual illness. Gardner makes a similar point when he says, "Freedom without moral commitment is aimless and promptly self-destructive. We must restore a vigorous sense of individuality *and* a sense of shared purposes" (Gardner 1961, p. 137).

To make my argument, I have oversimplified both the adjustmental and self-actualization points of view. Both have had enormous influence on education, much of it constructive. Yet, it is time to go beyond these limiting theories. Our task is to both adjust and self-actualize—and more than both. Our task is to develop a student's educability so that he becomes the agent of his own adjustment and self-actualization.

Part IV

The
Humanistic School

A Carnegie Corporation study of the schools concluded that the reforms proposed by James Conant had had little effect because they

> . . . made simplistic assumptions: If only we could attract better people into teaching, or give teachers more "subject" courses and fewer "method" courses, or break the power of the old educational establishments, all would be well with the schools. But this ignores the fact that the way public schools are organized destroys spontaneity, initiative, and love of learning among teachers as well as students . . . The public schools are quite literally destructive of human beings . . . I think they are the most grim, joyless places on the face of the earth. They are needlessly authoritarian and repressive—not because teachers and principals are stupid or venal, but because nobody ever asks why: why the rules, or why the curriculum? (Silberman 1969).

Another recent study, based on visits to "260 kindergartens through third-grade classrooms in 100 schools clustered in or around major cities of thirteen states" concluded that a decade's educational ferment has created little significant change in the classroom:

> We were unable to discern much attention to pupil needs, attainments, or problems as a basis for beginning instruction, nor widespread provision for individual opportunities to learn. Most classes were taught as a group, covering essentially the same ground for all students at approximately the same rate of speed. Teaching was predominantly telling and questioning by the teacher, with children responding one by one or occasionally in chorus . . . When small groups of students worked together, the activities engaged in by

121

each group member were similar, and bore the mark of the teacher's assignment and expectations. Rarely did we find small groups intensely in pursuit of knowledge; rarely did we find individual pupils at work in self-sustaining inquiry. Popular innovations of the decade— non-grading, team teaching, "discovery" learning, and programmed instruction—were talked about by teachers and principals alike but were rarely in evidence . . . teachers and students did not appear to be intensely involved in their work. Only occasionally did we encounter a classroom aura of excitement, anticipation, and spontaneity; when we did, it was almost invariably a kindergarten class (Goodlad 1969, p. 60).

What an indictment! "The public schools are quite literally destructive of human beings . . . the most grim, joyless places on the face of the earth." Or "teachers and students did not appear to be intensely involved in their work."

Few schools have ever been exciting and joyful places. Yet, their suppressive and conforming effects have been accentuated in the fifties and sixties by the imposition on them of the academician's telescopic view of how children need to grow. We have permitted the university mentality to pervert our educational goals. Our children have been replaced by the curriculum as the focus of our concern. We listened to the university consultants who misidentified the important determinants of a child's growth. They pushed consolidated schools, increased specialization, educational television, wall-less classrooms and other fads of salvation that may only dilute further those critical humanistic conditions that make healthy growth possible. We kowtowed to the expertise of the psychologists who have so bent their research efforts to the acceleration of intellectual development and the rapid acquisition of information that the growth of our children has been warped. In the process, our own morale has been destroyed. We are told by experts to do what violates our wisdom and integrity. Many of us, particularly nursery and elementary school teachers, know that a child has to grow wholly to grow healthily rather than to be pressured to read earlier. With only a few conspicuous exceptions, for instance Lois Murphy (1962), psychologists have not studied the rich complexity of growing children. This imbalance in research on the growth process has been recognized by Dr. B. S. Brown of the National Institute of Mental Health. Upon assuming its directorship, he said, "I believe that the chief area which needs a great deal of expansion from its current level is child mental health" (1970, p. 3). And we have allowed ourselves to be manipulated by the admission requirements of universities and terrorized by the SAT dragon. The teachers of every school I've visited feel robbed of their autonomy and freedom to educate students as they believe they need to grow because, ironically, they may not get into college otherwise! They are rationalizing of course, but that's how they feel and behave.

The great weakness, as well as potential strength, of our schools is that most of them are not monasteries. A monastery has powerful psychological effects because it controls all of the time of its members. More importantly, it is organized around a core of values and expectations made visible in the lives of its superiors. Thus, a consistent and integrative psychological ethos is created from which there is no escape.

Despite the efforts of some schools to be like monasteries none can wall out the influence of the family, mass media, and peer culture. So a school is only one of a number of competing and conflicting forces in a child's life. The effects of one frequently work against and undermine those of another. A child who is being cajoled, seduced, buffeted, threatened, hurt, hated, and crushed outside of school brings all of that with him to class. Even the most loving and skillful teacher in the most concerned and humane school may not be able to reach such a child. A school's power to further the educability of its children depends more upon what happens outside of its walls than most of us yet understand. We arrogate more power to our walled-in schools than they actually have. As a consequence, we blind ourselves to forces that often limit, but could enhance, the educability of our students. I return to that problem later.

A school that seeks to have powerful maturing effects on its students will do the following: create an educative atmosphere; secure a core of mature adult models; and develop shared, consistent, high, and humane expectations.

Chapters Eight, Nine, and Ten deal with these matters in turn.

Chapter 8

An
Educative Atmosphere

Education for educability goes on both within the classroom and throughout the school. Each of us creates an atmosphere in our classrooms: relaxed, secure, tense, expectant, casual, reflective. But the atmosphere of the entire school also sets the tone, the mood, the spirit for a youth's day. How does one sense, not to mention "measure," the educative atmosphere of a school? Those who have visited many schools need no illustration. Schools differ dramatically in their ethos and style. Little things tell you.

As you approach the school, is it cold, gloomy, and dark? Is the playground asphalt and barricaded behind wire mesh fences? Are there bright curtains on the windows? Are the corridors barren and impersonal? Do they remind you of the antiseptic tiled corridors of mental hospitals? Are there flowers in the offices and pets in the hallway? (Every school should have pets around.) Do the secretaries and children smile and greet you with, "May I help you?" Are the walls lined by gray lockers, each with a combination lock, or are there open cupboards with books, papers, and coats of students visible? Are the bulletin boards neatly ordered with official notices and announcements from the principal or are there student messages and comments haphazardly scattered on them. Are there rugs in the classrooms? Are the desks neatly ordered facing the teacher? Is it a school for children in which they obviously live, or is it an adult's school which children attend?

Does the principal first want to show you the new science lab and the new boiler in the basement or does he express concern about Jimmy who just told him in the hallway his parents are getting divorced? As you walk through the corridor with him, do the children freely come up to you and interrupt to tell him something? Does he call them by their first names? Does he affectionately kid them about not interrupting or does he remain sour, aloof, and frowning? What do the children call their teachers,

"Sir," "Mr.," or do they use their first names? Is there a lively interchange between teachers and students walking down the hall or do students and teachers ignore each other? Are the students relaxed and expressive? Do they hum and sing and cavort in the halls or do they stolidly push past you, blankly staring at you as just another stranger in the school? Do they move from class to the auditorium in quiet, regimented lines or do they find their own route at their own pace? Are they assigned to seats or do they sit where they wish? Are the sexes segregated from each other? Are they restless, distracted, resentful, or eager and listening as you talk? And do they ask questions when you are finished? Or doesn't the school give them time because of the "schedule?" Are the students direct, evasive, critical, open? Do they ask personal questions or make comments about their school or classes? Do the students talk about "our" school or do they describe it as a thing "out there?" Is it difficult to sense whether or not you would like to be a student in that school?

I think of Billy who was one of eleven hundred children in a beautiful new elementary school whose atmosphere progressively stifled his growth during that first year. It took him an hour every morning to get to school on the yellow bus. Although a very mannered and quiet fourth grader while in school, he exploded so violently on the bus going home that his parents were constantly being called by the principal to discipline him. Resistant about going to school, fearful of his teacher whom he said "screamed" at everyone, assigned to sit at a lunch table with seven other children none of whom were his friends, lost in the large crowd during recess, subdued by a principal who insisted the children be quiet in the halls, unhappy about not being in the first reading group, his principal joy in school was gym, particularly when he was allowed to play kick ball at which he excelled. He said he didn't mind his gym teacher's insistence that they line up in straight lines, be quiet, and follow instructions exactly. But he did dislike the fifteen-minute lectures this former army sergeant would predictably make about the long-haired boys who were becoming juvenile delinquents. Much of the year in gym, and occasionally during recess and after school, Billy and a selected group of others were given precision military drill exercises for the spring benefit performance. In class, his demanding, tense, and perfectionist teacher marked him down for his sloppy handwriting. She used competitive verbal and numerical games to encourage her children to learn. Several parents complimented her about how she was keeping their children on their toes. Billy, however, fell further behind throughout the year. By itself, the demanding competitive classroom atmosphere might have been tolerable—even enjoyable—to him. Instead, the atmosphere of the rest of the school only aggravated and intensified it beyond his ability to restrain his natural exuberance once he escaped the school. At home he was a different child: mischievous, playful, and explosively outgoing. What will happen to Billy next year and the following year in such an atmosphere? He'll be well-prepared to adjust to the even larger, more impersonal, and authoritarian junior high school. But he won't be more educable.

What makes an educative climate in a school? Let's begin by describing what it is not. Some of my favorite indices are:

1. The principal runs his school through the intercom. Classes are ceaselessly interrupted by crisp announcements and commands.
2. The principal doesn't trust his teachers. He checks each day to see if a teacher has completed his lesson plan.
3. The curriculum is rigidly specified and leaves little choice to individual teachers. A teacher of English cannot select with his class the books they would like to read—even in these days of inexpensive paperbacks.
4. Students have few opportunities to select the topics for their own papers or class discussion.
5. The schedule is king!
6. The corridors are deathly quiet. So are those classrooms that can be controlled. Or the corridors are a crescendo of chaos as are some classes.
7. Children need a pass to go to the bathroom.
8. The office knows where each child is each moment of the school day.
9. Teachers are selected primarily for their academic expertise and not for their educability and maturity, excitement and vitality.
10. The school is so strongly departmentally organized that a history teacher cannot assign a novel without jealousy occurring.
11. Teachers are forbidden to visit the homes of their students.
12. Children are always sitting on the punishment bench outside of the principal's office.
13. Lunch time is 23 minutes long.
14. Teachers spy on the girls smoking in the girls' room.
15. Teachers dread faculty meetings.
16. The lecture method dominates throughout the school.
17. It takes too long to secure supplies.
18. The playground is locked after school.
19. Children don't help each other to learn.

   To create an educative atmosphere in schools, at least four interrelated steps must be taken: limit the size of the school, clarify the school's purposes, develop an intercommunion of basic values among its members, and hire humane and mature adults (The Four School Study Report 1970; Heath 1968*b*; Tamminen and Miller 1968).

School Size

   I know no way to escape what is now an established fact. A humanizing educational environment requires a small-sized school. To build a large school for this generation in these times, regardless of how compelling the financial reasons may be, is to fashion a joyless prison. For fifty years, it will have the viral potential of alienating most of its children. Those districts now cursed with large schools are finding it difficult to escape their bureaucratic atmosphere to create a humanistic one. Current attempts to break up schools of a thousand or four thousand students into "houses" or smaller academic units within existing factory-like structures will be generally unsuccessful. A charismatic, powerfully persuasive and dogged principal may be able to suppress some of the psychological handicaps of large size. But what happens when he leaves? The underlying bureaucratic mentality seeps out of the woodwork.

   What is a "small" school? My rule of thumb is that no school should have more students than every adult and most students can know and encounter in some activity during the week. But what number? Probably not more than a few hundred. Research suggests that a high school between four and five hundred borders on being too large. Beyond that size a bureaucratic atmosphere readily emerges (Tamminen and Miller 1968). Such a school is not too small to meet the needs of its students. Even James Conant, a prime mover for school consolidation, said that a comprehensive school could be maintained with a hundred students in each class. Other groups, like the Educational Commission, the National Commission on School District Reorganization, and the White House Conference on Education have stated that schools could be as small as three to five hundred students and still offer a comprehensive education (D.D. Heath 1971). Are small schools uneconomical? That's a myth. Studies of the Minnesota public schools suggest that schools that graduated fewer than 38 or more than 175 seniors a year were less economical than those that graduated some number in between — which averages out to about four hundred students (Tamminen and Miller 1968). Moreover, if we were clearer about our educational priorities, we could well be much more economical than we now are.

In a small school, a youth knows everyone whom he might eat with, meet coming to school, or play with. He knows when a stranger enters the school. In such a school, every teacher knows something about whomever is discussed in faculty meeting. The school's small size makes it a conscious act to ignore a student. It's large size makes it a conscious act to know one. I don't believe teachers realize how importantly the structure of a school affects their perceptions of students. A small school makes it possible to consider a youngster as an individual and not just one of 150 faces seen in classes each day. Teachers do not have to be so specialized; they can teach several different courses to the same students and so understand them in a broader context than is possible otherwise. Obviously, in a small school, teachers and students can participate readily in each other's lives, in decision-making, and in the formation of expectations and the management of discipline. Only in a small school is it possible for most students to break out of the age-segregated strait jacket we impose on them. Only in a small school will children be able to encounter a number of adults in a diverse range of activities.

No significant improvement in the education of black children in large city schools will occur until most of the schools are abandoned. Too many of them are so bureaucratically rigid, removed from the lives of their youngsters, and staffed like prisons, even to the point of placing a policeman on each floor, that no educative or humanistic atmosphere is even conceivable. It is criminal to put several hundred deeply frustrated, hurt, and angry youngsters together in one building. We must begin back at the beginning—where the kids are. Create small "store-front" schools in each block. A child should be able to walk safely to school. He should be able to play with the same kids he sees in school. The school should have large windows. Parents should be able to visit and participate in the life of the school. Secure a mature and educable master teacher who can teach more than just arithmetic or reading or spelling. Free that teacher of curricular, bureaucratic, and secretarial restraints. Keep the same teacher with the children for several years. Use new teachers, parents, and older children as assistants to provide a range of alternative older persons for children to relate to. Trust them to create that humanistic climate that is critical for wounded and despairing children. Encourage the introduction of more informal activity-type programs that permit movement and involvement (Silberman 1970). Abolish age-segregated grades. Rotate the few specialized teachers needed among the local group of schools. Provide a mobile van complete with a medico-psychological-social worker-educator diagnostic team to be on call to a group of local schools. Perhaps combine middle and high school — but keep them small. Give up the frills. Keep the schools close to home base. Keep alive a caring, community-school atmosphere. Radical and logistically complex? Sure. But until a drastic reform is made in the size of our schools, our children will continue to be crippled in our school-prisons.

Clarity of Purposes

A second essential ingredient of an educative atmosphere is the clarity of the school's goals. Most educators don't know what kind of school they want. Silberman says that much of our education is mindless (1970). I agree. "What's wrong with school is not that teachers don't know what they're teaching, but that they don't know why they're teaching it" (Silberman 1969).

The author of the elementary school survey said, "Neither principals nor teachers were able to articulate clearly just what they thought to be most important for their schools to accomplish. And neither group was very clear on changes that should be effected in the near future" (Goodlad 1969, p. 61).

How can one create an educative atmosphere in a school when one isn't certain how a child needs to grow? What happens, of course, is that education gets watered down to the least common denominator. Teachers become preoccupied with what is easiest to do: impart information and teach a limited number of academic skills. Most schools are simply a collection of isolated classes and activities whose effects frequently undercut each other.

Let me go back to Billy and ask you, as a teacher, what your goals would be for him? The principal goal of too many teachers would be to teach him to spell or speak French, not to further his growth as a human being in the ways I've described in Chapter Six. A teacher dedicated to furthering his educability would answer my question this way: Billy needs to learn how to put his vitality into his academic work, even if he becomes temporarily disruptive in the classroom as a result. The discrepancy between his controlled mannerliness in school and his exuberance at home needs to be reduced. He also needs to learn how to make friends, to begin to think of himself as able to achieve, to learn to enjoy school, *and* to improve his spelling. Such a sensitive teacher would be alert to the effect of gym upon his educability in the classroom, let him sit with his friends at lunch, and find a way to get into his world to understand how he felt about her. She would realize that his handwriting is too trivial an issue to fuss about. She would be alert to how he responded to her competitive games and team him with others to dilute the possibility of individual

failure. She would visit his home and ask his parents for their advice about
how he should be growing. At the faculty meeting, she might question how
recess could be handled differently. She would talk with the gym, music,
and art teachers about his needs as they saw them: What did they think
could be done to help him express himself more spontaneously and integratively. Her goal is clear: To help Billy become more educable and mature. What would a school be like with a principal and teachers who
shared such a similar goal? It would have a powerfully educative atmosphere.

Intercommunion of Values

Neither a small school nor clarity of purpose makes an educative
atmosphere if there is no intercommunion of purpose among the people
in the school. Cardinal Newman long ago identified intercommunion of
purpose and value to be a determinant of a powerfully educative community (1852). But the intercommunion of purpose that created distinctive
and distinguished schools in the past is being eroded away by the turbu-
lence of rapid change and the challenge of younger teachers and youth
itself. Increasingly, faculties are divided about their purposes and the
worth of their traditions. Much of the divisiveness is occurring between
those who advocate only self-actualization or individuation and those who
defend an adjustment or socialization point of view. Should a school value
expressiveness, freedom, self-determination? Should its students be allowed
to swear or wear whatever they want, attend class when they want to, decide what they want to read or what the dormitory or social codes are to
be? Does it really make any difference if a youth spells and writes sentences correctly as long as he can be understood? *Or* should a school value
order, guided development, and preparation for the real world? Should
students learn to accommodate themselves to the sensibilities of others,
particularly adults, to accept responsibility for others, and to honor what
older, more competent persons require?

How do we create greater intercommunion of purpose? Secure educators and not just administrators to be the head of a school and of its
principle departments—educators who have a vision of what a school could
be and what kind of youth the school is to produce. Then carefully select
teachers, not just for their competence, but also for their temperamental
resonance with that vision. Don't try to be all things to all people. Diversity in a faculty may be centrifugal; a school also needs a core of faculty
that provides unity and coherence. Next, develop structures that provoke

periodic reflection about how the school is transforming and fulfilling its vision. Create an atmosphere that expects teachers and students to communicate with each other, but not just about the state of the weather, the football team, or the other Mickey Mouse topics that let us shield ourselves from confronting significant issues.

Create patterns that stimulate meaningful communication. A faculty lounge where coffee is served and chit-chat occurs is not enough. Don't expect intercommunion to result from a typical faculty meeting, in-service training program, or a committee charged to decide "Our Goals for the School." Concepts and abstractions frequently distort what we actually do. They get in the way of understanding *until* we have shared some common experience or action together.

So develop structures that enable faculty to work together on the problems of a boy like Billy, for example. Help teachers share their feelings of inadequacy and despair because they can't reach every kid in their classes. Create a regular consultation period during which teachers get together to discuss specific children. Find ways to help Billy's teacher talk with his gym teacher. Better yet, encourage them to observe how each works with children. Create ways in which teachers can work cooperatively together with Billy and the other children—and then reflect about what they did. Make the educability of Billy the focal point of the communication. Then the abstract issues of freedom, permissiveness, and discipline will lose some of their polarizing effects, because teachers will discover what amount of each a Billy needs.

But, you may say, "Your examples are of elementary school teachers. They are more progressive and flexible than any other group of teachers. How do you develop an intercommunion of purpose among individualistic academicians—say the specialists of your own school?" Fair question. I certainly would not begin by provoking a discussion about the meaning of liberal education. That would result in a collective, abstract ego trip. I will describe an on-going effort of my own school that may produce in time greater commonality of purpose. The faculty recently abandoned most of the formal course requirements for underclassmen that had defined "becoming liberally educated" at Haverford. Instead, it instituted an *inquiry* at the end of a student's second year to assess how he had used his freedom to become educated.

A pilot study was proposed, the heart of which was the creation of faculty-senior teams of five people to assess the growth of ten to twelve students. Each student was to submit a folder that included an essay describing his intellectual growth since matriculation, an example of his best work (a sculpture, a play, a research paper), his grade record, an evaluative statement from his advisor, and, initially, scores from an ETS-designed examination. Both the team and the student would then collectively assess his performance and development to determine how he needed to grow in the future.

What happened? Predictably, many of the faculty were not very enthusiastic about the proposal. Abstract, tendentious objections were raised about almost everything. They were unclear about its purposes, insecure about how a team could conduct a meaningful inquiry that didn't terrify and paralyze students, and uncertain about how to assess liberal education. But the pilot study was undertaken. The results? The students appreciated the attention and advice of five faculty and senior students. The seniors enjoyed working with the faculty and, in fact, often proved themselves better examiners. The faculty stumbled onto a number of insights. They could not make a definitive judgment as to whether one student was more "liberally educated" than another. They learned that students were much more complex and varied than their methods could objectively measure. Glimpsing how students thought and felt about their own growth at the college, some of the faculty for the first time expanded their ideas of what it meant to be a student. The teams recommended that the inquiry be converted from formal examination into a counseling–assessment session to be given at the end of the freshman year. Freshmen about whom there were reservations were to be assessed again at the end of their second year.

Another important result was that the faculty had inadvertently created a new structure for working together on a concrete problem. To participate with an economist, a physicist, an artist, and a linguist to fashion a meaningful, comprehensive discussion with a student proved to be liberally educating to the team itself. Each learned how others viewed the same problem from a different perspective.

The Staff

The dominant impression I get from the schools I've visited is that the key to a school's atmosphere is the style, the "presence," of the influential adults of the school. But what kind of "presence?" Is the principal stiff, brusque, authoritarian, and negative with his teachers? Are the key faculty responsive, concerned, and warm people not easily put off by the life style of some radical students. One senses almost immediately what the adults are like: the way they ask a question, the kinds of questions that concern them, the adjectives they use to describe students. The right kind of adult is deeply committed to the healthy growth of students. The system and the curriculum are not allowed to get in the way. Such attitudes require a high degreee of educability and adaptability to change.

I am increasingly asked how a humanistic atmosphere can be created in a school. The soundest and quickest way is to create a core of educable adult models.

Chapter 9

Educable
Teachers

The key to significant change in schools is the liberation of teachers. The only way to humanize schools is to change the system so that teachers can become more educable and mature persons. Then real education can begin. But not before.

I don't care how many television sets there are in classrooms, how recently the social studies curriculum has been revised, how many modules of time are available to create flexible schedules, or how elaborate the communication studio is. It is human beings who make an educative atmosphere. If a school does not have educable and mature teachers, no innovation will create any significant educational growth.

Our highest priority in the seventies is to liberate ourselves. We need to be freed from the suppression of our affectionate and caring feelings, from the stifling of our imaginations, from the blocks to our initiative.

So the issue is: how do we provide experiences that further the growth of teachers? There are two principal ways: first, alter our structures to force new adaptations, and second, provide more effective forms of teacher-growth experiences throughout the life span of the active teacher.[1]

Alter the System

Psychologists have underestimated the extent to which a person's educability and maturity are limited by the roles he must "play," by the demands of the physical environment in which he works, and by the routinized ways of thinking and doing that he has fallen into.

[1] I ignore one of the most critical formative influences on the educability of teachers, namely, the type of preparation our schools of education provide for beginning teachers. Silberman has spoken fully to this issue (1970).

134

The stereotyped role of the teacher is suffocating and immaturing to a vital and creative person. A teacher must be morally impeccable, sober, subservient, a political eunuch, noncontroversial, "straight," judicious, cool. A teacher must always be conscious that he is a "teacher." He can't take off his shoes and teach sitting on rugs in the classroom and use meditation or movement exercises. He can't play with children—of any age. He can't wrestle, dance, hike, socialize, work with, or even touch students. He can't enter into the world of the kids he must educate. He must always appear to be that dignified, sober, controlled, stuffy puritanical adult. Children seldom experience their teachers as human beings. Many of us have so internalized these and other expectations of what the life style of a teacher should be that we are aghast at even the thought of holding a class on the floor of our classroom. To protect ourselves from our own youthful needs and feelings, we cower behind our masks as teachers or wear them as if they really were our own. For some, their roles as teachers are their own. That's good. But if our lives are only masks, then gradually our students experience less and less a joyful, spontaneous, adventurous, fun-loving teacher able to abandon himself to childish caprice and adolescent passion. We teachers become models of control and sobriety—of boredom and death.

I want a school in which a teacher can be freely himself. I'm not advocating that every teacher now take off his shoes when he enters his classroom. A teacher must maintain his own integrity but, I hope, playfully so. Otherwise, he risks becoming a manipulator of students or an obvious phony. I want an atmosphere in the school that accepts, liberates, and does not condemn humane impulses and feelings. Our stereotyped expectations of a teacher are like a sieve: they sift out all that is idiosyncratic, expressive, colorful, spontaneously delightful, and tender. We need to stop channeling our teachers so narrowly. We need much greater psychological diversity in our adult models. Children need to know adults with whom they resonate and can identify. So let's abandon the role of playing "teacher" and learn how to be more fully human with students.

I was not aware of how much my own teaching style and mode of relating to students were affected by the physical structure of the classroom until I brought rugs into my classes on which students could sprawl if they wanted to. Several decades ago we took the bolts out of the desks that kept them in straight rows facing the teacher. We have yet to take the psychological bolts out of such classrooms. When twenty-five students sit facing us, what happens? We become the focus of attention. The desk in front of us is our physical symbol of authority as well as the barrier to spontaneous ways of relating to students. Our fragile egos may be bolstered by such an arrangement, but what are the other consequences? We are forced to be more active and directive. The responsibility for the class becomes exclusively ours. If we have a discussion, it is initiated by us and is a collective dialogue. We ask Jimmy a question, then Mary, and then Susie. Since it is easy for a student to hide in a group of twenty-four others, our discussions usually involve only four or five students at best. Students can't see the faces of the others anyway. Just heads. It's much easier just to drift off into obscurity and daydream if one can interact only with a droning teacher or the backs of heads. Why do students have to sit in chairs for several hours a day? Why can't those who would be more comfortable lie on the floor? Why can't they take off their shoes, stretch out, and sprawl as they wish? They'll become more educable. They'll be less self-conscious about risking a question and more argumentative. The traditional physical arrangement of our class assures a teacher-dominated classroom. It enhances passivity, dependence, boredom, interpersonal isolation, and noninvolvement.

The traditional classroom arrangement also affects our teaching style and constricts our imagination. It forces us into an information-dispensation or lecture role, the easiest of all the modes of teaching. We physically tower over the students; they must look up to us. I became aware of the subtle psychological effects of this physical relation when I sat on the floor looking up to some of my students. Some of them were able to talk more fluently when they were able to look down at me.

With a circle of students, it's harder for a student to lose himself in the group. To imaginative teachers, an open space in the middle of the class opens up other teaching possibilities: psychodrama, role-playing, smaller and larger circle discussion techniques, and other experiential forms of learning. We educators need to examine much more critically how the physical environment of the school constrains our humanness.

If we want to wake ourselves up, force ourselves to adapt and grow in new ways, then let's change our physical environment to liberate us from our habitual and deadening ways of teaching. As an experiment, get rid of three quarters of the desks in your school tomorrow, place rugs in each room, and feel the frustration that is necessary to new adaptations. But don't make a fetish out of such a change. Be adaptable. Flow with the needs of yourself and your students. In one class I taught, we moved six different times in the first six weeks of class until we found the particular setting that appealed to most of the group. There may be many arrangements for those teachers confined all day to an assigned classroom.

The last structural determinant I want to mention briefly is the unconscious routinized habits of thought that have imprisoned us for decades.

There is no more insidious barrier to becoming more educable than to *know* that what we believe is true and what we do is right. Arrogance destroys educability. Most of our educational truths and practices are myths and rituals. We embody them, for example, in the sacred schedule (I will look at the holy curriculum later.)

The fact is that our schedule of seven forty-five minute periods a day dictates our priorities and teaching methods. The fact should be that our priorities and methods dictate our schedules. Let's see. We have seven periods a day. That means a student can have one free period for study hall, band practice or other activity. That leaves six periods. There's time for his five major subjects each day and three minor ones that can be alternated with assembly and gym. We stuff our knowledge into forty-five minute packages and then transfer five of these bundles each week to our students. Of course, there is no evidence whatsoever that this particular schedule is an effective way to make students educable. But since we have always done it this way, it must be right.

What is the consequence of this schedule for teachers? We too must fill up our seven periods. We must convey similar bundles of information to four or five groups of students each day. If we put too much energy and enthusiasm into transferring our packages, we are very tired by the end of the day. But since we must correct homework assignments and prepare for the next day, to conserve our energy, we operate in low gear. Who but a manic can maintain his enthusiasm, excitement, and involvement day in and day out with 150 students, most of whom he will never know well? I couldn't. I could never survive as a high school teacher emotionally. After several years of this dampened transferral process, teaching becomes routinized and boring—to us and to our students. But we've always done it this way; it's natural and right.

What can a teacher do in forty-five minutes? By the time the class has settled down, announcements made, and papers returned, there may be 39 minutes left. So you initiate a discussion. The argument begins to get focused and the students involved. Brrrrrr . . . the bell sounds. Off dash the students to the next class to repeat the same teasing game. The argument is unresolved. You turn to the next class. Soon you find this process too frustrating and wearing. It's easier to occupy the time talking at the students. They find that easier too. They don't have to be prepared. Our schedule teaches students not to get involved.

I have been a victim of the schedule in a different way. I'm asked to speak in assembly for thirty minutes and answer questions for fifteen. By the time the stragglers are seated, announcements and introductions made, and my profound message delivered (which is always longer than necessary), I have six minutes left for the potentially most rewarding part of the 45 minutes. Just as we launch into a question that challenges a point or seeks to clarify an ambiguity, the bell rings. "We are so grateful that Dr. Heath has spoken with us today. We must close now, but those who have a study hall next period can remain if they wish!" Who of us willingly would organize our day like this if we were trying to help youngsters become more educable?

There are other myths and rituals we know to be true and right. A student should take four or five major and three minor courses simultaneously, although they may so fragment him that no integrative intellectual experience is possible. A college-bound student must have several years of German even though he has no talent for it, is bored, and is becoming deeply resistant about learning any other language anytime. We have always taught year-long courses in secondary school though we risk boring a student by such an inflexible curricular plan. We staff our courses with experts when increasingly students need models of how a wise nonexpert goes about mastering a field he himself doesn't know much about.

We have so enshrined our myths and rituals in our system that to challenge them is to confront God himself. Some adventurous faculties are freeing themselves of these myths and rituals. More of us must do so if we are going to make the changes necessary to meet the growth needs of this generation. The following chapters assume that the schedule reflects rather than dictates our priorities.

We don't become more educable and mature unless we confront a problem. What a marvelous problem we could confront ourselves with if we lengthened our class hours to 75 or 90 minutes. Why not teach science three or even two times a week for an hour and half each time? Why not stop lecturing and, instead, hand out ditto copies of what we had planned to say and then divide our classes into small simultaneous discussion groups? Why don't we really take a fresh look at our curriculum instead of tinkering with it by rearranging little chunks here and there? We never get to the heart of the matter: how to so disrupt our own lives that we become more educable and alive persons in the classroom.

Let's assume you teach history. Tomorrow, play charades in class using the names of historic characters or incidents. You will begin to free your students of their inhibitions about expressing themselves in front of others. The day after tomorrow, take off your tie and roll up your sleeves and begin to feel comfortable—if this is what would make you more spontaneous while teaching. And the day after that, begin to question your colleagues about the sanctity of *the* schedule. The next day exchange classes with the English teacher and deal with the poem he was going to deal with. Why not be really way out the next day? Follow some of your students through their schedule. Discover what they go through day in and day out. Learn how your students function in other courses. You may never think about Betty again in quite the same way. She may come alive when she demonstrates her competence in biology. You will begin to understand your students as human beings.

Continuous Growth Experiences

Schools have failed to provide structures for helping teachers continue to mature and become more educable during their teaching careers. Let's be honest. Such rituals as sitting passively through another boring in-service, two-day workshop or taking another trivial course during a hot sticky summer change the behavior of very few teachers.

Those adults who are already educable will read books like this and try some of the new ideas out in the classroom, but how do we help our colleagues who don't read such books to be open to continued change for the next twenty years of teaching? The first prod, namely, the "shock, confusion, perturbation, uncertainty" of which Dewey spoke, is already at hand. I don't agree with the critics who say that most teachers are hopelessly uneducable. Most teachers are not close-minded and arrogant. True, some may *appear* to be. But when I get by these defensive stances, I discover few teachers who believe they are doing the best job possible for today's youth. Instead, I find much uncertainty and discouragement that are potentially healthy if they can be channeled into constructive change.

To repeat the message of Part III: to become more educable is to risk being shook up personally, to reflect, to be willing to explore new alternatives, to form tentative lines of action, to test their viability, and then to use the best in the classroom.

The problem is not that most teachers are not potentially educable and receptive to change. The problem is we have not developed powerful enough forms for helping teachers to help themselves become more educable and mature.

What types of growth-experiences might we explore? I will talk primarily about those I have had experience with, for I know some of their effects and defects. I order my suggestions in terms of their increasing power to involve teachers in examining their own attitudes, motives, and styles. Any powerful experience challenges our myths and rituals and disrupts us personally. It is a threat to our stability. Therefore, any program to further educability may create defensive resistance in immature teachers as well as encourage healthy growth in mature teachers. The more powerful growth experiences require professional guidance.[2] For ethical reasons, I believe these more powerful procedures should be offered only for volunteers who are aware of their purposes and general procedures.[3]

Of the suggestions I have, the least powerful is to bring someone to the school to be a catalyst for change. An outsider who is not identified with either the administration, faculty or students can provoke more open communication and reexamination among the groups than can be generated by anyone within the school. To stir up faculties, I might talk on a theme for twenty minutes, like boredom, and then ask the faculty to break into groups of four or five to examine the implications of my comments for their own classrooms. I ask them to share with each other, if they feel comfortable doing so, several things they do which may bore their students or suppress spontaneity in their classrooms or in the school. After twenty minutes or so, the groups reconvene. I proceed, say, to discuss rootlessness. Twenty minutes later the faculty breaks again to examine how the structure of their school may accentuate feelings of isolation and loneliness in their youngsters and themselves. I then follow the same procedure with the topic of meaninglessness, after which I ask them to discuss among themselves the implications of these forms of alienation for themselves personally and as teachers. By this time, some groups are so involved in exploring issues that many have never shared with each other that I become superfluous. In fact, it is sometimes difficult to get some groups to come back to the larger group after the first small group discussion. I don't think there was resistance because I was too threatening—or boring.

What does such a procedure accomplish? Most teachers, like their students, need a forum that sanctions and accepts without criticism open and direct self-revelation about their concerns. From others they may learn more about their own less-conscious apprehensions and hang-ups. Teachers also may learn how to listen more actively and critically during the talk, for they know they will shortly be discussing its implications with each other. And they are also securing some training about how they might break up their own forty-minute lecture to cultivate more active involvement by their students.

Another potentially powerful method to help teachers become edu-

---

[2] To induce enduring changes in a school is much more difficult than my comments indicate. Not just individual teachers but their patterns of relationships (the system or organization itself), must be so modified that means of self-renewal become integral parts of the system. For insight into the problems of changing organizations, see Benedict, Calder, Callahan, Hornstein and Miles 1967; McElvaney and Miles 1969.

[3] For an excellent discussion of the ethical issues involved in sensitivity sessions, see Lakin 1969.

cable is to create small experiential workshops. Their explicit purpose would be to induce and provide support to their members to change their own teaching style and relations with their students. We teachers have not learned how to develop mutual self-help educational forms. It is a myth that it takes a professional to help another person become more mature. A small group of teachers who feel comfortable with each other might create a weekly two-hour session to discuss a common reading about education. For example, a group might work its way chapter by chapter through this book to draw out its inconsistencies, ambiguities, and implications. Better yet, a group of faculty and students might do the same thing, but explore its implications for their relationships with each other and for how their own school might humanize itself. As the members of such groups felt a growing acceptance of each other, they might become oriented to deliberate self-change. Might not such a group provide guidance and support to a teacher who was struggling to respond maturely in her relations with a Billy? Might not it provide invaluable support to new teachers who get practically no professional assistance during their critical first years? Eventually, the group might explore role-playing and other group procedures by which each could help the other learn how to deal with their classes more effectively (G.I. Brown 1971).

But you ask, "Where do I get the time to read a book and participate in such a supportive group for two hours a week?" Such a group is a form of in-service education. Time should come from the hours you work in school. I'm serious. Our highest priority is to find ways to help teachers become more educable. Schools must free their schedules so that every teacher has the opportunity to participate in personal and professional self-development during the hours school is in session. Teachers should not avoid the challenge of confronting their own development by correcting student papers or retreating to the smoking lounge. They need the stimulation, guidance, and support of other teachers. To create such a group is to begin to create an educative atmosphere in the school. To release groups of teachers for such an experiential workshop, we could, at the very least, give more responsibility to students to monitor their own study halls in the afternoon, assist in supervising young children on the playground, or conduct classes. Education can go on when we are not in the classroom.

A third way to encourage greater educability in teachers requires professional expertise. I myself have been reluctant to provide more personal self-revealing and growth experiences by using encounter group procedures with faculties for reasons I discuss later. But I have found another way that preserves a teacher's right to his privacy, but gives him the opportunity to participate freely in exploring his understanding of students and hence himself. A school identifies a child who represents a typical management or educational problem, who is known by most faculty, and whose parents assent to the procedure. I visit the school, observe a child like Billy in class, read his records and test scores, interview the teachers who know the child, and then interview and test the child with a selected group of psychological tests. I draw the material together for an intensive faculty workshop. I describe my understanding of him, how he needs to become more mature, and what I observed about the school that might accentuate his difficulties. I then suggest, very tentatively, some changes that could be tried in the classroom and the school that might further his educability. I don't pretend my understanding of that particular child is accurate, for there is seldom time to make a careful analysis. The material is used only for illustrative purposes about how to understand a child and how a school might meet his needs.

The meaningful point in the workshop comes when the teachers feel comfortable enough to talk about how angry and desperate Billy has made them. By focusing on a real live itch in the classroom and exploring their ways of scratching that itch, some teachers begin to develop more skill in understanding and coping with their own personal hang-ups about certain types of children. They begin to understand the complex causes of behavior. Also, new communication patterns are formed between teachers who may have never talked with each other about their feelings before.

Obviously, such professional assistance is expensive and not readily available. Schools say traditional psychiatrists are not too useful. They seldom observe a child in the classroom, know little about education, and are ignorant about the real problems teachers face in coping with twenty-five to thirty-five children in a class. No saint could follow the recommendations I have read in some children's folders.

So where are we to secure the professional expertise for this type of growth-experience? We need to generate it within the school itself by radically redefining the goals of our guidance counselors and school psychologists. I have urged elsewhere that a counselor should be the expert about the educable and maturing effects of the school's atmosphere (1968a). The primary focus of his efforts should be to help the adults of the school become more educable and more understanding of children. Obviously, to fill such a role, counselors need a different type of training, which they should be able to get.

A fourth way to develop more educable adults in a school is to use the controversial methods developed by the human potential movement, best represented by the Esalen Institute (Gustaitis 1969), National Training Laboratories (Bennis 1967), and Carl Rogers (1969, 1970). The sensitivity and encounter groups, gestalt therapy procedures, marathons, and sensory awareness sessions encompass many diverse techniques. In any detailed critique of the human potential movement it is essential that careful distinctions be made between the different techniques. I do not intend to make such an analysis here. Besides, too little adequate research has been done on the procedures to determine what types of persons might benefit from them, what the principal effects are, how long such effects persist, and how to modify the environment to maintain such effects. I confine myself to some general comments and recommendations, with which many may disagree.

What happens in an encounter group? There is no standard procedure. Different leaders have different styles and encourage different types of activities. Central to any group, however, is the mutual exploration of each one's feelings about the others and the development of healthier ways of relating. The focus of the group is on what is happening at the moment between the members. A variety of techniques may be used to encourage increased awareness and to confront a person with his less-conscious interpersonal styles: physical contact, sensory awareness exercises, role playing, more specialized techniques associated with gestalt therapy, meditation, movement, and dance.

Here are several recommendations. First, many of the specific growth-inducing and releasing techniques now being developed in such centers can be integrated into the work of the classroom. I discuss them in later chapters. Second, I do not recommend at this time the use of typical encounter procedures for groups of teachers from the same school except under special conditions. Third, I urge that each school district make available the opportunity for a teacher to participate, if he so wishes, in an educational encounter-type workshop conducted elsewhere that extends over a number of weeks. Fourth, I strongly urge that regional, readily accessible, educational growth centers be established where the development and testing of new experiential learning procedures can be carried on. Principals, school psychologists, and key faculty who are models for other teachers and students could visit such centers for leadership training.

I don't recommend that encounter groups be used within a school for its faculty at this time—simply because the procedures are potentially more powerful than most schools may be able to take. To participate in an encounter group can be a disruptive emotional experience, particularly for intellectuals who don't live close to their feelings. Consequently, the effects of a group cannot be confined to the group itself. Faculty who resist joining such groups may be resentful about the "in group" atmosphere that develops among participants. It would be difficult to preserve the confidentiality of what goes on in a group if many, but not all, of the teachers of a school participate. Latent divisiveness within a faculty could be accentuated. Because members of such groups may learn that they can release tightly suppressed competitive and hostile feelings, particularly toward authority, they may become more assertive toward department heads and the administration outside of the group. My hunch is that those teachers who are almost exclusively intellectual could become centers of very strong resistance within a group and generate much antagonism. Yet, if they remained outside the group, such persons would be predisposed to be deprecating and sarcastic critics. Finally, while such procedures are primarily for basically healthy and stable persons, it would be difficult to exclude an unstable and neurotic colleague insistent on participating. A school must continue to function. But if its ordinary fabric of interpersonal and working relationships becomes emotionally shredded, its students suffer.

In time, research may clarify what encounter procedures are appropriate growth-experiences for a school to provide for what teachers under what conditions. I would feel more comfortable recommending encounter procedures within a school for faculty volunteers if: the principal and a few key faculty have participated earlier in similar workshops; other faculty have been psychologically prepared for becoming emotionally involved and more open by participating in other growth-experiences like some I've been recommending; there is faculty-wide acceptance that such procedures may be disruptive and that some nonparticipating faculty may feel resistant and excluded; the faculty is willing to endure and use the potentially disruptive effects as the incentive to make significant changes in the atmosphere and style of personal relationships within the school; and most important, there is a highly qualified leader available who is sensitive to the institutional complexity of a school.

Since a school has an obligation to help its teachers become more educable and mature, it should give them the opportunity to have an intensive educational-encounter group experience. Teachers from different schools could apply for evening sessions of three hours each that might run for ten to twelve weeks. Four to five such groups of twelve to fifteen adults could be set up. About two hundred teachers could thus participate in any one year, which would make it economically feasible for a district to get a competent leader. I would recommend that two or three teachers from the same school participate in encounter sessions at the same time in order to develop a mutually supportive core group within a school. I would also recommend that the encounter procedures incorporate many experiential educational techniques as integral parts of the sessions. The teacher might be encouraged to adapt some to his own classroom teaching.

Every faculty has its unstable and less mature members. Teachers are human, too. We become depressed, suicidal, fretful, suspicious, hostile, overly sensitive, sadistic, lonely, withdrawn, cold, unapproachable, and tight. Such teachers can have destructive effects on students as well as on the atmosphere of the school. Who enjoys working with a bitchy, hostile, complaining colleague? Just as schools should provide growth-inducing experiences, like encounter groups, for healthy and stable teachers, so should they provide opportunities for less healthy teachers to get intensive psychological assistance. I would not rely just on individual therapy; I would encourage the experimental use of group forms of therapy. Why pay thousands of dollars to teachers who warp and destroy kids and refuse, for a fraction of the money, to provide resources that might help them become healthier adults?

The most urgent recommendation I make is that educators learn more about what sensitivity procedures are most appropriate for promoting educability within a school. As is true of any "movement" that explores new ways of promoting maturing, many bizarre and morally unconventional activities will be advocated and defended. Devotees, faddists, proselytizers, and charlatans obscure and distort the genuine merits of the many different techniques. *Life* magazine can create an unfortunate image of an Esalen by vividly picturing only its mixed nude bathing in its sulphur baths and portraying nude sun and moon worshippers. The movie *Bob and Carol and Ted and Alice* makes us laugh at the "movement," but profanes its spirit. Despite this sensationalism, I found Esalen to be a deeply moral experience. The search for integrity involves much suffering and pain, scrupulous honesty and reflection. We need regional educational growth centers that are not afraid to be in touch with the avant-garde, to test the educative power of new techniques, and to determine their appropriateness in the schools. These regional centers could serve as demonstration units of new experiential forms of education to which principals, school psychologists, and key faculty could go, not just to observe or listen to another lecture, but to become more educable by directly experiencing new group techniques. The center could also provide consultants who could help those schools from which several representatives had come adapt what was learned at the center to the specific school setting.

A critical unresolved problem about the encounter group procedure is whether its effects endure when a person returns to the old setting and long-established, conventional patterns of relationships. One way to stabilize one's increased educability is to form a small group of those who have had encounter experiences. Such a group can provide mutual support, the security to be vulnerable, and the opportunity for periodic resensitization. Once a core of teachers has participated in such an experience, then the atmosphere of the school may become more acceptant and supporting. If such an educative atmosphere begins to develop, then the school itself becomes the support that maintains the growth of those who participate in subsequent encounter groups.

Chapter 10

Shared
Expectations

A school helps young people become mature by sharing with them the process of developing high, consistent, and humane expectations of what they are to do and to become. Noble goal. But this prescription is a Pandora's box of hidden, complex, emotionally charged issues that demand another book for clarification. So I must be selective. My purpose here is to describe an attitude to take toward educating students. The next chapter describes more concretely my own efforts — and failures — to fulfill the prescription.

Frankly, I am unsettled about the wisdom of asserting that expectations are central determinants of healthy growth. On the one hand, my own research tells me that of forty different causes of a youth's maturing in my own school, the expectations of its faculty ranked between third and eighth in importance (1968b). Self-determination and autonomy are not synonymous with self-expression and willfulness nor do I believe that a permissive environment (where there is an absence of expectations) nor an authoritarian environment (where there is an absence of the freedom of choice) promotes healthy autonomy. Finally, I am temperamentally a person who holds students to very high expectations.

On the other hand, I can't ignore the affirmation of Fritz Perls, founder of Gestalt therapy,

> I do my thing, and you do your thing.
> I am not in this world to live up to your expectations
> And you are not in this world to live up to mine.
> You are you and I am I,
> And if by chance we find each other, it's beautiful.
> If not, it can't be helped (1969, p. 4).

147

Nor can I close my mind to the power of Neill's Summerhill (1960), the humanity of John Holt's passionate defense of individuality (1964), the experience that supports Carl Rogers's nondirective mode of teaching (1969), the spirit of the Free School movement, and Laing's insistence that we do violence to another when we hold an expectation of him (1967). Each says that our expectations—externally imposed rules, academic requirements, prescribed courses, and schedules—stifle a youth's maturing and snuff out his curiosity and vitality.

Perls, Neill, Rogers, Holt, and Laing are sensitive, perceptive, persuasive people. Their ideas have created the controversy and inspiration that is the growing edge of much educational change today. But note a curious fact. With the exception of Holt (greatly influenced by Neill), each man has had many years of psychotherapeutic training and experience. They have extended their therapeutic insights about healthy growth to the school and the role of the teacher.

But is a teacher a therapist? A therapist a teacher? No. A few gifted persons may be both. But to teach is not to do therapy.

To teach and to do therapy are both arts. Both have the same goal: to assist another person become more educable and mature. Both involve complex and subtle activities difficult to describe. Neither can be proscribed by specific "do's" and "don'ts." Both are relational activities. Both involve at least two different human beings in direct, persisting communication. Teachers and therapists usually are more mature than their students or patients. Each has skills, knowledge, and wisdom that the students or patients seek to take advantage of or make their own. What we learn from teaching and therapy may assist us to understand how to release blocks and stimulate growth. (Therapists and teachers can learn from each other, although until now it has been the teacher who has been more influenced by the therapist.)

Despite these similarities, teaching and therapy are not identical. Teachers work primarily with students who are still educable and growing; therapists primarily with patients who are severely blocked, even regressing. Teachers focus more on confronting a youth with external reality; therapists more on confronting a youth with inner reality. Teachers are trained to communicate knowledge, cultivate specific adaptive skills like reading, and provoke involvement with substantive issues. Therapists are trained to be sensitive to the nuances of their relationship with a patient and to help him become more aware of himself as well as more open to his feelings about other people.

Teachers work with preformed structures: organized information, sequential curricular patterns, and the school itself. Therapists work with amorphous structures: wishes, fantasies, and motives. Teachers tend to value societal authority and view their task as preparing a person to adjust to society. Therapists tend to value individual autonomy and view their task as helping actualize, that is, individuate, a person to be in harmony with himself.

What distinguishes a teacher from a therapist are his expectations. True, both expect a student or patient to become more mature. But a teacher's expectation is that his students will learn that knowledge and become more mature in those intellectual skills, attitudes, and values that promote his adaptation. A therapist's primary expectation is that his patients will alter their concepts of themselves and develop more mature relations with others. At times, a teacher must act like a therapist using the educational resources at his command. So must a therapist act like a teacher with what resources he commands. Of course, teaching and therapy are not mutually exclusive. A person grows healthily by growing wholly. Therefore, how a youth is growing in his personal relations affects what happens in the classroom; how he is growing in his intellectual skills affects what happens in the therapy hour. How a person matures wholly is the basis of our understanding of him. A teacher works with one of the figures emerging from the background; a therapist with another. But each figure is only part of the ground. *That* is what a teacher-therapist deeply understands—and never ignores.

When prescribing for teachers, Neill, Holt, Rogers, Perls, and Laing emphasize the therapeutic orientation. Neill and Holt strongly reject societal authority and the traditional structures of the school. Neill even rejects the importance of books. Both assume that a youth will grow more fully if his freedom is not restricted by expectations, even by an expectation that he learn a skill like reading. Both Rogers and Laing emphasize the pursuit of the self rather than the world "out there." Both also reject the legitimacy of external authority, emphasizing the importance of the development of individual autonomy. Perls emphasizes "do your own thing." All blur the distinctions between therapy and teaching. They devalue the socializing function of teaching to extol its self-actualizing function.

The Free School movement, which is a test of these ideas is worth examining here. Dissatisfied with the suppressive and crippling effects of the public schools, as documented by Silberman (1970), hundreds of small parental groups are developing their own schools in which the teacher is ideally a resource person. A child chooses for himself if he wants to learn to read, what he is to do during the day, what class, if any, he is to attend.

The Experimental Schools Corporation of Arizona said of its elementary school, "We will not attempt to 'teach,' per se but instead will provide an environment within which children will have the unrestricted opportunity to explore and create at their will. The only basic restrictions center around the notion of destruction of one another and the destruction of the materials and facilities" (*New Schools Exchange Newsletter,* No. 43, 1970). The Second Foundation School puts it this way:

> The rejection of the traditional role of teachers is based on the idea that people are naturally curious and are basically interested in the world around them. They are also capable of teaching themselves; and, in fact, this is the best way for them to develop their individual potential. Our goal is to gear teaching to the needs of the students in an atmosphere of freedom, openness, and honesty. The teachers are resource agents in an environment adapted to what the students attending find worthwhile. Initiatives for study will come from both staff and students. There will be no mandatory testing or grading; attendance at all activities of the school is voluntary (*New Schools Exchange Newsletter,* No. 41, 1970).

Such schools are the flowering of the commitment to self-actualization as the primary goal of education. I have earlier rejected such a goal, as it is usually defined, primarily on theoretical grounds. It may enhance self-centeredness and hence limit subsequent integration, stabilization, and automatization. If such occurs, then a youth will be limited in his ability to make mature adaptations that take into account the expectations and needs of other persons. He may become unhealthily, rather than healthily, maladjusted to his society.

My rejection may be premature or unfair. It is more important to look at what the proponents of self-actualization actually do when they "teach" children than what they say their abstract goal is. The validity of their assumptions about the conditions that promote healthy development will be settled not by belief, but by empirical test. The Free Schools offer that test. I will support more strongly the Free School philosophy or other child-centered approaches if it is shown that they do produce *healthily* maladjusted students.

But what is the evidence to date? Only anecdotal comments similar to those offered by the proponents of encounter groups are available. "We have found that this kind of experience allows children to learn how to learn, enabling them to move into unexplored areas of knowledge and quickly achieve a level of competence that most educators tell us is impossible (Experimental Schools Corporation of Arizona, *New Schools*

Exchange Newsletter, No. 43, 1970). I know of no *adequate* evidence I
could accept as a researcher about the long term maturing effects of the
Summerhill approach and the teacher-only-as-a-resource mode of relating
to students (Hart 1970).

So what stance should we take toward the ideas of Neill and Holt
while they are being tested by the Free Schools? First, no one mode of
teacher-student interaction is *the* healthiest mode for all students. Therefore, we should vigorously encourage the Free School movement and other
radical critiques of our traditional ways of nurturing healthy development. We need greater diversity in our schools. I want small neighborhood schools that differ in philosophy and approach within the same
school district. I want a youth to have the opportunity to attend a school
outside his immediate neighborhood at public expense if it might encourage his maturing more effectively.

Second, we should demand adequate follow-up assessments of how
students in the Free Schools learn to adapt. The test of their adaptation is
not *how* they respond to the environment of the Free School itself, but to
the larger society. I don't doubt that the schools will help students become
maladjusted Many of them already are or else they wouldn't seek out such
schools. The issue is whether the Free Schools help them become healthily
or unhealthily maladjusted.

Third, even if the Free Schools do nurture maturing effects, we must
remain skeptical about what their proponents claim were the critical causes
of such effects. The same questions should be asked of the Free Schools as
of the educational technologists, team-teaching enthusiasts, encounter
group adherents, and other innovators. Are the effects due to the enthusiasm and personal commitment of the adults, or to the idiosyncratic
charisma of teachers like Neill, irrespective of the modes of teaching they
use? Does the school obtain the same effects five years after its inception
as it does in its first few years when novelty and enthusiasm are greatest?
Are the effects due primarily to the school's setting rather than to its
methods? After all, the evidence seems clear that small school communities
do provide more maturing and less alienating environments.

Fourth, what types of students are Free Schools most appropriate
for? My hunch is that the compulsively rigid or suppressed child may benefit most from the freedom from adult expectations permitted in a Summerhill (Neill 1960)—if he doesn't collapse completely when given such freedom.
As therapists have known for years, a secure, permissive, unstructured environment is the treatment of choice for inhibited children. It certainly
doesn't necessarily follow that it is the most favorable growth-inducing
mode for a healthy child. It probably is not the educational method of

choice for impulsively uncontrolled children, like many in our center city schools, who need the security of stable, warm, but *firm* adults to help them master their impulses. Neill doesn't tell us how many of his students couldn't cope with Summerhill's freedom and so had to be asked to leave.

Fifth, my hunch is that the Free School methods will be most useful for helping young children mature but less useful in assisting mature youths to continue to develop. The integrated day program used in some English elementary schools suggests that less structured and more individually centered learning is effective with many young children (Silberman 1970; Yeomans 1967, 1969). But an older and more mature youth has the autonomy to accommodate to expectations and demands without being suppressed in other areas of his development. A more structured program may be a more efficient way for him to master information and skills rapidly. A student unable to accommodate to expectations and structured programs has many fewer options available to him. And a measure of a student's freedom is the number of real choices he has created for himself.

Finally, the assumptions made by the Free Schools about why healthy development occurs are romantically simplistic. Children vary enormously in the degree of their "innate curiosity." Other needs, like those for security and affection, may become dominant and limit a child's curiosity. I know no evidence that demonstrates that "freed" curiosity necessarily leads to sustained mastery of a skill in children without considerable stimulation, guidance, and much reinforcement from adults. Development just does not "unfold." A child is not innately "wise" about what skills he needs for his survival as an adult in our society. Healthy growth is the result of a continual interaction between the child's potentials for acting and the environment's expectations about, stimulation of, and response to those potentials. Growth can be facilitated by providing an organized environment appropriate to the child's developmental level. An art of teaching is how to arrange the environment in orderly sequential steps that help a child make progressively systematic differentiations. The brochures of some Free Schools read as if a child is to be presented with a rich, but only randomly organized, environment out of which he is to wrestle his own meaning and organization.

So I predict that after the first flush of enthusiasm, the Free Schools will become increasingly more structured, their teachers will initiate more guidance and direction, and their expectations about how a child develops will become more visible and consciously implemented.

Neill and other critics have over-reacted to the suppressive, authoritarian and conformist expectations of many schools and have ignored the fact that expectations can stimulate and guide healthy growth. They see a child's curiosity as the only determinant of his development. But the desire to be like an adult is another impetus to growth. So is an encounter with a problem, difficulty or challenge that produces "shock, confusion, perturbation, uncertainty." An expectation is a challenge that, through frustration and tension can initiate the adaptive process.

I like to think of an expectation as an anticipation of a potential to be realized. We can best further a youth's educability by developing shared, high, consistent, and humane expectations of how both we and our students are to function in class.

All of the qualifying words are important, but most critical is "shared"—the similarity of the teacher's and the students' expectations of how they are to grow. If my expectations prevail, the students see me as responsible for the course. It is *my* course. It is *my* assignment. It is *my* expectatiion that they write papers. One way to "get back at me" is to fail *my* course. If students respect me and agree with my expectation, they might internalize them and learn to assume the responsibility of fulfilling them. More often than not nowadays, a student does not feel it his responsibility to complete a teacher's expectation. Increasingly, students feel that they work for somcone else; they feel suppressed. The expectations are the system's, not theirs. No wonder they fight to eliminate grades which tell them who's running the show. Increasingly, students are not going to accept our arbitrarily imposed expectations. They will demand that we justify what we require of them. We confront a widening cleavage between our expectations and those of our more sensitive and able students.

What do I mean by sharing expectations? For many years, I have asked students to determine how we were to assign grades for my courses. Out of one hundred points, how many should be assigned in the final grade for papers, different examinations, class participation, and so on. But this past year, a student said, "But you say that tests and papers aren't an adequate measure of what we might get from this course. Who knows? We may grow in other ways. Why don't we leave 25 of the 100 points unassigned to be given for growth in other ways?" We agreed that at the end of the course, each student and I were to evaluate independently his growth. If we disagreed, we would try to reach some consensus. But then I wondered just how I was to evaluate what thirty different students were getting out of the course beyond what I saw in their exams and papers. We needed to clarify our expectations about what we meant by "growing in other ways." A committee was formed, meetings were held, and ten criteria (called *queries* at a Quaker college) emerged. The class didn't like some of them and returned them to the committee to be reworked. We next submitted eight queries. Still unsatisfactory. Finally, the class agreed that the *Six Queries Plus A and B* (on page 155) were to be our expectations for the course. *Plus A and B* were criteria some students vigorously claimed were inappropriate for an academic course. So we agreed that those students who wished to include A and B as optional criteria for their growth could do so.

If an expectation is to initiate growth, then it must demand behavior that is neither habitual nor beyond what the student can reasonably learn. A principal function of a teacher is to hold as high expectations of a student as he is able to meet. That is, we need to help the student develop a realistic vision of what he can become. Since our intuition of his potential may be incorrect and since it is his decision anyway what level of expectation he wants to achieve, we have to work toward consensual agreement about our joint expectations of each other. The development of a "weness" attitude between teacher and student will make it easier for each to say "no" to the other if either's demands are excessive. One student exasperatedly told me one day, "Don't push me. I'm right on schedule." I stopped pushing. He knew where he was.

How can we develop ways to get such feedback to minimize disagreement about our mutual expectations? Why not ask students to evaluate their own classroom performance or their own papers after they have completed them? Why not have students assess our comments about their papers? Why not have students write on the backs of their examinations their estimate of how well they did, which we see only after we have corrected them? Why don't we develop rotating committees each week that meet with us to assess how the classes went for the week and how we need to change? If there are too great discrepancies between our evaluations and theirs, we know we both need to clarify our expectations. In other words, we should try to get within the student's frame of reference to determine if our expectations are too low or too high. We also need to allow students to get within our frame of reference. I don't teach as well as I could. I fail too often to make my expectations clear and to determine if they are similar to those of my students. Recently, some of my students have volunteered to help me grade examinations. Students said they never realized before what I expected an A answer to be. They were also surprised by the range of responses that can come from a group of thirty students. Some understood my problems as a teacher a little more sympathetically.

Grades have been the traditional method for informing students about how closely they have matched expectations. Grades become an issue for many reasons. They may be unjust or may communicate too little information about how a person has not met expectations. They may be

Six Queries Plus A and B

1. To what extent have I become engaged in the course material and course activities?
    Have I mastered basic concepts and terms? (Refer to diagnostic exam and other indicators.)
    Have I actively participated in extra sessions?
    Have I discussed the content of the course outside of class?
    Have I integrated the content of this course with material in other courses?

2. To what extent have I developed intrinsic intellectual interest in the course?
    Have I extended myself beyond the regular class work and done outside reading, writing, and thinking?
    Am I motivated by other than external factors, like grades?

3. Have I contributed to the effectiveness of the class?
    Have I been actively involved in class discussion and not allowed myself to become simply a passive observer?
    Have I maintained a sustained interest in the course?
    Have I sought to keep discussion focused and to the point?
    Have I been willing to challenge points of view in discussion?

4. Have I been willing to take initiative?
    Have I given the teacher adequate feedback?
    Have I let the teacher know when I am resisting his expectations?
    Have I encouraged student-faculty interaction?
    Have I used the opportunities for evaluation and criticism of the course?
    Have I been willing to express my own ideas?

5. Have I come to class adequately prepared?
    Have I attended class regularly?
    Have I kept up with class assignments?
    Have I come ready to ask questions and discuss assignments?

6. How sensitive have I been to the needs and feelings of others in connection with the course?
    How often have I participated in and profited from cooperative learning experiences?
    Have I shown proper respect for other members of the class?

A. Have I become increasingly aware of the dynamics of interpersonal relationships?
    Have I questioned my thoughts, attitudes and assumptions about other people?
    Have I learned to deal with conflicts in interpersonal relationships?
    Am I better able to relate to other people?
    Am I more aware of the feelings and thoughts of others?

B. Have I allowed the course to influence my values and attitudes?
    Has my outlook on life been changed by this course?
    Have I been open to new information, especially when it conflicts with and contradicts previously held values and attitudes?
    Has my outlook on other courses been changed?
    Have I become more educable and mature?

used competitively, either by teachers or students, in a way that alienates students from each other, or to punish students, or to maintain expectations whose legitimacy students question.

The key issue, it seems to me, is how to provide accurate feedback to students and ourselves about how they and we are meeting shared expectations. A related issue is how to help students monitor and assess their own progress, so that they won't be dependent upon someone else's judgment. Consequently, from kindergarten on, we should develop means to encourage children to assess their own progress. By the end of the sixth or seventh grade, they could write their own evaluations to be attached to those of their teachers. By the time a student is in senior high school, he could not only assess his own growth, but could also give himself a grade (if we must use such a system). Better yet, the students and the teachers could work together to reach a consensual description and evaluation. I do this in some of my courses. When a student's grade and mine differ by less than five points or so, the higher estimate prevails. If the discrepancy is greater, we talk. I have found that where there is a "we-ness," the development of shared expectations, openness in feedback and in assessment, then grades are not so much an issue with students.

An expectation that does not induce tension or confusion will not initiate the adaptive process. A student reacts automatically and habitually. Therefore, our expectations should create a wide enough discrepancy between what is habitual and potentially possible so that frustration and tension occur. Growth is a continuous process of modifying or breaking up old habits and acquiring new ones. This process inevitably means some confusion and disorganization, even pain and anxiety. To be anxious indicates a potential that has yet to be fulfilled. To avoid frustration and anxiety is to avoid the possibility of realizing new potentials. The growing number of youth who can't tolerate frustration, anxiety, or pain are limiting their educability and actualization.

In contrast to those educators and increasing number of students who believe that learning should be joyful *without* frustration and pain (and work, too), I believe that personal disorganization and its pain are inseparable—from healthy development. Our dilemma is how to create expectations which induce tension and confusion yet do not induce so much disorganization that a youth becomes imaginatively deadened, autocentric, defensive, defiant, and less educable.

What are the signs that distinguish between a healthy and an unhealthy disorganization (Heath 1968b)? Our expectations are too high when a student's tension level disrupts other activities. Billy's school expected so much of him that his tension was displaced to the bus. They are too high when a student's confusion persists too long and interferes with his adaptation. Billy's disruptive behavior continued for weeks; he made no attempt to cope with the pressure at school in a different way. When a youth loses his joyfulness and enthusiasm, when he is tied up in knots, and when he feels suppressed, then he is unhealthily disorganized. Billy's growing dislike of school was symptomatic, though his effusive and delightful prankishness at home suggested that he was not too seriously disorganized. Another sign that disorganization may be limiting educability is when behavior becomes defensive, exaggerated, compensatory, and not readily reversible. If Billy's teacher and school altered some of their expectations, but Billy still blew up on the school bus, then his explosiveness might be symptomatic of a deeper disturbance.

Some students will resist any attempt to form an expectancy contract which may disturb their current equilibrium. If our assessment of their potential is realistic, then we need to explore why they are content with a partially fulfilled life.

Obviously, expectations by different teachers, the peer group, or one's family that conflict with those that we and the student have formed may lessen the power of a particular expectation to induce growth. One characteristic of a maturing environment, as Chapter Four described, is that its expectations are consistent and coherent. Too often, teachers do not share the same expectations of a student and so place him in conflict. I recall a senior I advised one year. He asked me what vocation I thought he should enter. I tried to help him explore his motives and preferences. The next day he was in a panic. A teacher whom he liked and respected had tried for several hours to persuade him to go to graduate school in his own area of specialty. Fearful of disappointing his favorite teacher, but mindful of my advice that he make his own choice, he fell apart.

More serious conflicts occur between the expectations of teachers and those of the peer group. The latter may say that it's square to ask questions in class or participate in discussions unless called upon or it may condone cheating and homework-copying. American educators have been singularly inept in learning how to work with the peer group to help shape mutually shared expectations. The Russians have been much more astute in integrating the power of the peer group with the expectations of the school. For example, group rather than individual efforts are frequently recognized (Bronfenbrenner 1970). I don't advocate manipulation. But we must learn how to use the power of the peer group if we want to fashion consistent expectations.

Another source of conflict is between expectations of the school and the parents of many students. Parents expect their fourth grader to

be taught French or given more homework. They expect discipline to be
strict or the school to "do something" about drugs. Children may be
buffeted back and forth by differences in expectations about dress, talking
to adults, swearing, or expressing anger. Communication between parents,
students, and teachers has become so tense in some communities that programs designed to bring the groups into closer contact are now in process.
One school has evening discussion groups to discuss different expectations
that parents, students, and teachers have. Why can't we be more relaxed,
like the teachers of English integrated day schools, about having parents
work with us? I have been dismayed by the number of schools that pro-
hibit teachers from visiting students' homes. The psychological walls we
build between ourselves and the family-community are bound to aggravate
conflicts in expectations.

What should we expect of students? Our principal expectation is
that they become educable and mature. Keeping that expectation clearly
in mind will protect us from imposing, consciously or unconsciously,
other expectations on students that are arrogant, irrelevant, or nosey.
What they wear, the length of their hair or hair style, the neatness of their
handwriting, or their sexual and social activities are not critical concerns
of the school. They may become concerns *if* it can be demonstrated that
they seriously interfere with the achievement of the school's principal
task. A school does have a responsibility to formulate a drug-use policy
in school because drugs can affect motivation and hence educability. A
school does have a concern if drinking parties are held during the week and
students come to school high or half asleep. However, I fail to understand
how the length of a boy's hair or his beard has any relation to his educability. Nor can I understand why a school, unless it is residential, should
concern itself with students who are sexually involved with each other
when out of school. These issues are much more complex, of course, when
specific problems must be faced. The path to their resolution in a human-
istically oriented school is through its means for collaboratively forming
and implementing expectations.

What happens when a youth does not live up to expectations? Questions like discipline, trials, punishments, suspensions or grades, failure,
detention and a host of other more or less legal issues come immediately
to mind.

Both psychological and institutional factors provoke young people
not to fulfill expectations. Some are just perverse and defiant, or for other
reasons may need psychological assistance. But many of our so-called
discipline problems occur because students do not share in forming expectations which we expect them to meet. By imposing our expectations,

we encourage resistance and defiance. A school dedicated to helping its students become autonomous will provide them as much opportunity to form their own expectations as they can responsibly fulfill. Unfortunately, few teachers ever think of helping children form their own goals and carry them out. We should begin in kindergarten. Children should work with the teacher to learn how to set goals, make decisions, propose consequences if the goal is not fulfilled, and suggest who is to decide if the goal is not reached and how the consequences are to be implemented. Of course, we begin with small steps that a child can be expected to make. Then we extend the opportunities as he becomes more mature. All concerned parties in the school should work with students to formulate consensually the rules and regulations that they have the competence to handle (Heath 1969*b*). They should also have the opportunity to experience the consequences if they fail to meet their obligations. It should be clear just what criteria constitute failure, who is to make this decision, and what the range of consequences will be. In contrast to Russian educators, Americans have not learned how to help youth develop more responsibility for their peer's behavior. Whereas Russian student judicial councils have considerable power to regulate discipline, American student councils are notoriously powerless (Bronfenbrenner 1970).

Effective self-discipline is not generated by fear of the vice-principal and his book of legalistic rules and regulations and threats of physical punishment and psychological torture. Such threats only push some adolescents to test their limits and, at best, only temporarily suppress willful defiance. A large school seldom will be able to provide effective conditions for developing self-discipline. Hence, we will have policemen stationed in corridors for years to come. A small school with an educative atmosphere and respected adult models provides the conditions for mutually formed expectations to be internalized. Genuine self-discipline emerges from the development of one's own expectations, which one accepts responsibility for.

I have been discussing, in effect, the development of an educational community (Newman and Oliver 1967). In such a community, each member, including the faculty, feels he belongs, values being a member, forms stable and intimate ties with other members, and knows that others are concerned about his personal development. By helping to formulate the community's goals and expectations, as well as the principal means of achieving them, its members are willing to assume responsibility for achieving them as well as for maintaining the vitality and educative power of the school. To humanize our schools is to make just such educational communities.

Part V

How to Humanize Our Schools Now

One elementary school principal recently berated me, "Just what am I to believe? Yesterday, it was the self-contained classroom. Today, the fad is team teaching. Tomorrow, we will return to the self-contained classroom modified along the lines of the British informal school. Why do we do what we do?"

That's the point of this book. To clarify the why. To construct a rationale for evaluating what we do and plan to do. Until we clearly understand how a person develops healthily and how students need to grow to be able to deal with what's coming, we will continue to stumble mindlessly from fad to fad.

If the analyses to date are valid, then how to change our schools is obvious. Clearly and accurately identified problems prefigure their solutions. The foundation and ground plan of our new school will include principles like these:

1. Boredom will be lessened by concentrating on learning experiences that integrate intellectual consciousness with emotion and action.
2. Belonginglessness will be reduced by creating smaller educational units in which people care for and cooperate with, rather than ignore and only compete with, each other.
3. Meaninglessness will be countered by a deeply experiential education that continuously confronts a student with his beliefs and values and helps him learn how to make mature choices.
4. The demands of our future society will be anticipated, in part, by encouraging the mastery of "skills of being," like learning how to change one's self as well as one's social institutions. Our curriculum will become more deeply contextual or problem-centered. It will cultivate a wider range of skills.

5. The educability of a youth will be stimulated and tested by diverse experiences not confined to the classroom. We will learn how to use the organization and activities of the classroom, school, *and* the local and wider community.
6. We will ceaselessly ask ourselves, "How does *this* youth need to develop to become more mature?" Neither a state's Department of Education nor a college's admission or departmental requirements nor a teacher's bias will be allowed to get in the way of his growth. We will provide greater diversity in learning modes and experiences in order to meet the needs of individual students.

Part V suggests how to create more humanistic schools. But the effectiveness of the specific changes I propose depends upon the development of an educative atmosphere, educable and mature adults, and shared expectations. It will be a futile gesture in the long run to introduce specific programs piecemeal if we don't change the atmosphere of the school. We first must create new ways to help teachers grow themselves and become more receptive to change itself. The effectiveness of an innovation ultimately depends on the institutional context in which it takes place.

Chapter 11

A
Personal
Vignette

This chapter describes where I am now with my own students. Maybe my effort to implement, however imperfectly, some of my ideas will suggest to others more powerful ways to educate.

So where am I now? I know that I'm discontent with what I do as a teacher. Research tells me that much of what we believe we do in our conventional classrooms and schools has little significant *enduring* impact on our students. I know that most of the information I insist my students memorize will be forgotten within months, if not weeks, after the examination, unless it has become functionally integrated with their on-going interests. I also know that some of the more important determinants of a student's educability and maturity are not understood and seldom utilized by teachers. As I've said at great length, the school's atmosphere, the coherence of its purposes, the quality of the personal relationships of the students, the ethos of the peer culture, the humanness, enthusiasm, as well as competence of the faculty are frequently more powerful causes of growth than are our formal curriculum and traditional teaching activities (Chickering 1969; Heath 1968*b*).

I have also become dissatisfied with the traditional, fragmented survey approach most textbooks and most faculty, including myself, use to organize our introductory courses. And I have increasingly found that the conventional didactic role of the teacher automatically sets me apart from students. So I have offered a course for twenty entering freshmen for several years titled *Contemporary Psychological Problems: Alienation and the Educational Process*. I had two goals: 1) To introduce seventeen-year-olds to how one psychologist identified, analyzed, and explored problems from a psychological point of view. I had no expectation that we would survey all the principal topics that define contemporary psychology. Nor did I care if they memorized most of the terms in the index of a contemporary textbook. I did want them to master some core psychological concepts and understand the principal methods used in psychology. More importantly, I hoped they would learn how to formulate meaningful and testable questions about human beings. 2) To challenge the freshmen to take a more active and responsible attitude toward their own growth in college by changing the traditional teacher-student relationship.

Since few students would know much psychology, I assumed the responsibility of defining the first topic. I selected the concept of alienation, a topic not even discussed in most psychology textbooks. By studying that topic, I hoped we could discover the assumptions that theorists from different academic disciplines make about man, and learn in the process how different disciplines define a problem. Then we would decide which assumptions to examine in more depth. Each question would lead to another. Where we would go, how we would go, and where we would stop were unknown to me. Similarly, the criteria for evaluating how each student was developing in the course, the "output" each was to produce, and its evaluation were other decisions we would make together.

My formal (though not psychological) preparation for the course was minimal, since I didn't know just what subsequent topics we would explore. I knew little of the literature about alienation itself and deliberately refrained from trying to become a quick expert in it before "teaching" the course. I ordered copies of the text that a concurrent Introductory Psychology course was using to have a ready background source available that illustrated the conventional organization of psychology. I also secured copies of several sociological articles on alienation, and ordered two films, Fellini's *8½* and the Perry's *David and Lisa,* that portrayed different aspects of alienation. The one required assignment I made for the semester was that each of us prepare and share at the first meeting of the class his reflections about what alienation meant to him.

I vividly recall that first three-and-a-half-hour class. Twenty young men and women, just out of high school, unknown to each other, squeezed into our living room. Many sprawled on the floor, puzzled and apprehensive about what was going to happen. No outline, no assigned readings, no papers, or scheduled exams. Just a middle-aged professor, twenty students, and the topic of alienation. I had a fleeting wish this were the last meeting of the class.

But I underestimated our mutual capacity to educate each other. We began by introducing ourselves by the name we preferred. If *they* felt comfortable calling me "Doug," that was OK with me. In our evaluation session fourteen weeks later, one young man said that that comment had really thrown him. He thought I was putting him on. It took him nine weeks to feel comfortable calling a college professor by his first name. Each of us, including me, talked briefly about our own feelings of alienation. Then I talked at greater length about some of the themes discussed in Part I. After refreshments, we organized ourselves to learn more about alienation. The class divided itself into four interest groups. Each was to discover how alienation was defined by either political-economic, sociological psychological, or religious thinkers and report its findings to the class in two weeks. Each group was also to alert itself to the psychological assumptions made by, for example, its economists or theologians. I had scheduled the film *8½* the next week to further probe our feelings about alienation.

So began the most hectic, busy, traumatic, and illuminating course I have taught in eighteen years. When each group met with me several days later, I asked how it planned to begin. Blank stares! An embarrassing pause. So began the first lesson of how to search out a problem. Within the first week and half, the groups had tracked down other faculty, even the Provost of the College, to interview them for information, discovered the library and that of neighboring Bryn Mawr College, learned that most academic disciplines have their own reference and abstracting sources, and discovered Marcuse, Marx, Fromm, Weber, Tawney, and Keniston. By the second week, the members of each group had read a great array of sources, understood much less of them, and were becoming quite anxious about what they were supposed to do with all the notes they had collected. The first weeks of college usually merge into one big confusing blur, anyway, but to decide for one's self to read Fromm's *Sane Society* and several other books and articles for just one course with no outline or idea of what the teacher expected was too much for some. Already they were worrying about how they were to be graded. So all that week, students dropped by to query me, "What am I supposed to do now?" or "What do you mean by 'psychological assumption or question'?", or "Are we supposed to get our groups together sometime?" After spending an hour with one student showing him how to analyze the psychological assumptions Marcuse makes in *One Dimensional Man* and another hour with a student interested in Cox's assumption about the relation of maturity to secularization in *The Secular City,* I learned I could not be a tutor for twenty individual students and teach other courses as well.

I hastily invited each group to meet with me again, asking each member to share briefly with the rest of us what he had learned. Out of that came plans for each group to organize its material and present it to the class in no more than forty-five minutes. I suggested that they integrate their material, prepare a common group outline, learn how to use ditto machines, and practice their talks beforehand.

In the meantime, we had seen *8½*, after which we had stuffed our twenty-one bodies into a student's room that also contained several distracting kittens. The movie was psychologically beyond the group. It's obtuseness threatened some freshmen who were very proud, and defensively so, of their own intellectual capabilities. But basically, they did not yet feel secure enough with each other to share the personal feelings that the movie induced.

I was proud of the students during the third weekly session. The individual or group reports were clear and succinct, though too cryptic at times. Some groups sparked crisp and critical discussion. Out of the evening emerged a plan for the next week. As I expected, we discovered the theorists had different and contradictory views about the nature of man's motivation. We decided to examine what psychologists have discovered about the role of instinct in man. The class assigned itself a number of chapters out of its basic text and some readings of Freud. I was to bring a case history of a student who had failed college to illustrate how to analyze an individual case of alienation.

And so we were off! From work on motivation we went more deeply into Freud. And from Freud we went into personality and abnormal symptoms. I was asked to lecture part of each class as well as assume the responsibility of conducting discussions. To conclude our topic on alienation, the class, in response to my urging, decided that each group would design a testable research project on alienation I illustrated how to design one. During the next week each group formed its own hypothesis, worked out its materials and procedure, and then reported its proposal to the rest of the class. The rest of us appointed ourselves as a review committee for the National Institute of Health to decide whether to fund the project or not.

Since it took so much time to plan each subsequent session and since we were having difficulty securing the books we needed, a special voluntary session was held to plan the rest of the course. The students relied more on me by this time to suggest readings. The class decided to study Jensen's controversial thesis that Negroes are genetically less able to deal with abstract thinking than whites. To prepare the group for his technical monograph, I taught the class some statistics and other background information. This topic led to the study of the development of thought and language. And from there we went into prejudice and the genesis of attitudes.

The persistent problem we all faced was how to assess the development of the members of the class. The class's petition to the faculty-student educational policy committee that grades for the course be waived was rejected. The students suggested that we assign everyone the same grade. I rejected this cop out and insisted we abide by the spirit of the college's requirement. So we were forced to decide just how grades were to be assigned. Eventually, the class decided that each person could produce what he wished, that is, submit at the end of the term whatever work he wanted to be evaluated. He would describe what he had done and then evaluate its quality by assigning himself a grade. I would evaluate his work independently. If our evaluations disagreed by only a few points, the student would receive the higher estimate. Otherwise, we would struggle for consensus. The class too quickly accepted the criteria I had drawn up in haste for defining their growth. In retrospect, such criteria were critical, and we should have taken the time to clarify our mutual expectations. The criteria included such things as responsibility for keeping the class alive and interesting, assistance to others in the course, the extent of non-assigned reading, the degree of involvement in the material as reflected by discussions with others not in the course, the mastery of the concepts and methods of psychology as demonstrated in their output, and so on.

Our most traumatic and illuminating episode occurred half way through the course when each student talked with me for half an hour about his expectations and work in the course. I asked each to evaluate himself on the criteria which the class had accepted, as well as describe the "output" he planned to submit during the rest of the course. About half of the class saw this discussion as an inquisition. Some felt I was tyrannical. Others thought I was running an experiment in which I was inducing stress in half of the group. About half of the group enjoyed the procedure, never having had a teacher review their work with them in this way before. I was forced to re-examine my own motives. Eventually, those who felt I was "persecuting" them worked through their feelings. The rest of our classes that semester, while not divisive, were more argumentative. I became aware of the psychological problems that can occur when the traditional teacher-student role is transformed into a cooperative "we-ness." It was I who experienced the most difficulty with my "role." I was not truly a psychological equal of the group. Although willing to share the organization, conduct, and evaluation of the course with the class, I was unwilling to abandon my belief that growth must be tested in action or by some output in some form.

I also believed, and still do, that students need to learn how to form sub-goals for themselves. Otherwise, as happened for about seven or eight students, some are unable to organize themselves when given the freedom to set their own goals. Many in the class would have preferred only to absorb passively and never produce actively. Many resisted the idea that we do not know that we know something until we produce it in action. The danger of a "we-ness" relationship is that it can degenerate into a conspiracy of nonexpectation, particularly if a teacher is not willing to risk acrimony and then work it out with the group. For several weeks, some students felt I had betrayed the spirit of the class by asking them to hold themselves to their expectations.

Under pressure from me and a majority of the students, we did decide to have an hour examination. Its purpose was to provide information about the precision with which students were mastering core concepts. Each student took the exam at his leisure and then met with his original group and me to review his own test. I never saw the completed examinations nor the grades the students assigned themselves, if they did. They later admitted they were shocked by how passively they had read the material. Almost all learned that they had not organized the material actively and therefore had not really thought very critically about what they had read. Continuous assessment is essential to prevent a student from deluding himself that passively skimming material is equivalent to thinking *or* learning.

About half of the class wrote short papers preparatory to longer ones which I edited carefully. Others decided they wanted a final examination. Although a third of the class took the exam, only a quarter decided to include it as one part of their "output" for the course. Other students read voraciously, incorporated their new understanding of psychology into papers for other courses (and became known as the psychological "experts" of their seminars), volunteered to work in a nearby mental hospital, and tutored some youngsters. Two of the students assumed the responsibility for baking cakes for the seminar each week.

How effective was the evaluation procedure? As I had discovered with previous classes with whom I had shared the evaluative-decision process, most students resist evaluating their own work. But when they do so, I usually independently agree, within a few grade points, with their estimates. Several could not organize themselves to prepare any output, though they had read extensively beyond the assignments made by the class. We agreed they would receive a minimally passing grade. I also anticipated that my judgments would differ considerably from those of a few students. Such was the case. Conferences were held with each of these. Eventually a compromise was reached after we had explored quite thoroughly our mutual assessment of the quality of work in the course.

What were the effects of the course? We did "cover" a wide range of topics, some much more intensively than the concurrent introductory psychology course did. Although those who took the final exam did exceptionally well, I doubt that many students mastered the number of facts and definitions which a traditional course is preoccupied with. The students felt they had learned a great deal of psychology; several students concurrently audited the regular course and believed they learned more in our seminar. Many of the students wished I had imposed more organization on the course. More than half of the students claimed that they had developed a strong enough interest in psychology to major in it—an unanticipated consequence. Finally, in a school in which most students "cut" classes quite faithfully if allowed to do so, not one student voluntarily missed a class for fourteen weeks, though attendance was not required.

These were not the critical effects, however. The students saw the course as the first they had ever had which they could organize and conduct as they wished. Actually, their freedom was not unlimited, for I did have expectations and did assume the leadership in conducting discussion and maintaining the pace of the course. Passive involvement by the teacher can readily lead to deterioration of a course—given the fact that most students lack experience in organizing their own lives, let alone the work of a group. More than half of the students experienced a disastrous drop in their motivation to work in the course about a third of the way through. They ruefully admitted they were just too accustomed to being told what, when, and how to do their work to be able to take responsibility for their own education. Most had recovered from this malaise by the end of the course or during the following semester. The experience provoked intense guilt in a few, with whom I struggled for many hours to help resolve. They no longer could blame the "system," the teacher, or something "out there" for their inability to work. It was not that they weren't interested; few said they were bored by the course or by any of the class meetings. They could still function if told to do something in their other courses. They just couldn't get themselves to do the reading or write the papers they had assigned themselves to do. The students, and I, learned how deeply entrenched is their dependency on external structure and incentives to keep themselves organized. The consensus of the final class was that this type of course was indispensable for students to have—but much earlier in their schooling. They agreed they were not yet mature enough to be able to manage the freedom the course provided. Much of the mid-term blow-up was caused by students who felt guilty about not fulfilling their own expectations. They projected their self-blame onto me, the "inquisitor," who reminded them of the discrepancy between their expectation and their accomplishment—and who may have unintentionally turned the screw too tight.

With only a few exceptions the students felt that the course had been one of the most profitable growth experiences they had had. As I recall, they unanimously recommended that a similar course be given in the future. What lingers in my memory as the course's principal effect was an incident several months later. A freshman rebellion was close to erupting about a major curricular change. When a committee agreed to meet with the class, only about 40 of the 175 freshmen appeared. Twelve of my former students were there; most of the more vocal members were from my class. I would like to believe that some of my students had been turned on to their own educational growth by their preceding semester's work. Had they become so involved in their own education and more autonomously self-directing that they were becoming healthily maladjusted—even to the system which I was helping to construct? Marvelous, if so. But perhaps it is just such students who volunteer for an experimental course anyway. I will never know.

What did I learn? I learned that expectations need to be clarified early in a course. Although there was more "structure" and organization to the course than the students believed, their subjective feeling of being "free" tended to make such structure unobtrusive. The pain and confusion that we mutually endured while struggling to organize the classes and to decide what our expectations were are essential experiences for a student to have. Of course, it would have been much less wearing on all of us if I had organized the course more directively. A youth needs, however, the opportunity to struggle with freedom to learn just how mature he is. Students overestimate their ability and motivation to direct and sustain their intellectual interests. They need guidance, group support and continued opportunities for self-assessment if they are to learn how to become more self-directing and responsible. Growth occurs in small steps, not giant leaps. I learned that to abandon the protection of the teacher "role" and some of its power puts a teacher in a more vulnerable, that is, highly educable, position that may at times be quite threatening. But I also learned that if a teacher wants to assist his students to develop in the ways I have urged in this book, then he must risk becoming vulnerable and growing with his students.

I doubt that any particular technique the class developed was very novel (Duberman 1968). After all, teachers have experimented with teaching methods since Adam and Eve were faced by their first child. But I now must draw out the rationale for initiating the specific procedures that were used. Recall that a youth matures in five mutually interdependent ways. First, he becomes more able to represent his experience, including his understanding of himself, symbolically. I tried to establish a reflective atmosphere for the course by the assignment to think about their own alienation, the use of provocative movies, the case study of a student, and more dramatically, as it turned out, the interview to confront students with their own motivation and expectations. Our constant reflection about the course and its organization also helped to make us more aware of the problem of educating ourselves.

Second, a maturing youth becomes more allocentric. He gradually internalizes the language and mode of thought of his culture. Mastering a new subject, like psychology, modifies one's thought, concepts and views of others. One criterion of growth in the course was the acquisition of a more precise mastery of the core concepts. Also, as a youth develops, he becomes less egocentric and more concerned about others as well as capable of relating to them. Again, one criterion of growth in the course was the degree to which he helped the class and other students and contributed to the effectiveness of his smaller group. Thus, I valued highly the efforts of one student who made the transportation arrangements for the class and of those who provided us with refreshments. They helped to create the atmosphere of the class. Small, task-oriented groups were deliberately used to facilitate more rapid understanding of others who might have similar intellectual interests. Two of the groups were unable to work well together, due in part to several students who were resistant to giving to or accommodating to others.

Third, a maturing youth becomes progressively more integrated. To establish an expectancy that human beings should be understood contextually, I chose a topic like alienation that could be analyzed from a variety of nonpsychological points of view. Throughout the course, I sought to relate the topics we were discussing to other issues. Another concern was the extent to which they integrated psychology with their other courses as well as the extent to which they discussed the course materials with others not in the course. Finally, the development of a "we-ness" relationship between us contributed to the emergence of a sense of class unity that helped to create an educative atmosphere.

Fourth, a maturing youth becomes more stabilized. The trial examination, the design of the research experiment, and the frequent papers (for some students) may have helped to "fix" some basic concepts and skills. I remained dissatisfied with the procedures we developed to encourage growth in this dimension. Our collective failure to agree about regularly practiced outputs and more systematic evaluation of their growth limited the stabilization of their knowledge of psychology. However, I persistently refused to accept more responsibility for organizing the classes, assuming the lecture role more frequently, and goading delinquent students. So the class had the opportunity to struggle long enough to organize itself for some students to begin to stabilize such skills. If only they had had similar reinforcing experiences in other courses. Finally, the closeness of the group and the relative openness of our relationship has resulted in lasting ties between some of the students and myself.

Fifth, a maturing youth becomes more autonomous. The criterion that students apply their knowledge to other courses recognized that the test of the autonomy of a skill or of one's knowledge is its use in different situations. A principal thrust of the course was to develop more self-determination and responsibility. My failure to hold students to their own expectations may have undermined the development of a sense of accountability in some. The collaborative formation of expectations, individual determination of his own output, and assessment of the quality of his own work also facilitated growth in autonomy.

I was chagrined by our failure to confront our values, examine alternative positions, and develop a more integrative psycho-philosophical view of man. But I comforted myself with the rationalization that perhaps the best teaching in this area is indirect.

This is not the end of the story. As researchers know too well, the initiation of any change, whether it is a new therapeutic technique, drug, or curricular innovation, may induce positive effects because of the enthusiasm that hope and novelty generate. To break with old patterns, to take risks, is disturbing, but it stimulates expectations, renews flagging efforts, and releases much vitality and excitement. The test of the worth of any innovation, particularly an educational one, is never its effects the first year; it is its effects the second, third and fourth years.

The second year was less glorious than the first—and instructively so. We began similarly, but this time some students had heard of the course and came with too high expectations. I felt too assured. I was not as apprehensive that first evening when the students piled into our living room. By the end of the initial session, however, I vaguely sensed that the class was different from the first, but did not make the effort to tell myself how. The students decided to have a voluntary sensitivity session to get to know each other better. A senior Psychology student, assisting with the class, trained in such procedures, led the class. The experience deeply affected some and helped to create a closer group earlier in the course, but several students didn't participate and remained psychologically on the fringe of the class the entire semester.

In the meantime, several groups had been ferreting out meanings of the term alienation. But in contrast to the previous year, the groups did not show the same initiative and involvement in their projects. Fewer students sought out the faculty or me. Fewer extended themselves to read beyond several articles or a book. A larger number of students didn't work well with the others, so the effort to create an effectively functioning group caused more frustration than seemed worthwhile. Rather than prepare one integrated report, each group decided each member should give his own—and who can remain interested for a three-hour evening session listening to other students give too abstract, occasionally disorganized, and exhaustive reports? The sheer amount of information that deluged us that third session contributed to an overwhelming sense of intellectual chaos. The class vigorously repudiated my attempt to limit each group to forty-five minutes. So half of the reports were postponed to the following week. I was torn in deciding how actively I should intervene. To be as critical as I should have been risked suppressing and alienating some of the students. To clarify some reports would have required so much time and assertive control by me that I risked reinforcing the impression I was *the* person responsible for the class. Besides, I was just as confused and ignorant as the others about the content of some reports. So I followed the lead of the class.

But the class was in difficulty. The sessions and interest were dragging. We weren't functioning well together. Fewer students took the initiative to help shape the class. Whereas more than half of the previous year's class had met voluntarily several times to plan the subsequent units of work, only two students appeared for our major planning session. My own inclination to take a decisive organizing role in my classes unconsciously took command. Although the topics were suggested by the students, the organization of the course became psychologically mine. I planned too far in advance, thus robbing the students of the opportunity to confront their own drifting interests and to struggle to fulfill them.

I early prodded the class to clarify our expectations for evaluating development in the class. The college's educational policy committee again rebuffed a petition to waive grades. The students decided to follow the same procedures that had been worked out by the previous year's class.

My interviews with each student about his progress on these criteria and anticipated output did not evoke any emotional blow-ups, but they did aggravate feelings of guilt, as I learned later. Like the previous class, most of the students struggled—with more tension and pain than seemed necessary—to define for themselves what their output should be. But more of the second class tried to get me to tell them what to do, what book to read or topic to study. They asked me to prepare an extended list of books they could read. I did. Several insisted I should set deadlines for their papers. I refused. We agreed to have a diagnostic exam midway through the course; several students refused to take it. Three students cut classes, read little of the material, did not participate in class, and produced little output. I talked at length with each to express my concern. How they used their freedom remained their choice—and responsibility. But, I said, I was at a loss about how I was to evaluate with them their growth in the course.

What were the effects of the course? The students claimed they had worked harder, were more actively involved, and learned more psychology than their friends had in the concurrent survey course. They urged that the course be given again. Like the first group, they said that they should have had such a course much earlier in their schooling. Some despairingly said they felt the course had come too late for them.

In our evaluative session, the students were preoccupied with their feelings of guilt and paralysis. To be given some freedom but not to be able to take advantage of it starkly confronted them with their illusions. Some students said they never really believed until the last few weeks of the course that I would not step in to tell them what to do. They vaguely felt they were supposed to meet *my* expectations, but didn't know what they were. Their written evaluations of their growth seconded the same themes the first group had described.

What did I learn this time? My impression was that fewer students had become as involved in the course as had the preceding year. Fewer sought me out as frequently. Fewer participated in the planning. The atmosphere of the class was less vibrant and expectant. The class was not as constructively rebellious as the preceding one. Eight students of the second group were so passive and uptight that they seldom participated, even though they claimed in their interviews that they felt comfortable and secure with the others. The presence of a substantial group of nonparticipating, seemingly distant, and even resistant students curbed the development of a sense of unity and common enterprise.

I didn't respond appropriately to the passivity and resistance of the large group of detached students. I moved unthinkingly to assume more responsibility for planning and conducting the classes, rather than confronting the students with their own inactivity and detachment. There wasn't an assertive enough "group will" to question and resist the organization I was inadvertently imposing on the class. It was too comfortable for the class to not have to define its own goals and question our procedures. Furthermore, by not taking the time to reflect frequently about each class and how we were functioning, the discontent of some was acted out by coming to class late and leaving early. The accumulating guilt of others resulted in paralysis. These feelings remained unexamined and so never were freed. To learn how to educate one's self requires continued reflective monitoring of the devious ways we have learned to avoid becoming more autonomous and genuinely free.

Finally, the experience was no longer as novel for me. I had become a prisoner of the "success" of the previous year's adventure. When asked, I was too quick to suggest what "worked" with the previous class. It was more efficient to rely on the procedures so laboriously generated the first year than to suffer the frustration and uncertainty of taking a really fresh stance toward the needs of the students the second year. Maybe that is why we "covered" so much more material and more topics the second than the first year. But I was not as enthusiastic nor as preoccupied about the second as I was about the first class. I dreamed about the first class at nights; I didn't the second. I was too comfortable.

To educate for self-determination means to risk uncertainty, frustration, and even hostility. But its rewards are thereby potentially much more intense: contagious excitement, a waking up to life, and even a joyful commitment.

I sent the following note to the students after the last session:

To: Fellow Colleagues
From: Doug

Some Thoughts for the Semester

1. Rollo May talks of neurotic guilt and healthy guilt. Neurotic guilt leads to paralysis, lack of interest, projection of responsibility onto someone else, and dependence. Healthy guilt spurs the inner perception of potentials unfulfilled, the initiation of action to fulfill them, and the acceptance of responsibility for what one becomes.
2. Freedom is not the absence of restraint or the abolition of structure. Freedom is the acquisition of skills, attitudes, and interests that increase a person's options for making choices.
3. Your life is yours to choose what you wish to do with it. It is not your parents', the college's, or mine.
4. Whether an experience has provoked growth cannot be told until that potential growth has been tested in other situations.

I hope each of you has expanded your choices and is now more willing to accept the responsibility for the choices you are making.

Chapter 12

Symbolization

Teachers are part of a system, curbed by schedules, sequential requirements, curricular programs, and the expectations of others. Most do not have the freedom I have to work with students in the way I do. They could. Our schools could become freer than they are now. We could become freer ourselves—*if* we took a fresh look at our assumptions and methods. The model of maturing provides a vantage point for taking such a look. It identifies what types of changes might help young people become more educable.

To go beyond educating just for knowledge and academic skills requires us to alter our curricular priorities and emphases. We need to free some resources and find the time and energy to venture along new paths.

Educational technology promises to provide some time and release some energy, but it is now too costly for what it can produce.[1] Hopefully, within a decade we will have the inexpensive technology to individualize and make more efficient the acquisition of some information and some symbolic skills. But the more fundamental questions will remain. Technology should be most useful in the *first* stage of the adaptive process— where we are now in most of our schools. But will we continue only to stuff students with unrelated bits of information and overdevelop a limited number of skills? Will we persist in making students even more lop-sided? Who is to decide what information is to be programmed? The companies that hire the programmers and consultants? What criteria decide what they program? Will they merely collate our existing texts and rob us of the opportunity to question more deeply what we teach? Will we really be any better off than we are now with our textbooks? Will schools have become more humane or *only* more efficient?

[1]See Silberman 1970, pp. 186-203, for a judicious assessment of the role of technology in the school.

Our dilemma is in deciding what to teach.[2] What in the world should a student know? He needs that knowledge most relevant to the *enduring* problems he is likely to encounter in his life. But what problems are those? What contemporary Delphic oracle can answer that question in this rapidly changing world. Hutchins is right. In days of such rapid change, knowledge to be learned should be deeply *general*. It should prepare a youth for anything—not *some* thing. One should know "those works of the mind which illuminate or are likely to illuminate human life *under any conditions that may arise*" [my emphasis] (Hutchins 1968, p.6). I will discuss later some types of information our youth should be, but aren't mastering in our schools today.

Sometimes it's easier to know what we don't want than what we do want. The same principle applies to the information we should teach. At least we can say what students don't need to know. Surely my daughter didn't need to spend hours memorizing Shelley's "Ozymandias" in the sixth grade or Housman's "To An Athlete Dying Young" in the eighth grade. She can't recall either now. Why did my son have to learn the names of all the countries in Africa or the names of all the counties of Pennsylvania?

Each school needs to create a means of insuring that each teacher annually reviews in detail the specific information students must memorize in his courses. We need to ask ourselves, much more self-consciously and regularly than we now do, why we require students to learn certain things. Is this information they will need five or ten years from now? Or is this information only illustrative and likely to be out-of-date within a few years? What constitutes the core information all students must know to become more educable? What are the reasons, the criteria, the principles we keep using to justify what we require? Are these criteria and principles justifiable themselves? Are they really appropriate for what should be done in the classroom?

We are on surer ground when we talk about knowledge of the self, whose burdens and delights we carry with us through our lives. We are our own enduring problem. That is why Socrates's dictum, "Know thyself," is eternally relevant. What of the student's self is the teacher's primary responsibility to illuminate and cultivate? Those skills and values that enhance a youth's educability.

Some guidelines might help us establish clear priorities about the skills to emphasize. Certainly, we need to provide opportunities for a

---

[2]I want to provoke questions and suggest a point of view for re-examining some cherished assumptions, not to become mired in the complexities of specific curricular problems.

student to find out what he can and cannot do well. Also, there are certain skills, like practical math, that are necessary for survival in our society. Finally, there are preparatory skills, like reading, that are necessary for obtaining and for facilitating the acquisition of other skills.

Unfortunately, there are less functional reasons that make us teach the skills we do: tradition, classical views of the liberal arts curriculum, and college admission requirements. Many requirements are archaic, motivated more by historic or political reasons than by valid educational reasons. It is time for colleges to develop more functional requirements for admission. The important question is not how many course credits a student has accumulated, but how educable he is to the particular demands of the college (Heath 1971*a*).

In terms of the above criteria, we place too much effort cultivating advanced mathematical, foreign language, and grammatical skills and too little effort developing skills like learning how to learn and judging complex situations.

Let's look first at mathematics—so central to our curriculum and so consuming of a student's time. Of course, students need to discover how apt they are in different types of mathematics. No argument. But for getting along in our scientific and technological society, I doubt most youth need to be proficient in more than the applied and practical math they got in their first seven to eight years of school. Just how useful are geometry and trigonometry for most people other than engineers, surveyors, and yachtsmen? Why do we make students take so much algebra? The only time I use the algebra I learned thirty years ago is when I help my children with their homework. Actually, by reminding me of what I have forgotten, they teach themselves. If adapting to our society were really a central guideline, we would require all students to have applied statistics, even some probability theory, perhaps elementary accounting, and techniques for balancing a monthly bank statement.

If we are honest, we will admit that even for the great bulk of our college-oriented youth, most of the math taken in high school is useless. Our dilemma is, of course, that we don't know with certainty which students may need advanced algebra, solid geometry, or calculus. We can make some educated guesses. Maybe 10 or 15 percent of the college-bound population?

But wait. Doesn't training in mathematics train the mind? What other subject cultivates abstract, logical, rigorous, and critical thinking as well? The answer has been "many others" ever since Thorndike studied the question in 1924. Training in mathematics does not necessarily improve the quality of thinking in other areas. The prime area of curricular improvement and acceleration in the past decade has been mathematics. No one has claimed that such accelerated training has improved the ability of students to think logically about personal and social issues, for example. My own limited data indicate that there was an increase in quantitative reasoning of our freshmen in the sixties. However, there was no comparable increase in their ability to think abstractly or conceptually with a wider range of information (Heath 1968*b*).

Other reasons may justify teaching advanced mathematics: their historic centrality to the liberal arts, their aesthetic elegance, their revelation of the power of the human mind, and so on. These are not compelling, however, if our goal is to educate for educability.

What should we do? Individual students should have the opportunity to discover the limits of their potential. Individuals vary in their readiness for mastering, say, the formal operations required by algebra. We must develop more individualized programs that permit students to progress with success at their own rate. When it becomes clear that a student is reaching the limit of his skill or patience, then he should not be required to continue. He should not have to complete algebra to graduate. Otherwise, we may exhaust his self-esteem. To require, as we now do, students to suffer geometry and algebra for years is to risk making them resistant to mathematics for the rest of their lives. They may become less educable for learning later in life the math they may need at that time. My hunch is that when we understand more about the determinants of learning math, we will discover that some people who could not understand algebra at age 13 and 14 master its principles very rapidly at age 20 or 30.

We should take a closer look at the relation between the mathematical abstract operations we require and the developmental phase of our students. I suggest that we be more flexible and allow some students to skip taking mathematics for one, two or even three and four semesters. Why should they take it every year, year in and year out, for nine, ten, and eleven years? For our administrative convenience? It's not evident that cognitive maturation parallels so nicely our sequential mathematical curriculum and pace. Growth occurs in fits and starts. If a student is having persistent difficulty and is losing interest, why not take the pressure off? Encourage him to resume when he and his teacher believe he is ready to.

It's poor pedagogical practice to teach the mastery of a tool too long before it can be used practically. Students complain that algebra and calculus are abstract games. They are. They don't need to be. Many students view typical homework problems as scarcely relevant to concrete problems they are concerned with. They are right. If we must begin teaching algebra in eighth and ninth grades, for example, should it not be taught with a concurrent *meaningful* laboratory experience or integrated with physical science in some way?

Our goal should be to teach students *how* they could teach themselves mathematics. Then, if a college student, say, decides he wants to be an economist, he will have both a desire and the skills to learn the calculus he needs. As it is now, we crush the desire, make students feel they are stupid, and don't teach them how to teach themselves what they need to know when they need it.

What about learning a foreign language? Our myths befog our understanding of its relevance to a student's educability. Every youth should have the opportunity to learn *how to learn a language* other than his own and, ideally, to develop the desire to learn a second language. Every youth should have the opportunity to test just how linguistically talented he may be in more than one language. In this global village of ours every student needs to understand and respect other people and their customs.

I know of no evidence that our current language courses either assist many students to master a language with any degree of proficiency or contribute much to these goals. I have the greatest sympathy for dedicated language teachers. They are burdened by the most unfavorable psychological conditions for teaching I can think of. Let's examine just how effective our current language programs are. Fortunately, we do have some very impressive information secured from national studies of 2,783 college seniors, randomly selected from the 12,000 concentrating in languages. Presumably, such samples include many linguistically gifted students. Most had had many years of language preparation. The proficiency level of the seniors was assessed for listening, speaking, reading, and writing. The principal finding was that "the median graduate with a foreign language major can speak and comprehend the language . . . somewhere between a 'limited working proficiency' and a 'minimum professional proficiency.' " (Carroll 1967, p. 134). The principal determinants of even this limited language proficiency were travel and residence abroad and use of the language within the parental home. Of secondary importance were foreign language aptitude; and, then only for French and Spanish, the time when they began to learn the language. Of significance is the conclusion that "those who do *not* go abroad do not seem to be able to get very far in their foreign language study, on the average, despite the ministrations of foreign language teachers, language laboratories, audio-lingual methods, and the rest" (Carroll 1967, p. 137).

Few students ever develop much proficiency in another language in our schools. Fewer still ever use that language for any length of time to justify the enormous amount of effort and time devoted to mastering it.

The harsh truth is that we don't know how to teach foreign languages well.[3] We know only very imperfectly how a child learns his *own* language, let alone a second one that he seldom, if ever, uses outside a classroom (Heise 1968). We also know very little about individual differences in educability for language learning. Although the current belief is that the audio-lingual emphasis is the "best" way to teach language, there is no evidence yet to document that hope (Hayes, Lambert, and Tucker 1967). This belief, when rigidly applied, may be, in fact, very destructive. True, children do learn their own language orally. But our students are not two years old. They have had years of learning visually and conceptually. Relying heavily on oral techniques can be damaging to a student's educability if he has a limited auditory memory span (as many do), erratic attention and concentration spans (as many do), and inhibited verbal facility (as many boys, in particular, do).

The Carroll study does not answer another very critical question. I know of no evidence that a student who has the aptitude to learn a romance language readily will also learn Chinese or Russian more rapidly than will a youth who just cannot master Spanish. I assume he could. I just don't know. Some students certainly can master French or Spanish more effectively than they can German. A school should provide a sampling of the principal families of languages so a student can test his potentials against several really different languages. Therefore, I would recommend that a school not offer two romance languages if it is limited in its resources. Instead, it could offer Spanish, German, and Japanese, for example.

I also know of no evidence about the *generality* of language training. That is, I don't understand why we believe that to teach a youth Spanish may help him learn Hindustani or Russian later in life. Since no one knows just what language a youth will actually need, if any, later in life, I have never understood why we spend unconscionable amounts of time and a school's precious resources teaching him four years of French, for example. Even the French and German requirements for the PhD will be obsolescent in most fields by the time any number of current high school students get to graduate school. And proportionately fewer students may go on to graduate school in the future anyway. So why the furor to teach French in fourth grade? If a thirty-five-year-old business man or sixty-year-old tourist needs French or Japanese, why can't he teach himself or take a Berlitz course? Our capacity to learn doesn't cease after we leave school.

---

[3]Readers interested in a major evaluative research program designed to assess the effectiveness of specific language teaching methods should read Hayes, Lambert, and Tucker 1967.

"Well," it is usually argued, "learning another language helps you understand how another people think. You can appreciate how a language shapes reality differently. A student needs to learn a language to transcend his parochialism." Fine. But how many students master a language well enough to appreciate the subtleties of another culture through its language? Not many, according to the Carroll report. It is an elitist myth that by learning German a student will better appreciate the character of Goethe. Is it worth a year of struggle to learn that Italian has no comparable word for our word "warmth"? Thousands of students become disgusted and intolerant rather than appreciative and respectful of another culture in their language courses. To not think of themselves as stupid, students devalue the language and its people, saying, "What stupid people to have so many different irregular verbs." And it doesn't do any good to point out our own hideously complex verb structures.

We should admit that learning a second language in our society is a dreadfully inefficient exercise because it is nonfunctional. To have a 45-minute French conversation in class and never hear or use French the remaining 23 hours and 15 minutes of the day is a ridiculous way to learn a language skill. No wonder most students think language courses are irrelevant to their lives. They are. No wonder the principal effects of most language courses (unless they are taught by gifted teachers) are boredom, feelings of inferiority and incompetence, and increased resistance to learning not only the language being taught, but other languages as well that they might consider learning in the future.

What should we do? Our highest priority should be to rechannel some of the wasted funds now going into teaching language into intensive research about how to help a child learn a general language facility. Our explicit goal should be to learn how to teach a youth to *want* to, and to know *how* to, teach himself the particular language he might decide he needs fifteen or thirty years from now. We should provide a greater range of languages for students to sample to discover their facility. We should eliminate all language requirements, beyond, say, a one-semester elementary course in secondary school. If a youth discovers he has an aptitude and interest, then he can proceed at his own pace. My hope is that some day we will teach a general linguistic course that provides the skills which can be later used by the student to teach himself the specific language he needs at the time. Like advanced mathematics, language should be learned close to the time that it can be functionally integrated into a youth's other activities. If we really insist that our college-bound youth should learn a language (and I think this is a mistaken goal), then let's stop kidding ourselves. Let's settle down, take the funds it would cost to teach him

Spanish for four years, and send him to Mexico or Spain for a semester where he will have to learn Spanish to survive. Better yet. Our fifteen- to sixteen-year-olds have difficulty now securing jobs during their summer vacations. Why not sponsor very intense language courses abroad during the summer, for which they could get academic credit for the proficiency level they achieve?

I will gladly modify these views when someone can demonstrate to me that any considerable number of young people become more educable by enduring current language programs. Most become less educable.

Of course, the ability to communicate clearly in one's own language is a highly desirable skill. We make students take years of English. But think of the myths that prevail about the importance of grammar as well as the art of teaching writing. As only a footnote to my comments about mathematics and foreign language, I quote without comment the following, taken from the *English Journal,* the National Council of Teachers of English publication for high school teachers:

> For the new teacher who is anxious to get started right, perhaps a review of what "should not be" in the English classroom is appropriate. In recent years, several studies have indicated that the majority of English teachers subscribe to the following theories:
>> that grammar disciplines the mind for logical thinking;
>> that more writing means better writing;
>> that vocabulary can be taught by having students learn words compiled from a spelling book or some other authoritative source;
>> that diagramming helps students understand grammatical concepts underlying sentence construction;
>> that the study of grammar helps students become better writers;
>> that English grammar serves as preparation for work in foreign languages;
>> that only the masterpieces of the literary heritage should be taught;
>> that identifying parts of speech in sets of illustrative sentences is a valuable activity;
>> that the analytic method is superior to the quick appraisal method in grading compositions; and
>> that pointing out errors in illustrative sentences is a valuable technique for explaining grammatical principles to students.
>
> All of the practices cited above are in *disagreement* with findings of research and professional writings in the field (DeVries and Tovatt 1970, p. 854).

One skill imperative for this changing world is to know how to learn. Most of us learn erratically and inefficiently. How can we help students to become aware of how they learn, to become aware of how haphazardly they organize their effort and time? Do we know how to help students outline and abstract complex materials or even read a difficult book?[4] Do we teach students how to memorize rapidly? For example, much language learning is by rote. Psychologists know a great deal about efficient ways of memorizing. But how many teachers take the time to teach their students such basic principles—or even know about them themselves?

Certainly, other skills central to educability are to know how to identify the important from the unimportant, how to ask meaningful questions, and then how to organize and focus one's knowledge, as on an examination, to answer such questions. For example, do we encourage our students to submit questions to be used on their own exams? Do we help them learn how to improve their questions? Do we help them learn how to organize their knowledge? One way is to encourage students to grade the examinations of the class. Why not break up the class into teams of three? Code each student's exam so it remains anonymous. Then review with each group the principal points a good, average, and poor answer might contain. Better yet. Prepare a ditto sheet with examples of the different types of answers. Each student of the team then reads and evaluates the answers of the entire class to the same question. The team members then compare their evaluations to agree on a final grade. What do students learn? They immediately confront the wide range of individual differences that exist in every class. They quickly identify the well-organized, perceptive answer. They discuss with each other the discrepancies in their evaluations, and in the process become much more aware of what a logical, coherent, and thoughtful answer is like. As one of my weak students said, "This is the first time I ever understood how a question could be answered well." Another said, "Now I know why teachers say my thinking is too vague and diffuse." Students invariably find the exercise self-revealing. They also discover something of the subjectivity of grading, particularly of essay questions, become more sympathetic towards the teacher, and may even become less suspicious that the teacher is "playing favorites." By participating with our students in their collective evaluation, we all get a much clearer picture of just what our real goals are. By sharing in the educational process, they become more interested in their own educational growth.

[4]Fortunately, texts like Boynton and Mack's introductions to the short story, the poem, and the play (1965*a, b,* 1969) are now appearing, designed specifically to help secondary school students develop such skills.

Another obvious skill is knowing how to go about solving a problem. By problem-solving I don't mean learning how to do thirteen arithmetic and six physics homework problems each evening. I am appalled by how limited our understanding is of the power of "sciencing." To know how "to science" is to know how to clarify a problem, search out alternatives objectively, fashion new solutions, make controlled tests of their adequacy, and then apply the verified principle to a new situation. Sciencing is only a systematic and self-conscious way of adapting. But we keep these insights from students. For example, my freshmen come from some of the more demanding schools in the country. They have had most of the basic courses in science, but few of them are able "to science." Some may know the Second Law of Thermodynamics, but they don't know how to act like a scientist. They don't know how to control irrelevant variables. They don't know what independent and dependent variables are, nor the distinction between a control and experimental group. They don't know how a scientist goes about exploring the natural world in less formal ways as well. Much has been made of "discovery" learning in the sciences. I have not yet noticed the effects of such learning. If students do have rudimentary "sciencing" skills, they don't know how to apply them to the issues of social science or to other areas of human concern.

Education is not a value-free enterprise. Integral to a school's purpose of furthering educability is the cultivation of certain values rather than others. To learn how to symbolize accurately is to encourage honesty; to be more allocentric is to be more objective, tolerant, and caring; to grow integratively is to become more flexible and consistent; to be more stable is to be more steadfast and persistent; and to be more autonomous is to be more courageous. If a school commits itself to developing educability, then it commits itself to developing values like honesty, objectivity, tolerance, and caring. It's a myth that education destroys conscience. Instead, it humanizes formerly rigid and authoritarian values (Feldman and Newcomb 1969). A youth's values become more deeply humanistic, I suggest, as a consequence of his becoming more educable (Heath 1968*b*).

We sometimes forget that there is an ethic to the pursuit of truth. Certain values are so intrinsic to intellectual maturing that the failure to develop them distorts the intellect. A person who falsifies information, consciously ignores contradictory facts, copies the work of others, and interprets what he has learned to fit some preconceived purpose other than truth is an intellectual psychopath. Regardless of how bright he is or how much he has learned, we have failed.

What about other values not intrinsic to educability? Values like those in the Declaration of Independence and the Constitution? Values of the corporate state or of the Judeo-Christian tradition? Now we encounter conflict and controversy. These values may conflict with those of educability. For example, Russian schools educate for allegiance to the state and therefore limit the development of autonomous values. American schools stress individualistic competition and often limit the growth of allocentric values (Bronfenbrenner 1970). Should schools seek to make students loyal to specific political or religious values? Of course not. Indoctrination limits educability. But students should understand and know in depth their own country's traditions. They should also be acquainted with alternative ways men have organized societies. But the school should not *coerce* its students to choose one rather than another.

I am *not* suggesting that schools abandon the religious values, for example, that make them distinctive. A school may indeed wish to indoctrinate and risk limiting maturing in some areas. That is its choice. I believe it is possible for a school to witness vigorously to specific values and still genuinely respect a youth's right to believe otherwise. To not advocate that schools make patriots or converts will disturb some people. My position grows out of the belief that an open and democratic society offers the most favorable socio-political conditions for the fullest growth of its citizens. Educable students will understand that. Therefore, I don't fear the subversion of the state by its citizens, if the state is genuinely open and makes the maturing of its youth its highest educational priority.

We don't further the maturing of a youth's values by requiring him to recite a prayer, pledge allegiance to his flag, sing the "Star Spangled Banner," stand when the teacher enters the room, or go to every pep rally to demonstrate school spirit. These are rituals and routines. They may affirm values, but they don't provoke reflection about values, unless, of course, they conflict with other emerging values of students—as is now beginning to happen frequently. Habitual activity of any kind is the opiate of increased awareness and a potential barrier to growth. We preserve such rituals to symbolize and strengthen a particular value commitment we have. Rituals *are* important. They should not be given up too casually. However, teachers delude themselves if they think that participation in such rituals stimulates the maturing of a youth's values. The primary spur to increased awareness is confrontation and challenge of what we believe (Heath 1968*b*). Each teacher should periodically recast some part of his course to confront students at all levels of maturity with its core value implications.

I am particularly dismayed about the failure of scientists to engage students in the social implications of their methods and content. It is the effects of science and technology that threaten our survival. The anti-science and anti-technology stances of students grow more out of emotion than judicious thought. Yet, most teachers never locate science within a larger cultural-historical perspective or assist students to explore its assumptions and value implications. Why don't we confront students with the ethical questions involved in the application of scientific procedures to the study of man and his society? How many biology teachers challenge students to consider the implications of contemporary discoveries for our society? Unfortunately, too many scientists, like the rest of us, are committed to the propagation of their subject matter, not the maturing of their students. At least some of our science courses should become more deeply general and humanistic if our society is to have an informed and wise citizenry able to deal with the critical problems science has unleashed.

It is easier, admittedly, to challenge the values of our students through the social sciences, which I discuss later, and the humanities. Humanities teachers are potentially the most powerful faculty of a school. Why? Because they have more direct access than other teachers to the universal human problems and conflicts that are at the heart of most value issues of our culture as well as central to the developing identities of young people. They also have available a wider range of media, like film, art, music, poetry, drama, novels, and short stories for involving and so confronting their students with sharply divergent and convincing alternatives.

The single most powerful curricular determinant of the educability of Haverford students for years was a freshman English course (1968*b*). Why? Because its principal purpose was to make them examine their values, particularly those close to their personal concerns. Its perceptive and deeply humane faculty knew where their students were. They selected books, poetry, and film that spoke to these concerns. They knew how to support students who were enduring the disorganization and confusion that always attend the close examination of one's values. Skills of composition and communication were sharpened as a *consequence* of students confronting themselves. Ken Macrorie (1970) insists that a youth can communicate powerfully and clearly when he has something to say. I agree. We must help him first discover what he has to say.

One warning. Increased awareness does not automatically lead to more allocentric or integrative values. It may disrupt and confuse—which is OK, too. What is important is what happens then. Even though too many of our youth seem lost today in their own confusion, the schools must continue to confront. But they must go beyond merely confronting. They must develop more powerful ways to further the allocentric and integrative growth of their students.

Chapter 13

Allocentric Development

Healthy growth is dependent upon the presence of other people whose loving care, stimulation, and expectations bring out a youth's poten tials. Piaget long ago identified the interaction of one child with another as the critical determinant of his development from autocentric to allocentric thought (1928). Other research has confirmed over and over the centrality of the quality of our relationships with others to healthy development at all ages (Ainsworth 1965; Chickering 1969; Heath 1968b; Rogers 1967). Chapter Seven suggests that our increasingly alienated youth seemed to be going awry in their development at the allocentric phase of the adaptive process. Significant educational change should begin, therefore, at that point. Part IV describes the humanistic community our schools need to become. What other specific changes can be made to enhance allocentric maturing?

Put another way, "How can we structure the patterns of interpersonal relationships within the school to further allocentric development?" I have talked at length about the relation of the teacher to his students and emphasized the imperative of moving toward a collaborative "we-ness" relationship. We also need to create "we-ness" between students themselves. Many of us are not aware of how terribly competitive the atmosphere of schools is or how it sows distrust and isolates one student from another. The use of competitive techniques to "motivate" students, the early segregation of children into ability groupings, the emphasis on grades, CEEB tests and college admission hurdles all place a premium on out-doing another student. Even independent study aggravates isolation. Each works alone on his own project. He never becomes involved in or even knows about what someone else is doing. In these and other ways, schools encourage narcissism and self-aggrandizement.

How might we provide more genuinely cooperative learning experiences, in which students learn how to interact directly with each other?

Obviously, we should abandon our *predominant* reliance on the lecture method. We can learn how to integrate a variety of group discussion procedures into our courses. For example, why not introduce a topic and raise a question in the first ten minutes of a class? Then break up the class into small groups of five or six students to seek a solution to the question. Each would be expected to report back to the class its own solutions. The teacher could circulate among the groups and be a resource person.

Because students do not know how to sustain a connected and organized discussion among themselves for more than a few minutes, I have discovered that I must give assistance to them about how to lead and organize one even for only ten or fifteen minutes. At the beginning of the course, why not agree with your students about the number of times they will each have the opportunity to lead a small discussion group? Let them keep track of how frequently they do. Prior to the day of a discussion, ask for five or six volunteer leaders. Meet with them briefly after class to sketch the types of questions they can use to provoke discussion. Suggest how they can prepare themselves with further reading. When the time comes, don't fret if the discussions wander, dry up, or generate frustration. It takes time to learn such communicative skills. Why not have each student evaluate his own growth as a discussion leader during the semester and then check his evaluation against what the other students think of his development? And if you are sharing the evaluation procedure with your students, include the consensual evaluation in a student's final grade for the course.

Another technique for involving students in class discussions is to ask a few of them to sit in the center of the room and discuss a particular issue. The others sit outside the inner circle and prod the group with questions. Or, if discussions falter because students don't come prepared, break up the class into small groups to review the principal points of the homework. Each student might brief the rest of his group about one aspect of the assignment.

An adventurous teacher, desirous of freeing students from the textbook, might enrich these discussions by working with the class to generate topics which individual groups could research themselves. Then, in class, each member could contribute something different, which the group could then organize to report to the class. If a secure and cooperative learning atmosphere has been created, then the class might evaluate how well each group had organized its material and presented it to the class. Both teachers and students need more feedback about their efforts; otherwise, how are either to know how to improve?

There are other ways group techniques can be used. I rely heavily on students to help me organize and conduct a particular class. I recall Bill who was to report to the class, but who was petrified about talking in front of anybody. A sensitive and shy person, he never spontaneously talked in class. When directly questioned, he replied so tentatively and briefly that other students became as anxious as he. I had been close to Bill and knew how he felt. So I asked him if I could try to help him when it was his turn to work with the class. Several classes before he was to report, I casually said that Bill was to give his report soon, and that we would have to find some way to help him do a good job because he was anxious about talking to the group. Just before his talk, I asked each student to describe how he felt when he anticipated giving his report to the class. I began by describing my own anxiety when I had tried a different teaching technique with the class the week before. One by one, each student briefly described how he felt, frequently in very personal and moving terms. Some spoke very directly to Bill, saying they felt as paralyzed as he. By the time it was Bill's turn, he didn't feel quite so alone and "on the spot." Although he didn't look at us, he spoke well, which the class acknowledged in its assessment of his report. Bill told me at the end of the semester that he had never spoken so much in any class before. He had almost felt comfortable.

We might try other ways to create allocentrically mature relationships. If we know that the educability of a youth is blocked by feelings of isolation and loneliness, we might create a small working group of compatible people around him. We might even risk pairing students who irritate each other to work together on a joint task to which each would have something special to contribute. Research has demonstrated that a powerful way to change a person's prejudices is to team him with the person he dislikes on some task in which he needs the other. In the process of completing it, each may discover qualities in the other not seen before.

Why don't we help students learn how to assist each other to learn? For example, why not have two or three students work together to write a joint paper? Why do we always expect each student to write his own paper? True, one student might write most of the first report, but in the process, the second might learn how to organize a paper. Each might visit the other's home, discover some common interests, and learn how to cooperate. Why not break up classes into small tutorial groups each of which is responsible for the growth of every member of the group. Each member, for example, could proofread the papers other members of the group wrote. If the group were responsible for the grammar, punctuation, spelling, and clarity of each member's paper, students would learn how to proofread more carefully. A student might be spurred to master writing conventions to avoid being embarrassed by his peers' discovering how sloppy he is. A teacher could be freed to concentrate on helping students improve their style and arguments. Why don't groups of students complete the same examination together?

Or why don't we team students when they first begin independent work? Each can help the other when one becomes blocked. From such shared collaboration, in which they will have to argue, share, and accommodate to each other, may come learning about how to carry out one's own project later on. In other words, why can't we develop allocentric learning forms that encourage students to teach each other? Or do we believe that only a professional like ourselves can educate someone else?

There are many other techniques we can use for helping students learn how to assist others. If a question or issue is raised which only four or five students in the class are prepared to answer or discuss, why not co-opt them as teachers for ten minutes? Reorganize the class into four or five small groups for these students to teach. As a test, have one of their students summarize the basic issues. Not infrequently, I have students who ask or answer questions so circuitously or vaguely that I am baffled about how to respond. I will ask another student to paraphrase very briefly what was said. If he can't, I'll try another, and then finally ask for a volunteer. In this way, I check how faulty my own understanding is. The student may learn from his peers that it is not just his teacher who can't understand him. Again, such interpersonal feedback from peers can be a powerful incentive to change one's mode of interacting.

Why do I emphasize cooperative learning? For many reasons, some of which I've discussed in Parts I and II. We have been blind to the power that the peer group and its expectations have upon the educability of students. We should find forms that will sanction and encourage one youth to help another grow. A student may be more sensitive and responsive to the expectations of his peers than he is to those of an adult. If a youth is lazy, doesn't contribute, sponges on his group, the others will let him know soon enough. A youth may become more involved in his own education if he knows that he works for his group and not for his teacher. Of course, a teacher must be sensitive to the dynamics of such groups. He must be ready to intervene, interpret, or reshuffle members if one becomes a scapegoat or his growth is being stifled by the mix of personalities in the group. In creating such groups, a teacher will have to emphasize that individuals contribute different skills to a group. He may have to create groups that will permit the contribution of a less assertive and intelligent student to emerge. He and the class must be patient. For many groups will not function well. It takes time to learn such skills. Hopefully, the atmosphere of the class will encourage reflection by everyone about the group process itself—thus bringing into the collective awareness how change needs to be made. It may even be useful to have one monitor for each group who continuously observes the group, alerting it to when it is wandering and avoiding issues.

Many schools face such severe financial retrenchments that they are compelled to make major changes in their programs. Let's convert such a backward step into a healthy step. Let's take the opportunity to rethink our curriculum. Let's learn the lesson every developing country has had to learn. Our greatest untapped resource is the potential of students to help each other become more educable. We need a self-help program in the schools.

Let's take seriously the following observations that make a self-help program psychologically desirable and necessary. Adolescents have few opportunities in our society to perform meaningfully responsible service to others. One learns how to care for others by caring. Adolescents need to be challenged imaginatively, motivationally, socially, ethically, as well as intellectually, to discover the range as well as limits of their competences. Our schools will never have the resources necessary to provide the care and attention each child needs in the humanistic school I propose. Research on the effects of adolescents' tutorial programs in reading suggest that both the tutor and pupil progress more than those who neither tutor nor are tutored (Cloward 1967a, 1967b).

Every student in the eighth through the tenth grades should have the responsibility for an entire school year of helping two younger children become more educable. This responsibility would be fulfilled during time released from the regular school day. It would not be added onto the existing schedule. We would revise our schedules as well as our curriculum to make this action-service program an *integral* part of a student's academic development. Each student would work cooperatively with the children's principal teacher who would supervise a team of ten to fifteen tutors. Ideally, adolescents from the eighth through the tenth grade would be working in the same classroom. The tutors would be given training in the skills they need by the supervisory teacher and the guidance staff. Each tutor would work with his two children together for one hour each day for four days a week. All of the students working with the children of the same class would meet together with their supervisory teacher on the hour of the fifth day. Guidance consultants would attend such sessions. At this time additional training, reflective appraisals, and group discussion of individual problems would take place. Since a person's educability is determined by factors other than just his academic skills, the tutors would become involved in other than academic activities. They would be encouraged to use their initiative, imagination, knowledge, and skills to help a shy child become more expressive, a restless, impulsive kid more focused, and an inse-

cure child more secure. If one of the adolescent boys is himself a troublemaker in class, let's give him responsibility for working with a younger
troublemaker. Perhaps in the process of learning how to help such a child,
he may learn how to help himself.

Adolescents have many talents. Some are superb athletes, others
excellent guitarists, some fine dramatists. All of them know how to read,
do their multiplication tables, and spell passably, at least at the second and
third grade levels. Others excel in handicrafts, some are very sensitive, and
some are marvelous organizers. Why can't we develop the educational
structure that will utilize such talents in the service of helping another
person grow? Adolescents have much to give; why must we compel them
always to receive?

I can hear the objections: "Chaos! . . . I wouldn't trust some of
my eighth graders out of my sight for more than 20 seconds . . . How
are we to get the students to the elementary school and back in time for
their next class? . . . But there's no room in the schedule . . . Parents
will object . . . What elementary school teacher wants to run a seminar
of twelve adolescents? . . . Besides, they will just make more work for
everyone . . . They'll mess up our classrooms . . . They might even
damage some children psychologically. In fact, they will." And so on and
on and on!

Of course, every imaginable thing that could go wrong will go wrong
if we expect it to and don't prepare for it. But let's test our adolescents by
discovering what they can do when given a meaningful responsibility. Let
them develop such a program with us. Let a joint faculty-student committee organize and supervise the logistics. Perhaps a number—maybe even
quite a number—of students will initially fall by the wayside. But perhaps
a number will come alive in their own classrooms, assume a more active
attitude toward their own growth, learn to care for another and find that
they can be openly expressive with little kids and then eventually with each
other. Perhaps they will begin to re-experience their own suppressed child-
like spontaneity and playfulness. Perhaps some may regain their self-confidence by discovering they can contribute to another person's development. Perhaps a few will understand how difficult the task is of being a
parent and teacher.

And the children? Perhaps for the first time, some will have a caring
brother or sister. Maybe some boys will, for the first time, form a sustained
relationship with an older male. Perhaps others will get the individual
attention and care from a big person that they have never had before.
(Adolescents can care if we allow them to.) Maybe a few will settle down
to work through several pages of a workbook if someone is there to help

them keep to the task. Perhaps others will learn how much fun it can be to work with an older person whom they may want to imitate.

And we teachers? Perhaps by the questions our adolescents raise some of us will be pressured to reconsider our goals. Maybe we will understand more of our children by observing how they relate to adolescents: will they work harder, accomplish more? Perhaps we will be stimulated by the catalytic agents some tutors will be. Maybe we will reflect more about children and how they need to be educated, expand our own alternatives about how to teach and test out some of the approaches we observe our adolescents stumble upon. Maybe we will become more educable too.

And the school? We will escape the psychological straitjacket our age-graded schools put on us. Adults will work with adolescents and children; adolescents with adolescents from the eighth through the tenth grades as well as with adults and children; and children will have the opportunity of relating to varied older educable models. Perhaps some of our disenchanted adolescents will identify with the school and begin to feel responsible for its vitality. Perhaps a mutual self-help program, where the children are helping their tutors too, will make a school more of an educational community.

Wistful hopes? Perhaps. But perhaps not. Schools are already initiating small-scale efforts and report the results as being very favorable to both the tutor and those being tutored.

Although I have been skeptical about the use of encounter and sensitivity procedures with adults from the same school, I am more sanguine about their *modified* use with adolescents. I know I seem contradictory, for adolescents may be more readily disorganized by such procedures than adults. Their impulses are closer to the surface, moods more unstable and controlling, and defenses less stabilized. Yet, the emotional and interpersonal inhibitions of so many are so deep and pervasive that more direct "releasing" types of allocentric experiences than those I've been discussing in this section are necessary. I propose that the educational growth centers described in Chapter Nine explore, develop, and try out different types of sensory awareness, sensitivity and even physical contact procedures and games to discover what may be appropriate to use with adolescents in our schools. Guidance counselors and school psychologists could then receive intensive and carefully supervised training in such procedures. They could be sensitized to their appropriate limits and the types of students for whom such procedures are unwise. Only upon certification by the center would a counselor be eligible to conduct such sessions in a school. The center might provide consultant supervisors in the first year or two of a counselor's use of such techniques. Student participation would be voluntary, of course, and parental permission would be required.

Sensitivity sessions have been held in a number of the schools I have visited, usually by professionally trained consultants. Principals report the atmosphere of their schools changed. Students are more open, relaxed, and spontaneous with each other. Their attitude toward academic work improves. I know of few evaluations of such claims or if such effects persist. However, the consistency of the claims suggests that sensitivity procedures could be powerfully effective in promoting allocentricism. Until we know more about their limitations, we should remain open-minded to their judicious introduction by competently trained people.

One obvious implication of my suggestions is that our guidance counselors and school psychologists need to be trained differently. Most of our traditional guidance procedures are not very effective anyway (Tamminen and Miller 1968). Counselors should work more with groups of students rather than predominantly with individual students. Students need to grow allocentrically; the stimulus to that growth will come from interaction with other students. Counselors need skills to facilitate group interaction. They should work with cliques, gangs, the "in" girls of a class who are scapegoating another girl, groups involved in drug activities, and so on. Counselors should be available as consultants in group dynamics to teachers who are open to the development of a "we-ness" relationship with their students.

Just as too accelerated symbolic development distorts growth, so too much emphasis on allocentric development undermines autonomy. We don't promote group and other cooperative activities at the expense of other types of growth. Our goal is the maturing of a youth, not just the acquisition of information or the development of cooperative skills. We must also provide integrative educational experiences that further a youth's identity and autonomy.

Chapter 14

Integrative Educational Experiences

Our middle-class values about what a youth should become are really askew. We overvalue his verbal ability, minimize his aesthetic and interpersonal skills, and actually devalue his practical skills. The traditional academic subjects are his "majors." "Bill. Don't you dare come home again with a D in English." Art and music are "minors." "Well, don't worry about getting a C in art. It's much less important than your math." Home economics, vocational training, gym, and extra-curricular activities are peripheral. "Don't worry. They don't really count for getting into college. What's important are your test scores and the grades in your major subjects." Most insidious is our attitude about vocational arts. A kid loses status in our middle class dominated society if he can't make the college preparatory course. He's stupid. He's only fit to learn printing or auto mechanics! The gap between our academic and nonacademic programs is a psychological chasm in most schools.

Such attitudes cripple the self-esteem of the nonacademically inclined student. They also breed intellectual arrogance and accentuate divisions among students. To help youth develop more wholly, they should be apprenticed to the discipline and romance of real problems that demand more of them as persons than just cerebral exercise. They now live in homes where there is no challenging physical work and no opportunity to develop physical skills; they live in cities of concrete separated from the opportunity of learning to live with nature; they live in schools and societies in which they seldom have the opportunity to play and study and work and worship with the same group of peers and adults; they live in a society in which they are given much more than they have the opportunity to give.

To educate more wholly, we need more than just an in-school tutorial program that teaches caring and other allocentric skills and values. We also need to heal the split between our heads and our hands. In particular, early adolescents need skills to relate to the real world. Hands are the most versatile extension of our brains. They are our tools. They can do much more than write. They connect us to others, things, and earth. They reach, carve, play, hammer, garden, pinch, hold, shape, repair, sew, massage, cook, saw, touch. They are our means to express, to create, and to love. A youth needs to know he can do something well, something that has consequences, that changes things. His hands communicate his growing power in very concrete, visible ways. Competence is power. Power brings self-confidence and self-respect which encourage educability.

What should we do? Bring our hands back into our curriculum. By early adolescence, every youth should be developing several practical and recreational skills that relate him to things, nature, and people. Rather than derogate such skills by labeling them as "minor," we should value them by requiring every youth to become so competent in at least one hand skill that he could earn a living with it if necessary. We should also find creative ways to integrate such skills with other activities of the school. Finally, we should follow Sweden's lead and not expect boys and girls to learn different skills. They may wish to, but that will be their choice. Our archaic stereotypes of masculinity and femininity limit the development of potential talents in young people. They also breed helplessness and are destructive to healthy growth (Heath 1970*b*). Many men must and do want to cook. Many enjoy cooking. Some even sew buttons on their own shirts. Cars get flat tires and stall even with women drivers. My wife learned what to do the hard way—when stuck in the backwoods of Maine one summer. Toilets overflow, fuses blow, and Johnny gets a bad cut. Plumbers are too expensive, the electrician can't come till next week, and the doctor's phone is always busy. There may be no man around. Why shouldn't men knit or weave? Why can't a girl carve wood or work on a lathe as a hobby? Men do create fashions and work in the garment industry. Women do work in machine shops and on assembly lines.

But what types of skills should we expect our youth to learn? Cooking, carpentry, plumbing, budgeting, electrical repair, driving, comparison shopping, sewing, nursing, child care, computer programming and key punching? Weaving, potting, camping, mountain climbing, tennis, scuba diving, judo, yoga, and dancing? Clearly, the list is practically endless. A school's resources aren't. A school must make choices.

What principles should guide our choices? First, I would offer those skills necessary to survive both physically and psychologically in our type of society. Certainly, household repair skills, automobile mechanics, cooking, typing, budgeting, and some recreational skills would be highly useful.

Second, skills should be taught that can be integrated with the academic aspects of the curriculum. Practical medical skills could be integrated with a basic course on mammalian anatomy and physiology. Electrical repair of motors and automobile mechanics could, if taught properly, provoke questions that might lead to an interest in general science and physical principles. Cooking and drug education might lead into principles of chemistry and physiology. Child care could be preparatory for the in-school tutorial program. In one Canadian college, physical education, particularly the calisthenics program, is the "laboratory" for learning certain complex mathematical group functions. Finally, a variety of expressive skills, like movement, dance, drawing, and yoga will become more integrated with academic courses as the latter become more experiential. My intent is not to be exhaustive, but to provoke our imaginations into seeing how we can integrate our hands with our heads—and with our hearts too. Dewey and Whitehead always repudiated the division between the academic and the technical-vocational as false. We should too. We know something when we produce it in action. Action requires skills—practical skills.

A second way to provide a more integrative education is to make the curriculum more experiential. Our students don't need just more knowledge; they need more experienced knowledge. We make our youth less educable by isolating cognitive from affective learning. We have constricted education to head learning. We need to liberate academic education to include all of the body. Don't misunderstand me. I do not propose that we convert our classes into emotional happenings or therapeutic catharses. I want an education that lets youth learn organismically, that is, intellectually, emotionally, motivationally, interpersonally, and ethically. I want emotionality integrated with intellectual discipline. I don't want just passion or just intellectualism.

Some examples? I teach a course in abnormal psychology in which students are responsible in the field work part of the course for tutoring disturbed adolescents in a nearby mental hospital. One of my goals is to help them become sensitive observers, not just of their patients, but of their own reactions to their patients. Another goal is to develop as quickly as possible a supportive group "unity" in the class so that if a student has a troubling experience with his patient or the content of the course he will feel comfortable sharing it with the class.

I'll describe the first class in detail. I notified the students before the course that we would try a variety of experiential procedures. A student who didn't want to take part in any of them didn't have to. A very apprehensive group of students came together that first class. I had placed rugs on the floor, moved the furniture aside, darkened the room leaving two candles lit near me. We took off our shoes, relaxed on the rugs, and settled down to a short period of quiet meditation. To sensitize them to their tensions, I guided them on an interior trip of their bodies, quietly encouraging them to relax and become aware of their own feelings. We then formed ourselves into random pairs to share our feelings of the moment with each other. I told Anne how anxious I was, for I had not used any of the procedures before. I didn't want to offend some students. She reassured me. Yes, she was apprehensive too. But she was too curious to not participate. To become familiar with the others in the class, we formed a circle, each member of the pair facing the other. Each of us then moved around the circle to the facing member of the next pair holding his hands for thirty seconds. Afterwards, we discussed what we had learned about each other from that momentary physical contact: how tight was the grip, was the palm sweaty, what texture was the skin, were the fingernails bitten down, was the hand "alive" or "dead"? I then blew out the candles, turned on some music, and asked each student to let himself just go physically to flow emotionally with the music. He could move, stretch, reach out, dance. My purpose was to prepare him to be looser physically and less self-conscious for the next exercise. Lighting the candles and turning off the music, I asked each student to dance or move with another for ninety seconds and then shift to another person he hadn't danced with before. I had learned at Esalen how powerfully self-revealing this movement exercise can be. One learns a great deal about another in a very short time when he must interact with him in a physically unstructured situation. Competitiveness, dominance and submission, muscular rigidities, gracefulness, expressiveness, emotionality, "at homeness" with one's own body, creativity and other personality traits emerge very saliently in bodily movement. Also, one learns very quickly with whom one "flows" and is simpatico as well as with whom one struggles or resists.

The group then separated itself into pairs that felt most comfortable with each other in the dance exercise. Each member of the pair told the other what he had learned about him from the dance. On the assumption that a person you feel physically comfortable with is a person you are more secure with, I asked each member to tell the other what being "abnormal" meant to him. They should feel free to be as personal as they wished. (A condition of joining the class was that the confidentiality of personal revelations be maintained.) The final procedure was for one member of each pair to form a circle in the middle of the room during which this group discussed what the words "abnormal" and "deviant" meant. The discussion actually generated many of the issues which we were to deal with later in the course.

In succeeding classes, we used other procedures, including role-playing of a schizophrenic mother relating to her sons, several methods of therapy, small group discussions about our patients, and various movement exercises to continue to sensitize ourselves to the subtleties of interpersonal relations.

What about a different type of course more narrowly focused on traditional academic content? I teach a course in Developmental Crises in the Life Span. Young men have always had difficulty empathizing with the early sections of the course that deal with infants and children. Although some became more alive when working in a nursery school, the class usually didn't jell until we reached adolescence and "their problems." So I needed some procedures for recreating some of the feelings of being a child.

Prior to the first meeting of the course, each student was to read an anecdotal diary kept by a mother of her infant son from the time of his birth to three years of age. I also asked each to bring a sheet with him to the first class. That caused some consternation. I began the first class with a period of quiet relaxation during which I asked the students to recall memories of being twelve years old, then five years old, and then their earliest memory. Then they tried to put their earliest memory into action.

Once the class had settled down, I asked each person to crawl under his sheet and assume a foetal position. I then guided the class through the principal stages of development and birth: quickening, limb movement, full body movement, labor, and birth. Even though the room was dark and each was hidden from the view of others by his sheet, we were amused by how difficult it was to utter the birth cry. Anyway, I asked them to stay under the sheets to forestall too great self-consciousness. I then read illustrative passages of different developmental stages from the mother's diary, which they acted out under the sheet.

The class then divided itself into small groups to share with each other their earliest childhood memory. Finally, some volunteers made a circle in the middle of the class and discussed among each other what "play" meant. They explored just how playful they could allow themselves to be, the most childishly playful thing they could see themselves doing, their reactions to our play in class, the functions of play. This discussion prepared them for some reading about play assigned for the following week.

The next week we began to study Erikson's theory of development. To generate experience with what he meant by trust, the students paired up during the week to take each other on a "blind walk." One student is blindfolded. The other leads him around to provide him with as many different sensory experiences as possible. Strong trusting feelings are readily aroused. So are feelings of mistrust in some. At the next class, we used other "trust" games and then discussed the meaning of trust before integrating the discussion with Erikson's theory.

"But these are psychology courses where it is easy to use such techniques. How can experiential learning be used in English, Social Studies, or foreign language courses?" Much experimentation is now underway to develop integrative modes of learning in these courses as well (Brown 1971). A technique developed by Hillman, an English teacher, illustrates one model. He asks a class to assume it has just crashed on a deserted island in the Pacific Ocean. What will they do now? For the next several hours, the members of the class struggle to define for themselves what they must do to "survive." Issues of cooperation, distribution of work assignments, leadership, procedures for settling disputes, and other interpersonal conflicts quickly emerge. Students become more emotionally involved than we might expect in trying to work out such issues. Hillman then assigns the class Golding's novel, *Lord of the Flies,* which describes what happens to a group of adolescents in a similar plight. Discussion and analysis of the novel take place within a common experiential context out of which personally relevant examples can be used to amplify the themes of the novel (Brown 1971, pp. 61-64).

Similar types of "experiential" exercises are being developed for social studies courses under the more familiar name of simulation games. Carefully worked out games are constructed that illustrate different historical crises, economic principles, governmental problems, social relations, and geographic problems. For example, the class may be divided into teams each representing a different nation that is confronted by a pre-arranged crisis. The game *Dangerous Parallel* is modeled on the Korean crisis, though the students don't know that at the time they play the game. The ministerial representatives of the different nations must make decisions, based on information given them, to which the Foreign and Defense Ministers and other staff of another country must decide how to react (Nesbitt 1968). The purpose of such simulations is to provide the experience of making complex and difficult decisions, to develop a deeper empathy and understanding about an issue, to learn how to cooperate with others, and to take another person's viewpoint or role.

Simulation games can also be used to help a youth develop mature values. Such games provoke decisions that reflect fundamental styles, motives, and values which students may be unaware of. Competitive, cooperative, dominant, submissive, self-centered, altruistic, aggressive, passive, and materialistic modes of resolving issues are frequently provoked. One game that can elicit just such motives and values has been developed by Community Change, Inc., a nonprofit group organized to train social change agents to work on problems of prejudice in white suburban areas (Seldon). The game simulates a metropolitan area facing an expanding deprived minority group. Twenty people are divided into teams representing the different power and interest groups of the area, like those who own much of the land, deprived minorities, laboring groups, city representatives, etc. Given information about its income, resources, and needs, each team decides its strategy and then in an assembled town meeting seeks to resolve the problems in terms of existing zoning laws, tax rates, availability of services, and so on. Teams that seek to sustain high land values and exclusive residential patterns force crowding in the cities that in turn eventually affects the economy of the suburb. At different stages in the game, the teacher can confront the participants with their own motives and values, illustrate the complexity of most value decisions, contrast the decisions being made in the game with those actually made in their home communities, and help students learn how to anticipate the consequences of their decisions.

Of course, imaginative teachers have always used a variety of methods to involve, motivate, or make a subject "live" for a student. Role-playing, psychodrama, field trips, and film, in particular, could be much more creatively used by all of us to provide a common experiential core out of which to generate the intellectual and value issues relevant to the course.

But there is another purpose for which experiential and sensitivity-type techniques could be used. Just one example. To master a language is not just to learn to listen, speak, write, and read. Learning a language involves attitudes, feelings, and gestures. How we speak reflects our shyness, insecurity, warmth, aliveness. To make language learning more integrative, we need to center it within the matrix of the body by means of playful action. Otherwise, language remains a disembodied "out there" academic subject that never becomes deeply internalized "in the bones," as some teachers say.

So what would I do that first French class? I'd play. I'd have my rug, a large open space, and maybe even some soft French background music. I'd converse with the class by gesture, pantomime, maybe even dance—and hopefully some more expressive students would spontaneously respond. I'd use only those French words descriptive of what we were doing. Groups of students could also play the game of communicating without English words with each other. They could communicate by drawing, gesturing, moving, or acting—or speaking in French. If I or the class became too tense, I'd laugh. A language class—any class for that matter—should be taught to laugh together very early. Some yoga exercises for reducing tension could be combined with commonly used French slang and gestures. Trying to communicate is frustrating. Let's provide students with the gestures and words (perhaps even a few mild French swear words) they need to express tension. As we acted, moved, pantomimed, I'd begin to attach short sentences to what we were doing and encourage the students to use them while they were moving and acting. Students should experience the sensations and feelings that a word or thought connotes. This is one of the lessons Piaget tells us by the way.

Because adolescents are self-conscious about how they come across to others, I would focus early on just this concern. I'd do a great deal of small group work. The groups could do different things during class. For example, one group might work with a tape recorder, playing back its burgeoning conversation to hear their own voices. Another might create in French their own skit to act out to the class. Of course it might consist more of pantomime than words, maybe even disconnected words at that. But that's all right. Another group might try to make the most horrendous or ugly or sweet French sounds it could. I could give them a variety of strange and familiar words for making the most egregious pronunciation mistakes. Any subsequent pronunciation mistakes they might make would be trivial by comparison. Another group might listen and try to mimic some French translations of a popular folk song. Another group might work on how they felt about their own voices, what they like and dislike about the way they express themselves to others, how they would like to be different, what they like and don't like about the way other members of the group communicate, when they feel most uptight in the class about talking, when they feel they can just let themselves go, and so on.

We don't necessarily assist a youth to overcome self-consciousness by ignoring it. We can help him in several ways. He can experience forgetting himself by becoming involved in action. Or he can learn how to become less sensitive to what he believes others will think of him. For example, by deliberately exaggerating his poor pronunciation we may help him to make a joke of it, thus reducing his anxiety. By mutually sharing his fears, we help him understand that he is only human. It takes considerable sensitivity, of course, to work in these ways with adolescents. That is why it is imperative to establish an open, frank, caring atmosphere in class so that students feel free to tell us when we inadvertently intrude too far.

The early Athenians never confined education to the academic. The educated Greek participated in athletics, sang and played the lyre, and danced the ritual dances. When Zorba the Greek wanted to communicate his joy, he danced. We should also find ways to integrate our bodies with our heads. Let's begin to incorporate movement and dance, meditation and yoga, music and art *into* our academic courses so that growth becomes an organismic experience and not just a head exercise. Why can't a course in writing use art as a means to capture visual images glimpsed during some yoga exercises? Why can't a course in modern American poetry use modalities like body movement, drama, and music as well as words by which to "experience" a poem? Some philosophy and religion courses might benefit from periods of meditation. In fact, why don't we stop talking so much in class, provide meditative periods for students and ourselves to think about a point or discussion, and use the quiet time to prepare mentally an incisive point. Let's break the strangle hold that abstract words have on the vitality of our classrooms.[1]

From my observations and limited use of experiential techniques, I have some "advices." Create and use procedures that have an integral relation to your purposes for the course. Don't play games just to play games. Always try to provide an opportunity to reflect at length about what has been experienced and then integrate such reflections into the intellectual content of the course. Unreflected-upon experiences do not necessarily lead to understanding or growth. Experiential learning takes time and patience. Don't be in a hurry to get through a lesson plan. Don't become anxious, as I have, if you don't complete all the work you had planned. Provide time for class discussion and reflection about the value of the experiences used in order to discover just how growth-inducing they may be. If there is a "we-ness" atmosphere in the class, students will, if encouraged, suggest their own forms of experiential learning. Some experiences may create resentment or anxiety. If so, such feelings should be discussed in the group. I find it necessary to have immediate feedback from students about how they are responding to the techniques. Some procedures may fail dismally. Let the class discuss why they did. But make education more playful.

Be prepared to become emotionally involved yourself. Such experiences do release feelings, create an aura of excitement, and produce intense emotional involvement in some. I have discovered that in only a matter of minutes some of the most intellectual persons can be drawn emotionally into group activity. Don't use procedures that you are uncomfortable with. Some of my students felt that it was my anxiety about some of the procedures I've described that made them anxious and a few resistant. One rule of thumb is not to ask your students to participate in an activity

---

[1]Brown's *Human Teaching for Human Learning* (1971) describes how educators have integrated Gestalt therapy, sensory awareness, and other affective types of techniques with classroom activity. Borton's *Reach, Touch, and Teach* (1970) provides a selective bibliography of other affective education procedures.

in which you would not participate yourself. Feel free to participate and let your students learn that you react like a human being too.

On the other hand, accept the fact that students will become apprehensive and anxious. Each of us risks exposure of ourselves to ourselves and to others when we become emotionally involved. As one senior said, "There was no other class that made me so anxious but there have been few others I enjoyed or learned so much from." Students have become so habituated, even drugged, and bored by traditional classes whose procedures they can anticipate five months ahead of time that they may be overly apprehensive about any departure from that style. What is important is not the anxiety we experience, but how we respond. Does it facilitate or inhibit adaptation?

In summary: be clear about your goals. Integrate experiential learning with the intellectual substance of the course. Be comfortable with the experiences you use. Realize that some will fail with some students. Risk becoming emotionally involved. Encourage everyone to let you know how they are reacting. Share with your students. But remember that you are not an equal among equals.

How do I evaluate this type of integrative learning? I have no good evidence about its effects. Research on the effects of simulation games, for example, confirms my observation that they are powerfully motivating and involving (Nesbitt 1968). However, like any educational technique, if they are not clearly associated with expectations about the mastery required of the content of the course, I doubt that they in and of themselves will suddenly produce measurable increases in traditional academic outcomes, like the acquisition of information. I believe that they will make more educable students. But I can't demonstrate that. They certainly help create a different atmosphere in the classroom.

One warning. Experiential education may make some students temporarily less educable. Most students are more emotionally suppressed than we know. They rigidly defend themselves against strong impulses. When suppressed feelings first emerge, they may be explosive and excessive. A few students may be threatened by the rush of their feelings and flee further behind their masks. Others may find their excitement so intoxicating they turn against bland, didactic methods. Our choice is clear: to play it safe, continue to bore students, and deepen their estrangement from their feelings or to venture and risk, wake up more students, and help them heal their inner divisions.

The last way to further the integration of a student is to develop a more contextual curriculum. I use the term "contextual" to emphasize complexity, multi-faceted, holistic, problem-centered approaches. Traditionally defined academic specialities break up the gestalt of experience. A youth studies medieval history, the art and music of the period in other courses, and its literature in another—and frequently each in different years.

Many signs indicate that schools are seeking to provide more contextual growth experiences. Some courageous colleges and departments are abandoning the traditional concept of a major that requires everyone to take ten to twelve specific departmental courses. They are now tailoring a major program to fit the needs and interests of the student. That's good. A committee of the National Association of Independent Schools has strongly urged a major overhaul of our social studies curricula to make them more contextual. Topical types of courses that aren't confined to any one traditional discipline are becoming more widespread. Some teachers have proposed that we reorganize our junior high schools, in particular, so that one or two teachers rather than five or six are responsible for the growth of twenty-five students for several years, relying on other teachers as resource people but having no specified curriculum. Such teachers would be wise nonexperts whose own educability and maturity would serve as models of how to go about learning material appropriate for this age group.

I have some curricular suggestions that I believe are more appropriate to the emerging world of tomorrow than some courses we now require. I'll sketch them briefly, for I want only to clarify the meaning of an integrative course, not justify a particular program.

One psychological effect of a more complex, interdependent, and incoherent society will be much greater frustration. Frustration breeds violence. Our students may well encounter much more violence in their personal lives than we have had to face. They will need to understand more clearly than we do now the causes of violence, techniques for resolving conflict, methods for modifying social attitudes and institutions, and in a more controlling society, their legal rights as individuals. We should create experiential, cross-disciplinary courses in *Aggression and Violence, Conflict-Resolution, Methods of Social and Institutional Change,* and *Principles of Individual Rights and Legal Redress,* to name but a few. Such courses would be central and not just elective. They could well replace some of our traditional history, English, and social studies courses.

A course on *Aggression and Violence in Man* could be designed to teach the causes of aggression, the direct and indirect forms by which it is expressed personally as well as throughout history, and the institutionalized forms different societies have developed to channel and contain man's aggressiveness. Another purpose of the course would be to confront each student with his own aggression, the types of situations that provoke his hostility, the defenses he uses to protect himself against his and other's aggression, and the values he has about aggression and its expression (Heath 1970*d*). Such a course could draw from a vast range of material. Biology, ethnology, psychology, anthropology, sociology, history, political science, law, and the humanities have concerned themselves with some aspect of aggression. Selected topical issues might vary from year to year, depending in part on what the class decided its interests were.

Many methods might be used to make the course experiential. A student might keep a daily journal in which he described how he felt when he was angry, analyzed the types of situations that triggered his anger or hostility, and tried to understand his typical reactions to aggression. Does he suppress it, but have nightmares, develop an upset stomach, withdraw or cool it, explode or punish himself, make sarcastic jokes or play extra hard on the athletic field? A teacher might use some of the experiential classroom techniques I've described to help his students learn how to share some of their negative feelings with each other. They would learn from others why and how they get angry, discover what each does that makes someone else angry in the class and, by means of role-playing or other techniques, learn how to master their aggression more constructively. Some of the simulation games that provoke aggressive responses in the context of a political crisis or war might be used as a diagnostic device in the classroom to facilitate the analysis of our individual and group hostilities and modes of handling them.

Other experiences might be to study the frequency and type of aggression students encounter during one week in their families, schools or local community, or on television. They might do a content analysis of their local newspaper about the frequency of aggressive themes. They might follow a small child around for a Saturday to identify the types of situations that incited aggression in him.

I would also provoke my students to grapple with their own values about both personal and societal forms of aggression. Selected novels like *Clockwork Orange,* films like *The Wild Ones* and reports of the Vietnam My Lai massacre could serve as complex situations for prodding students to clarify, search out alternative moral positions, and come to some tentative position for themselves.

A coordinate course might be titled *Conflict-Resolution.* We do almost nothing in our schools to help students learn how to resolve conflicts constructively. The purposes of such a course would be similar in principle to those for *Aggression and Violence.* Selected topics might include the different types of conflicts, sources of conflicts, including both biological and social intra- and interpersonal modes of dealing with conflict, illustrative case analyses of personal, interpersonal, national, and international conflicts, historically sanctioned ways of suppressing or resolving conflicts, case studies of strikes, arbitration procedures, collective bargaining, negotiations and wars, and concepts of justice and institutionalized means within the law for resolving conflicts.

Again, such a course could draw upon a wide range of sources, including literary descriptions of intra- and interpersonal conflicts, films, clinical case studies, psychological and sociological studies, historical, economic, and political case materials and writings. It would be instructive to visit or even study a magistrate's court. A more instructive experience would be to follow daily a nearby jury trial. In class, the different positions might be acted out, questions raised about the legal argument and process, and an independent decision arrived at prior to the verdict of the court. Students might become immersed in a local labor dispute, visit a marriage counselor, talk with a diplomat, and sit through some debates at the United Nations or the Senate.

A number of more direct experiential procedures might be used to confront students with their own personal conflicts and modes of resolving them. In addition to some of the simulation games that provoke interpersonal conflicts, I would design other procedures with my class. For example, each student might identify his most troubling interpersonal conflict. His assignment for the unit would be to analyze its sources, development, mode of expression, and then develop new adaptive ways to resolve it.

A third course that we could put into the curriculum is titled *Principles of Social and Institutional Change* Just what are our schools doing to help students learn how to induce constructive change in schools and other institutions? Nothing or very little. The purposes of such a course would be to understand why social change does and does not occur and to develop skills for creating institutional change. The course might focus on the development and persistence of habits, attitudes, and prejudices and their relation to the maintenance of different customs and institutions; the dynamics of power; the reasons for the rigidities of bureaucracies; the problems of decision-making in any hierarchical organization; various mechanisms now used to produce institutional change; the historic role of revolution and violence in inducing social change; the role of law, democratic and dictatorial methods for creating change.

A class could generate its own resource materials. Civil rights and SDS literature, revolutionary tracts, Mao's *Red Book,* underground newspapers, and case studies of how developing nations have changed might be analyzed for principles of change. Socio-psychological studies of attitudinal and institutional change, interviews with community change agents, books written by reformers, analyses of contemporary student modes of changing their schools, and studies of the power of the mass media and advertising could illustrate the complexity of the factors involved.

I hesitate to suggest one of the more relevant experiential means of learning how to change an institution. Some embattled principals might not appreciate a course whose laboratory was the school itself. *But* it is time we learned how to use our own schools as communal laboratories for helping youth become educable. Might not a class develop its own mechanisms for inducing constructive change, not just in its own members and classroom, but within a school as well? Many students are doing this now on an *ad hoc* basis in opposition to, rather than in collaboration with, the adults of their schools. What better laboratory for learning how complex, frustrating, and painfully tedious it is to change one's self and others? Of course, a class might select a highly specific target it wanted to learn how to affect, like persuading a local town council to clean up its stream or provide adequate garbage service.

Another priority course is the *Principles of Individual Rights and Legal Redress.* Students should be much more conversant with the rights and responsibilities of being an American citizen and have some basic knowledge and skills for making constructive use of the law. We need to alert young people to the encroachments on their freedom that a technologically sophisticated government can make. We should examine with them the issues involved in national data banks, credit ratings, wire-tapping, FCC policies that tend to prefer conservative, and discriminate against liberal, television stations, monopolistic control of sources of information, and the myriad other activities that are used to control in many subtle ways our thoughts and so our freedom. Every high school student in this country should be given an elementary course in the principles of law, his rights in relation to the police and the courts, court procedures, bail bond and preventitive detention practices, county jail and prison philosophy. Such a course could be easily made experiential.

The principle of integrative and experiential learning is, I hope, clear. We could have an exciting curriculum if we broke out of our subject-matter way of thinking about education and our narrow academicism that protect us from being personally involved with the motives and values of our students.

If education is confined primarily to the manipulation of ideas, we are never challenged to grow wholly; we are only a walking head. It is only when we transform an idea into action, that is, produce some output, that we can know the validity and value of our idea. The laboratory is indispensable to the physicist; the studio to the sculptor; the market place to the economist. So I look to some form of action-involvement as the potentially most powerful integrative educational experience a youth can have. Until we find ways to integrate knowing with doing, ideas with action, our students will remain deeply divided and alienated (MacDonald 1969).

Chapter 15

Stabilization
and Autonomy

The power of a model of healthy growth is that it provides a ground plan, a blueprint, that can guide the introduction of specific changes into schools. The model I have used suggests that healthy development proceeds systemically. The dimensions of maturing are not independent of each other: the development of one affects the development of another. For instance, curricular innovations to stimulate integration also may enhance a student's ability to symbolize or to think allocentrically. Whether an integration has become stabilized or not is determined by a test of its efficiency. If a new skill can be applied to a situation different from the one in which it was learned or stabilized, then it has become autonomous.

We do make limited tests of the stability of some of the skills we teach, like those for reading and number proficiency. We can determine their autonomy by how effectively they are used to master a social studies text or a science assignment. But as a youth grows older, the value of our tests for determining educability diminishes rapidly. Studies suggest that some of our most precious measures, like grade point averages, have little predictive value for almost any subsequent healthy adaptation a graduate may make. In an unpredictable world, which places a premium on educability, our traditional tests of growth are increasingly irrelevant. To test the stability and autonomy of a student adequately, we must extend the range of tests beyond the walls of the school while students are still in school. By testing how students adapt outside our sanctuaries, both we and our students will discover in what ways we can help them in the remaining time they are in school to learn how to adapt maturely. I must emphasize again that I do not intend to describe a detailed program for testing students. I seek only to challenge us to think more imaginatively about the whys, whats, and hows of testing their educability.

I have already suggested one such diagnostic test for use outside of the classroom, though also for use within the school. The in-school tutorial program not only may further a student's allocentric development, but also test his educability. It will become very clear from such a program which students have the stick-to-it-tiveness, motivation, other-centered values, interpersonal skills and adaptability to fulfill such a responsibility. Both students and we will discover which adolescents have not yet stabilized various skills and values and who is not very independent. And we will be shocked. Some of our A students will fail abysmally and some of our D students will succeed far beyond their own or our expectations. We will have found a way for academically weak students to bolster their self-confidence for such a test requires more than just abstract ability. We will find out how each student, including our proud academicians, needs to grow in the following years. We will also be learning how to use the school itself as a means to stimulate and test student educability as well as encourage the development of a sense of school community.

I have refrained from specifying details of the programs I suggest, since I don't want to obscure the principles behind them. One such principle is that if an adolescent demonstrates considerable maturity in his tutorial program, he should be given additional responsibility the following year. He may become a supervisor of a small group of eighth-grade tutors, for example. Or the school may develop a different type of action-service project for its more mature students. Another principle is that he should not participate in a relatively unsupervised activity until he has shown that he can function well in a closely supervised one. All such tests, of course, should be *integral* parts of the school's curriculum in which all students participate. Alternative, less demanding action-service programs should be available for those students who have unsuccessful experiences. Some students may need an additional year or two of such programs before the school can "certify" to the community that they are ready to function independently.

It should now be clear why I restricted my earlier tutorial proposal to students in the eighth through the tenth grade. A sixteen-year-old should be ready for a more challenging test of his maturity. I do not believe that schools have the resources necessary to provide such tests for most of their eleventh and twelfth graders. They must turn to the community. To facilitate a youth's stabilization and autonomy, therefore, requires at the secondary level a guided program of graded community tests.

What do I propose? I talk first of a typical eleventh grade and then a twelfth grade test.[1] I propose two tests appropriate for the maturity of

---

[1] If educability is our goal, then certain structural changes are imperative in schools: ungraded secondary school classes, more flexible schedules for easy movement into the community and back into the schools, and the development of more functional requirements than number of course credits amassed for graduation.

the typical eleventh grader, though there may be some eleventh, and even twelfth, graders not yet ready to participate. First, each qualified sixteen-year-old should work for the equivalent of two hours a day in some service agency of the community for four days a week or for one full eight-hour day, depending upon schedule contingencies. Similar to the tutorial program, such a program would be an integral part of the curriculum and would not be "added" on as a frill. A youth might work in a nearby hospital, day care center, nursery school, family service agency, OEO program, old age or nursing home. On the fifth day, he would participate in a two-hour reflective seminar with ten to twelve other interns, his supervisory teacher, and a guidance consultant to discuss the interpersonal, ethical, and other issues that have arisen during the week. Placement in the intern setting would depend upon skill, interests, degree of responsibility required, and might be coordinated with one of the integrative courses I have just discussed. A student, for example, taking the course on *Aggression and Violence in Man* might intern at a reform school or in a court agency. The agencies would be expected to provide an evaluation of each of its interns which could be used for determining how a student needed to grow the following semester or year. All such assessments should be frankly shared with the students.

Such a program is clearly practicable. Spring Valley, a commuting suburb of 42,000 people within the New York City area, has introduced a judiciously designed pilot project for one hundred of its tenth through twelfth grade students similar in principle to what I've described. Such a program was initiated by Alan Sugarman in response to the deepening alienation of the suburb's students. It has received enthusiastic support from teachers, parents, and students. An excellent succinct review of similar intern programs, their rationale, problems, and effects can be found in Sugarman's proposal (1968).

A community education program may be less practicable for large public schools. I have proposed elsewhere (1969b) that numerous small residential centers should be created in different parts of the country and abroad to which groups of mature high school students could go for twelve weeks to participate in an action-service educational experience. Carefully selected, mature adults would accompany them. Including the summer, four groups of students and teachers could attend the center each year. The purpose of such a center would be to challenge and test the educability of students to be able to adapt both to the practical problems of living with their peers as well as to the demands of the center's program. A permanent resident teaching couple would develop an integrative experiential program appropriate to the mission of the center. For example, at such a center in Appalachia students would learn about the ecology, geography, economy, political structure, literature, and music of the area. As one integral part of their experience, students would assume the responsibility of continuing some service project for the local community. Other educational centers might be located near migrant camps, center city recreational centers, factory-industrial, rural agricultural, musical-artistic, or political areas like Washington, D.C. A number of language centers might be established in countries like Mexico or cities like Quebec where students could stabilize their language skills while working in some service activity. Some of our language teachers would have to abandon their prejudice about the proper Spanish or Parisian accents.

Schools are already initiating similar though less ambitious types of programs. One public school has a travel seminar. The class moves from one part of the country to another seeking out new learning experiences as it goes. Others send classes for six weeks on archeological expeditions to Central America or to work on Indian Reservations. Another school takes its entire junior class to an ecological wild life preserve for two weeks. And of course many others have sponsored shorter types of field trips to different sections of the country. Such educational centers are practicable if we insist that they remain primitive and simple. Students could help construct and maintain the centers as well as be responsible for much of their operation, including housekeeping, cooking, educational, and entertainment arrangements. They are practicable if resources are put into personnel, not into fancy sleeping quarters, parking lots, or permanent buildings. The students are there not to loaf, but to work; not to do their own thing, but to serve others; not to be academically spoon fed; not to be coddled, but to be tested. Let's provide the opportunity for them to learn *how* to grow up by confronting them with the problem of their own psychological survival.

Such programs would be intrinsically rewarding to many adolescents and be exciting incentives to them to grow maturely enough to be able to participate. They will disrupt students and their accompanying faculty, confront them with many new problems, particularly interpersonal, and test their stability and autonomy in ways our schools and society aren't now doing. The program would also meet the needs of increasing numbers of youth for a commune-like experience for testing not only their practical and recreational skills, but also their interpersonal skills. Furthermore, our society needs to create new occupations more congruent with the emerging life style of some of our youth. The centers would provide a new type of vocational opportunity. The staff positions would strongly appeal to generalists deeply committed to the improvement of our society and the education of youth. Finally, such action-service educational programs will radically alter the relations of the students and their teachers.

If a student demonstrated that he had the maturity to handle his own growth, then I would abolish his senior year in high school. The senior year is now a wasted year psychologically for many students who are just marking time. They are satiated and bored. Those who are college-bound have their SATs behind them, their applications to college submitted, and only time to fret until they hear their fate. Much of what is taught in their senior year is not necessary for their subsequent adaptation to college. Failure in college is due more to the inability to handle its freedom and to direct one's own growth than it is to inadequate academic preparation. What our adolescents need to learn before they reach college is how to use their freedom maturely. Those who are not college bound need to grow similarly. They need sanctioned opportunities to explore with guidance several different occupations without being committed to them permanently.

We should convert the senior year into one or two apprenticeships in which the community can test, in a sense, how successful the school has been in educating its youth. With the school's help, each qualified student would locate a nonpaying 36-hour-a-week apprenticeship. He would return to school once a week for an intensive reflective three-hour seminar organized by a school-community supervisor. His former teachers might participate in such seminars to secure information about the effectiveness of their own earlier efforts. What might a seventeen-year-old do? He could work in a laboratory, municipal court, hospital, grocery store, gasoline station, body-welding shop, real estate office, lawyer's, doctor's, principal's office, or with a carpenter, policeman, electrician, or college teacher. Many students might also serve their apprenticeship in center city schools upon invitation by the local communities. Their earlier extensive tutorial work in their own school will have provided them with the necessary skills and knowledge; their intern work in their local community will have tested their sensitivity and maturity to work responsibly in such settings.

A youth would work in the community with its adults, who in exchange for his services would seek to further as well as test his educability. The work would not be defined as exploitative nor menial, but true apprenticeships in which the "master" assumed responsibility for guiding the continued growth of his apprentice. Such apprenticeships would be under the care of the school, which would continue to provide guidance and support. It can be a shelter in case a student fails to meet his responsibility or encounters traumatic or troubling experiences. He may have to abandon his apprenticeship to return to the school program. Detailed descriptions and assessments of how each apprentice developed would be expected and shared with each apprentice.

Practicable? There are many problems. *The* problem is the availability of positions that would not compete with or reduce the number of jobs available for adults seeking work. But until our society creates ways to help youth relate more functionally to adults at some point in their schooling, it risks estranging them further from the adult world as well as from themselves. Adolescents need to be tested in responsible action.

The effects? Students would have sustained working relationships with diverse adults. Adults would be drawn more intimately into the world of adolescents and begin to feel more interested in and responsible for their schools. Students would expand their competence, learn directly some of the realities of the world at work, and encounter real problems whose consequences were irremediable. Some might even gain a greater appreciation for their education and be stimulated to take charge of their own growth more assertively. Quite a number might become bored, discouraged, restless. Fine! They need to confront these possibilities as well, while they still have other options available to explore. From the results of similar programs, I'm convinced that most would show sudden spurts in their maturity and self-confidence.

The sixties have been years of turmoil and tragedy, of increasing despair and futility. In retrospect, they have been the years of the great American awakening to the potential suicidal effects that our affluent, impersonal and complex society was creating. Somewhat perversely, I feel encouraged, even hopeful. Despair can be healthy. If it forces us to confront the real problems of youth, schools, and society, then we are ready to adapt more maturely. Despair can be unhealthy too, if we bury our minds in the past and refuse to confront the challenge of our alienated youth and our emerging Big Brother society. There is an extraordinary amount of creative ferment in many parts of the country. Not just among the young. Not just in our human growth centers. Not just in our Free Schools. But in the attitudes and values of many people. There is movement in local communities and schools. Maybe not much yet at the state and national level. But at the roots, there is change beginning. More of us recognize the necessity for change. How radical such change must be for us to survive as a healthy people we don't yet know.

Our dilemma is: what type of change? Will we in typical fashion run off in all directions, experimenting mindlessly, and so create no enduring change? If we do this, we kill the emerging questing spirit.

We need clarity. Clarity of understanding of the needs of our youth, of ourselves, of our times. And clarity of goals. Clear goals prefigure their solutions. My analyses and suggested goals are intended not to end but to provoke searching and thoughtful argument, plans and action.

Such searching needs to be done in all our institutions. I talk only of schools because I know them best. We have much rebuilding to do to humanize our schools. Let's begin by learning how to liberate ourselves to become more mature persons, open to venturing and risking. Let's help our youth live more wholly now so they will be able to create a healthier society for themselves and their children tomorrow.

References

Adelson, J. January 18, 1970. What generation gap? *The New York Times Magazine.*

Ainsworth, M. D. S. 1965. In *Child care and the growth of love,* by J. Bowlby, 2nd ed. Baltimore: Penguin.

Allport, G. W., Vernon, P. E., and Lindzey, G. 1960. *Study of values.* Manual 3rd ed. Boston: Houghton Mifflin

Almy, M. Research reported in *The school as a model of society* by J. S. Grannis. Undated manuscript.

Astin, A. W. December 20, 1970. Survey for American Council on Education. Reported in *The New York Times.*

Bandura, A., Ross, D., and Ross, S. 1963. Imitation of film mediated aggressive models. *Journal of Abnormal and Social Psychology* 66: 3-11.

Barker, R. G. and Gump, P. V. 1964. *Big school, small school: high school size and student behavior.* Palo Alto, California: Stanford University Press.

Bell, D. 1966. *The reforming of general education: The Columbia experience in its national setting.* New York: Columbia University Press.

—— 1967. Toward the year 2000; work in progress. *Daedalus* 96, no. 3.

Benedict, B. A., Caldor, P. H., Callahan, D. M., Hornstein, H. A. and Miles, M. B. 1967. The clinical-experimental approach to assessing organizational change efforts. *The Journal of Applied Behavioral Science* 3: 347-380.

Bennis, W. G., ed. 1967. Biography of an institution. *The Journal of Applied Behavioral Science* 3: 119-150.

Bennis, W. G. and Slater, P. E. 1968. *The temporary society.* New York: Harper & Row.

Bereiter, C. and Englemann, S. 1966. *Teaching disadvantaged children in the preschool.* Englewood Cliffs, New Jersey: Prentice-Hall.

Berkowitz, L. 1962. *Aggression. A social psychological analysis.* New York: McGraw-Hill.

Birren, J. E. and Bengston, V. L. March 1969. The young, the old, the in-between. *The Center Magazine* II.

Borton, T. 1970. *Reach, touch and teach.* New York: McGraw-Hill.

Boynton, R. W. and Mack, M. 1965a. *Introduction to the short story.* New York: Hayden.

—— 1965*b*. *Introduction to the poem*. New York: Hayden.

—— 1969. *Introduction to the play*. New York: Hayden.

Bronfenbrenner, U. 1958. Socialization and social class through time and space. In *Readings in Social Psychology,* eds. E. Maccoby, T. M. Newcomb, and E. Hartley. New York: Holt, Rinehart & Winston, pp. 400-425.

—— September 1968. The split society: children versus adults. *Cornell Alumnus News.*

—— 1970. *Two worlds of childhood: U.S. and U.S.S.R.* New York: Russell Sage Foundation.

Brown, B. S. July 1970. *Memo from the director*. National Institute of Mental Health.

Brown, G. I. 1971. *Human teaching for human learning: an introduction to confluent education*. New York: Viking.

Buckley, T. June 21, 1970. The student moves into the 14th C.D. *The New York Times Magazine.*

Bureau of Labor Statistics 1970. *Occupational outlook handbook*. New York: Bureau of Labor Statistics.

Burns, R. W. 1968. Objectives and content validity of tests. *Educational Technology* 8: 17-18.

Callahan, D., ed. 1966. *The secular city debate*. New York: Macmillan.

Carroll, J. B. 1967. Foreign language proficiency levels attained by language majors near graduation from college. *Foreign Language Annals* 1, no. 2, pp. 131-150.

Chickering, A. W. 1968. *Project on student development at selected small colleges.* Third Annual Report, NIMH.

—— 1969. *Education and identity.* San Francisco: Jossey-Bass.

Cloward, R. D. 1967*a*. Some unwanted results of evaluation research. *Issues in Community Action Research,* Research Dept., Community Council of Greater New York, pp. 19-25.

—— 1967*b*. Studies in tutoring. *The Journal of Experimental Education* 36, no. 1.

Coleman, J. S. 1966. *Equality of educational opportunity.* Office of Education.

Cox, H. 1966. *The secular city. Secularization and urbanization in theological perspective* (1965). New York: Macmillan.

Crozier, M. 1969. A new rationale for American business. *Daedalus* 98, no. 1, pp. 147-158.

Cummins, T. J. January 25, 1969. Letter to the editor in *Saturday Review.*

DeVries, T. and Tovatt, A. September 1970. This world of English. *English Journal,* p. 854.

Dewey, J. 1922. *Human nature and conduct.* New York: Henry Holt.

Douvan, E. and Adelson, J. 1966. *The adolescent experience.* New York: Wiley.

Duberman, M. 1968. An experiment in education. In Students and politics, ed. S. R. Graubard. *Daedalus* 97, no. 1, pp. 318-341.

Erikson, E. H. 1959. Identity and the life cycle, *Psychological Issues* 1.

Eurich, A. C. ed. 1968. *Campus 1980.* New York: Delacorte.

Feldman, K. A. and Newcomb, T. M. 1969. *The impact of college on students.* San Francisco: Jossey-Bass.

Feur, L. S. 1969. *The conflict of generations; the character and significance of student movements.* New York: Basic Books.

Flacks, R. 1967 The liberated generation: an exploration of the roots of student protest. In Stirrings out of apathy: student activism and the decade of protest, ed. E. E. Sampson. *The Journal of Social Issues.* 23, no. 3, pp. 52-75.

Fleming, T. July 5, 1970. West Point cadets now say "Why, Sir?" *The New York Times Magazine.*

Four-School Study Report 1970. *16-20: The liberal education of an age group.* New York: College Entrance Examination Board.

Fromm, E. 1947. *Man for himself.* New York: Holt, Rinehart & Winston.

—— 1955. *The sane society.* New York: Holt, Rinehart & Winston.

Gardner, J. W. 1961. *Excellence. Can we be equal and excellent too?* New York: Harper & Row.

Glatthorn, A. A. 1970. *Students, schools, and the tides of change.* New London, Conn.: Croft Educational Services.

Goodlad, J. I. April 19, 1969. The school vs. education. *Saturday Review.*

Gustaitis, R. 1969. *Turning on.* New York: Macmillan.

Harris, L. 1970. Survey for American Council on Education.

—— January 8, 1971. Survey for *Life.*

Hart Publishing Co. 1970. *Summerhill: for and against.* New York.

Hartmann, H. 1958. *Ego psychology and the problem of adaptation* (1939). New York: International University Press.

—— 1960. Towards a concept of mental health. *British Journal Medical Psychology* 33: 243-248.

Hayes, H. S., Lambert, W. E. and Tucker, G. R. 1967. Evaluation of foreign language teaching. *Foreign Language Annals* 1: 22-44.

Heath, D. D. 1971. *School size. The effect on adjustment and social contact of high school seniors.* Unpublished Ph.D. thesis, University of Pennsylvania.

Heath, D. H. 1965. *Explorations of maturity.* New York: Appleton-Century-Crofts.

—— 1968*a*. But are they more educable? In *Innovations in counseling,* ed. R. E. Van Atta. 12th Annual Counselors' Conference, Austin: The University of Texas pp. 3-29.

—— 1968*b*. *Growing up in college: liberal education and maturity.* San Francisco: Jossey-Bass.

—— 1969*a*. Secularization and maturity of religious beliefs. *Journal of Religion and Health* 8: 335-358.

—— 1969*b*. *To educate for today's needs: why a Friends school?* Wallingford, Pennsylvania: Pendle Hill.

—— 1970*a*. Better educated: less educable? In *The time has come today,* ed. S. S. Letter. New York: Teachers College Press, Columbia University pp. 35-49.

—— Summer 1970*b*. Is masculinity becoming obsolescent? *The Journal* (Boys' Club of America), pp. 4-11.

—— 1970*c*. Student alienation and the school. *The School Review,* Chicago: University of Chicago.

—— 1970*d*. What education for a more violent world? *American Association University of Women Journal* 63, no. 4, pp. 160-165.

—— 1970*e*. *Proceedings,* Second Research Conference on Religion and Mental Health, Academy of Religion and Mental Health.

—— Winter 1971*a*. Education for what? *New England Association Review,* pp. 1-81.

—— May 1971*b*. The emerging religious vision of today's youth. *Nexus.*

—— 1971*c*. Research in progress.

Heise, E. T. 1968. Language methodology: an order of priorities. *The French Review* XLI: 853-860.

Hicks, D. J. 1965. Imitation and retention of film-mediated aggressive peer and adult models. *Journal personality and social psychology* 2: 97-100.

Himmelweit, H. T., Oppenheim, A. N., and Vince, P. 1958. *Television and the child.* New York: Oxford University Press. Published for the Nuffield Foundation.

Hoge, D. 1969. *College students' religion: a study of trends in attitudes and behavior.* Ph.D. thesis, Harvard University.

Hoffman, P. E. December 12, 1970. Survey for American Jewish Committee. Reported in *Philadelphia Evening Bulletin.*

Holt, J. 1964. *How children fail.* New York: Dell.

Hutchins, R. M. 1968. Permanence and change. *The Center Magazine* 1.

Jencks, C. and Riesman, D. 1968. *The academic revolution.* Garden City, New York: Doubleday.

Jung, C. 1961. In *Memories, dreams and reflections,* ed. A. Jaffe. New York: Pantheon.

Kahn, H. and Wiener, A. J. 1967. The next thirty-three years: a framework for speculation. In Toward the year 2000: work in progress, ed. D. Bell. *Daedalus* 96, no. 3, pp. 705-732.

Katz, J. and Associates 1968. *No time for youth.* San Francisco: Jossey-Bass.

Keniston, K. 1967. The sources of student dissent. In Stirrings out of apathy: student activism and the decade of protest, ed. E. E. Sampson. *The Journal of Social Issues* 23, no. 3, pp. 108-137.

Kennan, G. G. 1968. *Democracy and the student left.* Boston: Little, Brown.

Laing, R. D. 1967. *The politics of experience* New York: Ballantine.

Lakin, M. 1969. Some ethical issues in sensitivity training. *American Psychologist* 24, no. 10, pp. 923-928.

Lipset, S. M. July 18, 1970. The banality of revolt. *Saturday Review.*

Lyle, D. December 1967. The human race has, maybe, thirty-five years left. *Esquire Magazine.*

MacDonald, J., The high school in human terms: curriculum design. In *Humanizing the secondary school.* eds. N. K. Hamilton and S. G. Saylor. Association for Supervision and Curriculum Development, National Education Association, Washington, D.C., pp. 35-54.

MacKinnon, D. W 1960. The highly effective individual. *Teachers College Record* 61: 367-378.

Macrorie K. 1970. *Uptaught.* New York: Hayden.

Mallery, D. 1962. *High school students speak out.* New York: Harper & Row.

Management Newsletter. September 30, 1968. *Electrical World,* pp. 109-112.

Maslow, A. H. 1962. *Toward a psychology of being.* Princeton, New Jersey: Van Nostrand.

May, R. 1969. *Love and will.* New York: W. W. Norton.

McElvaney, C. T. and Miles, M. B. 1969. The school psychologist as a change agent: improving a school system through survey feedback methods. *Professional School Psychology*, Vol. III. New York: Grune & Stratton, pp. 20-50.

Miller, G. A. 1967. Some psychological perspectives on the year 2000. In Toward the year 2000: work in progress, ed. D. Bell. *Daedalus* 96, no. 3, pp. 883-896.

Monahan, W. 1965. *Teachers knowledge of students related to urban high school size.* Unpublished Ph.D. thesis, University of California.

Murphy, L. B. 1962. *The widening world of childhood*. New York: Basic Books.

Neill, A. S. 1960. *Summerhill*. New York: Hart.

Nesbitt, W. 1968. *Simulation games for the social studies classroom, New Dimensions*. New York: The Foreign Policy Association.

Neugarten, B. L. 1967. The awareness of middle age. In *Middle age*, ed. R. Owen. London: British Broadcasting Corporation.

Newman, J. C. 1891. *The idea of a university, defined and illustrated* (1852). New York: Longmans, Green.

Newman, F. M. and Oliver, D. W. 1967. Education and community. *Harvard Educational Review* 37, no. 1, pp. 61-106.

Orwell, G. 1949. *1984*. New York: Harcourt, Brace and World.

Paschal, E. 1968. Organizing for better instruction. In *Campus 1980*, ed. A. C. Eurich. New York: Delacorte, pp. 220-235.

Perloe, S. I. 1970. Authoritarianism, antinomianism, and affiliation among college students. *Proceedings*, 78th Annual Convention, American Psychological Association, pp. 325-326.

Perls, F. S. 1969. *Gestalt therapy verbatim*. Lafayette, California: Real People Press.

Peterson, R. E. 1968. *The scope of organized student protest in 1967-1968*. Princeton, New Jersey: Educational Testing Service.

Piaget, J. 1928. *Judgment and reasoning in the child*. New York: Harcourt, Brace.

—— 1950. *The psychology of intelligence* (1947). New York: Harcourt, Brace and World.

Platt, J. November 28, 1969. What we must do. *Science*, pp. 1115-1121.

Plimpton, C. 1968. *Report of the President*. Amherst College.

Reich, C. A. 1970. *The greening of America*. New York: Random House.

Rogers, C. R. 1959. A theory of therapy, personality, and interpersonal relationships, as developed in the client-centered framework. In Psychology: A study of a science. Vol. III, ed. S. Koch. *Formulations of the person and the social context*. New York: McGraw-Hill, pp. 184-256.

—— 1967. *The therapeutic relationship and its impact: a study of psychotherapy with schizophrenics*. Madison, Wisconsin: University of Wisconsin Press.

—— 1969. *Freedom to learn*. Columbus, Ohio: Charles E. Merrill.

—— 1970. *Carl Rogers on encounter groups*. New York: Harper & Row.

Roszak, T. 1969. *The making of a counter culture*. New York: Doubleday.

Rousseau, J. J. 1911. *Emile* (1762). New York: E. P. Dutton.

Sanford, N. 1968. The college student of 1980. In *Campus 1980,* ed. A. C. Eurich. New York: Delacorte.

Seldon, H., Community Change, Inc., Wakefield, Massachusetts.

Seligman, B. B. 1966. *Most notorious victory. Man in an age of automation.* New York: The Free Press.

Silberman, C. E. January 26, 1969. Interview reported in *The New York Times.*

—— 1970. *Crisis in the classroom. The remaking of American education.* New York: Random House.

Silver, A. January 30, 1969. Who cares for Columbia? *The New York Review of Books* 12: 15-24.

Skinner, B. F. 1948. *Walden Two.* New York: Macmillan.

Smith, M. B. August 31, 1968. Morality and student protest. Psi Chi Invited Address, American Psychological Association, San Francisco, California.

Steele, M. June 9, 1968. Student voices. *The New York Times Book Review,* p. 2.

Sugarman, A. W. April 5, 1968. *A proposal for a senior high school program of school-community service in Ramapo Central School District Number 2, Spring Valley, New York.* Application to the Commissioner of Education for State Aid.

Suhm, L. L. April 1964. *A national employment adjustment plan. A proposal.* Center for Leisure Resources Development. University of Wisconsin Extension Division, Wisconsin.

Sullivan, H. S. 1953. *The interpersonal theory of psychiatry.* New York: W. W. Norton.

Tamminen, A. W. and Miller, G. D. 1968. *Guidance programs and their impact on students.* Office of Education and Pupil Personnel Services Section, Minnesota Department of Education.

Thorndike, E. L. 1924. Mental discipline in high school studies. *Journal of educational psychology* 15: 83-98.

Tickton, S. G. 1968. The magnitude of American higher education in 1980. In *Campus 1980,* ed. A. C. Eurich. New York: Delacorte.

Tiedeman, D.V. 1970. *Report of the Commission on Tests.* Vol. I: Righting the balance. New York: College Entrance Examination Board.

Trilling, L. 1965. *Beyond culture: essays on literature and learning.* New York: Viking.

Tyson, J. C. 1957. *A comparative study of teacher-pupil relationships in small and large high schools.* Unpublished Ph.D. thesis, University of Virginia.

Yeomans, E. 1967. *Education for initiative and responsibility: comments on a visit to the schools of Leicestershire County.* National Association of Independent Schools.

—— 1969. *The wellsprings of teaching.* National Association of Independent Schools.

Index